Pearson Education
Test Prep Series
for
AP® HUMAN GEOGRAPHY

To accompany:
The Cultural Landscape

AN INTRODUCTION
TO HUMAN GEOGRAPHY
AP® EDITION, 13TH EDITION
James M. Rubenstein

Prepared by
Ann Linsley
Bellaire High School
Houston Independent School District
Bellaire, Texas

Courseware Portfolio Manager: Christian Botting
Director of Portfolio Management: Beth Wilbur
Content Producer: Lori Newman
Managing Producer: Michael Early
Courseware Director, Content Development: Ginnie Simione Jutson
Courseware Editorial Assistant: Sherry Wang
Rich Media Content Producers: Ziki Dekel, Chloe Veylit
Mastering Media Producer: Todd Brown
Full-Service Vendor and Project Manager: SPi Global
Supplement Cover Designer: SPi Global
Accuracy Reviewer: Linda L. Hammon
Rights & Permissions Project Manager: SPi Global
Rights & Permissions Management: Ben Ferrini
Product Marketing Manager: Alysun Estes
Manufacturing Buyer: Stacey Weinberger
Printer/Binder: LSC Communications, Inc.
Cover Printer: Phoenix Color/Hagerstown
Cover Photo Credit: hadynyah, Getty Images

Pearson   www.PearsonSchool.com/Advanced

ISBN 13: 978-0-13-523404-4
ISBN 10:   0-13-523404-2

Contents

Introduction to AP Human Geography

Advanced Placement (AP) Human Geography is an introductory college course covering a broad range of topics in human geography. The exam assumes that you have taken the equivalent of one semester of college-level preparation, with the understanding that many high schools will teach the course across an entire school year.

The AP Human Geography curriculum covers the depth and breadth of a typical introductory survey college course in human geography. The curriculum is reviewed and evaluated by geographers and college geography professors to ensure that it maintains both a rigorous and challenging preparation. Members of the AP Human Geography Development Committee select all exam material based on the curriculum. The AP exam administered in May is representative of the curriculum material and considered an appropriate measure of skills and knowledge needed in the field of introductory human geography. The exam questions are reviewed and statistically evaluated to ensure an introductory college level exam.

The purpose of this course is to introduce you to the systematic study of patterns and processes that have shaped human understanding, use, and alteration of Earth's surface. As a geography student, you will look at the Earth to analyze humans' organization of space and the environmental consequences of their decisions. You will examine patterns across the cultural landscape, identifying trends and anticipate future phenomena that might occur across the landscape. Additionally, you will explore different methods and tools used in their science and practice. The focus of any study in human geography is to understand the spatial patterns and processes of human actions and interactions within and around the world.

Goals of AP Human Geography

AP Human Geography course was established in 1999, with five college-level goals in mind. These goals are aligned directly with the National Geography Standards that were developed in 1994. Upon successful completion of the course, you should have developed geographic skills that enable you to:

Use and think about maps and spatial data.

Maps and spatial data are essential in discovering patterns on Earth's surface that reflect and influence physical and human processes. Learning to use and think critically with these tools will allow students to use real-world data to solve problems in various situations on Earth. Thinking critically about what is obvious and also that which is hidden on various maps provides students with the understanding needed to successfully use maps and spatial data.

Understand and interpret the implications of associations among phenomena in places.

Geographers look at data and map sets in order to understand changes in the spatial organization of Earth's surface. They are particularly interested in focusing on how phenomena (*an observable fact, occurrence, or circumstance*) are related to one another in particular places. Students should be able to not only recognize and interpret patterns but also to identify the nature and significance of the relationships among phenomena that occur in the same place. In addition, they should understand how a culture's values and tastes, political situations, and economic conditions contribute to the creation of unique cultural landscapes.

Recognize and interpret at different scales the relationships among patterns and processes.

Geographic study also requires that students view patterns at different scales. Geography is a matter of scale. It is essential for students to understand that a phenomenon that occurs on a local scale could very well be influenced by circumstances occurring at another scale—national, local, or even global. Geographers look for the connections operating at multiple scales when trying to explain geographic patterns and arrangements.

Define regions and evaluate the regionalization process.

Geography is not only concerned with identifying patterns across the cultural landscape but also with analyzing how they came about and what they mean. To successfully make such an analysis, the patterns have to be broken into smaller parts or categories, referred to as regions. By looking critically at regions of the world, geographers are able to consider how and why the regions emerged and hypothesize the implications for future development of Earth's surface.

Characterize and analyze changing interconnections among places.

To obtain the true depth of the geographic perspective, students must understand that events and processes occurring in one place can have a profound influence on other places. Students must analyze places and patterns as part of a whole, not in isolation. Be aware that relationships on Earth are in constant motion, they are continually changing, and it is necessary to figure out how and why this change occurs.

Topics in AP Human Geography

I. Thinking Geographically

This course emphasizes geography as a field of academic study and gives a brief overview of geography in nineteenth-century Europe. This overview will show how the discipline has evolved into the study of diverse cultures and unique areas organized around some key concepts.

Students are introduced to the importance of spatial organization—the location of places, people, and events on Earth to evaluate global connections of places and landscapes of human activity across Earth's surface.

Location, space, place, scale, pattern, regionalization, and globalization are key concepts integrated throughout the study. These concepts are essential for understanding spatial interaction and spatial organization of Earth's surface. Students should be able to successfully analyze human population growth and movement, cultural patterns, economic use of the Earth, political organization of space, and human settlement patterns especially urbanization. In addition, students will use and interpret maps to analyze spatial patterns and interactions that connect the units of study. The course applies mathematical formulas, models, and qualitative date to these geographic concepts in order to make educated predictions. Students are asked to make regional analysis of various phenomena and create appropriate regions to illustrate certain processes.

Ultimately, this course should demonstrate the relevance of academic geography in everyday life and decision-making. Students will apply these key concepts when looking at current events and policies of the world and should be able to ask yourself the following questions: "If I were a policy maker for the United Nations, why would this information be important? How would I use it to develop public policy that would impact humans in sub-Saharan Africa, Europe, and North America?"

II. Population Migration

An important geographic concept is how populations are organized across the Earth's surface. This part of the course provides the demographic foundations for the cultural, political, economic, and urban systems. By analyzing demographic data such as infant mortality rates, crude death rates, crude birth rates, and migration, students will understand the distribution of human population at different scales: global, continental, national, state, and local community. Students will be able to explain why populations are growing or declining in certain places and not others. Analysis of where and why fertility rates have dropped in some parts of the developing world but not in others is important to understanding development factors and global interactions. Age-sex structures (population pyramids) are different in many regions of the world and explain the political, cultural, and economic implications of these differences. A key component of population geography that is important in today's world is the understanding of refugee flows, immigration (both internal and out-migration), and residential mobility (movement to the Sunbelt) in order to appreciate the interconnectedness of our world. The relationship between refugees and political boundaries is also important, especially where refugees have no access to political power because they find themselves "on the wrong side of the line." Another key concept related to populations is that of environmental degradation. With increases in regional populations, many stresses occur on the environment, thus causing rapid out-migration and urbanization. Rapid immigration to certain parts of the world can exacerbate anti-foreigner sentiment because of the imbalance that occurs in wages, employment, and political power. Comparing different models of population change, including demographic and epidemiological transitions and government population policies, provides further analysis for evaluating factors and influences on development. Upon completion of this unit, students should be able to evaluate the role, strengths, and weaknesses of major population policies and make recommendations regarding them. For instance, is education essential in lowering fertility rates? Should females be empowered to accomplish this?

III. Cultural Patterns and Processes

The ability to analyze and predict various components of regional cultural patterns and processes is critical to understanding the distribution of human geography. Understanding the what, where, and why of cultural patterns provides a spatial understanding of the cultural landscape. Organizing culture groups by their language, religion, race, ethnicity, and gender creates a spatial pattern to observe changes over time and spatial diffusion throughout the world.

Students must look at cultural patterns from a variety of geographic scales, from local to global. Diffusion is a key concept when looking at these patterns. For example, the location of certain agricultural processes, or housing types, or where certain religions or languages are practiced and determining how these traits get from point A to point B? Analyzing these patterns of diffusion based on cultural characteristics provides an understanding to the centripetal and/or centrifugal factors that may be operating in a place.

In this analysis, the concept of folk culture versus popular culture will emerge. This is an important way to differentiate among cultures. Folk cultures tend to be isolated and will only diffuse through relocation, like the Amish culture. Popular cultures are global and relocate through many different types of diffusion. Distinguishing among the languages and dialects, religious practices, ethnic and universalizing religions, and the popular or folk culture of a group contribute to understanding the influence of cultural patterns on the human constructed landscape.

One important aspect of this section of the course is to look at the way culture shapes human-environmental relationships. The root word for culture is *cultus (to care for);* analysis of what a cultural group cares about is revealed in how they use, misuse, and regard the environment around them. If someone visits a major city in the United States, what would that person see—museums, sports facilities, recreational venues, and eclectic neighborhoods? This cultural landscape reflects what people in that culture do with their spare time and money. Would the landscape look the same in different regions, like the Middle East or Europe? Landscapes tend to reflect the cultural values, tastes, and sets of beliefs of a group of people. Cultural traits, such as the language and religion of a group of people, can be identified by looking at these landscapes. This identification helps build a cultural map of the group. Where did they begin, where did they move to, where are they now, and where will they be in the future?

IV. Political Patterns and Processes

This section of the course will introduce the political organization of Earth's surface at a variety of scales. Consider that the political boundaries that have been drawn over the years reflect somebody's view of how Earth should be divided. This view is sometimes in conflict with others' views of where a boundary should be, and thus problems can occur.

The main emphasis is on the concept of a state or country. How did the current world map emerge? What political entities were at play to get the boundaries we have today? By looking at the world in historic terms, one can analyze boundary changes over time. For example, the impact of colonialism on boundaries, as well as the devolution of the former Soviet Union, demonstrates that often there is no correlation between ethnic, economic, or environmental patterns and the contemporary world map. Also, consider forces that are changing the role of individual nation-states in the contemporary world, such as ethnic conflicts, supranationalism, economic globalization, regional economic blocs, and the need to confront environmental issues that know no political boundaries.

To truly understand the complexities associated with political boundaries, examine the issues at different scales, such as political units above and below the state. Political units above the state level include regional alliances, such as NATO, the European Union, or the United Nations. Political units below the state examine the function of entities like city boundaries, ethnic boundaries, and voting districts and how specific policies affect the spatial organization of cultural and social life.

V. Agriculture and Rural Land-Use Pattern and Processes

Patterns and processes of agricultural and rural land use explore four basic themes: the origin and diffusion of agriculture, key characteristics of the world's agricultural regions, reasons why these regions function the way they do, and the environmental impact of agriculture. It is important to examine where domesticated agricultural practices began and understand the diffusion of these practices around the globe. Understanding how changing diets, energy use, and new technologies impact the emerging sedentary societies reveals the influence of agriculture as it changes over time.

Earth's major agricultural production regions include extensive activities (fishing, forestry, nomadic herding, ranching, and shifting cultivation) and intensive activities (plantation agriculture, mixed crop/livestock systems, market gardening, factory farms, and horticulture). In addition to the "where" and "what" is produced, geographers are concerned with land survey systems, environmental conditions, and cultural values that create and sustain these patterns to provide food for the world's population.

One theory that will be important to the understanding of the location of agricultural activities is von Thünen's agricultural land use model. Other agricultural activities such as the impact of factory farming on food supplies and the distribution of crops and animals are also emphasized. The need to increase food production in the technological period of the third agricultural revolution includes developments in alternative farming methods and industrial and scientific influences in the development of sustainable production.

VI. Cities and Urban Land-Use Patterns and Processes

The urban geography unit focuses on the development and character of cities, and the internal structure and landscape of urban areas. To better understand the dynamic processes occurring in cities, geographers look at historical and current locations of cities, as well as their political, economic, and cultural functions. Analyze transportation and communications within and between cities, and begin to understand why there are differences in the growth of cities. Many of these differences will be tied to their political, economic, or cultural traits. Theories that will be examined during this first part of the unit will be Christaller's central place theory, the rank size rule, and the gravity model. Quantitative information, such as demographic data, migration, zones of influence, or the effects of job creation programs are used to analyze changes in the urban hierarchy.

The second focus will be on the internal structure and landscapes of urban areas. The study of large cities includes understanding land-use patterns, racial and ethnic segregation, architecture patterns, cycles of development, and transportation systems within the city.

The use of qualitative data from the census bureau, and qualitative information from narrative accounts and field studies, provides the foundation for analyzing how cities function, grow, and die. Models of internal city structure—the Burgess concentric zone model, the Hoyt sector model, and the Harris-Ullman multiple nuclei model—contribute to understanding how cities change over time. When studying these models, it is important for you to look at the architectural history and emergence of transportation within the city to truly appreciate the city's cultural landscape. New trends in urban development, such as the emergence of edge cities, New Urbanism, urban renewal, the gentrification of neighborhoods, and the move toward sustainable cities, link the city from the past to the future.

Although most urban geographers focus on North American cities, it is important to compare urban structures in other parts of the world. The study of European, Islamic, East and South Asian, Latin American, and sub-Saharan African cities illustrate the cultural values and economic systems of different regions.

VII. Industrial and Economic Development Patterns and Processes

Economic activity can be analyzed by looking at the interaction of natural resources, culture, politics, and history in specific places. It is this interaction that provides a spatial perspective of areas across our cultural landscape. By looking at these key concepts (natural resources, culture, politics, and history), we can appreciate why resources have different values in different societies around the globe. These values give regions comparative advantages for development over other regions.

The economic development models of Rostow's stages of economic growth, and Immanuel Wallerstein's World Systems Theory (core-periphery), are analyzed with the location theories, such as Weber and von Thünen, in order to understand the ever-globalizing world.

Contemporary issues that surround economic activity are evaluated at various scales to see how new patterns of economic inequity emerge. Management of pollution, energy needs of certain communities, and the need for some countries to improve quality of life are investigated. The impact of deindustrialization, the disaggregation of production, and the rise of consumption and leisure activities on the community, the country, and the region are evaluated to determine patterns over time and stages of development.

The AP Exam

The AP Human Geography exam is 2 hours and 15 minutes in length and includes both a 60-minute multiple-choice section and a 75-minute free-response section. The multiple-choice section is 60 minutes, has 60 questions, and is 50 percent of the exam score. The multiple-choice questions will emphasize the analysis of quantitative and qualitative sources. The questions will consist of five to eight sets of two to three questions with a quantitative or qualitative source. One or more of these question sets will include a paired set of sources.

The free-response section is 75 minutes, consists of three task and stimulus type questions, and is 50 percent of the exam score. The task and stimulus types will remain consistent from year to year. The students are asked to do the following: (1) Describe, explain, and apply geographic data to a situation or scenario (no stimulus). (2) Describe, explain, and apply geographic data using data, image, or map (one quantitative or qualitative source). (3) Describe, explain, and apply geographic data using data, image, and/or map (two sources, qualitative and/or quantitative). Each question will be standardized to be worth 7 points. Each part a student is asked to do in an FRQ is worth one point (© 2019 The College Board). For example, in an FRQ in the urban unit, one might be asked to: a. identify a place, b. explain the location of a place, c. describe the interaction of places, d. explain how the places are different, e. discuss how one of the places is attracting a new population, f. explain why one place has a greater connectivity to other places, and g. explain how the social needs of the population will have to change if new high-tech industries were to move into a place. Each item is worth 1 point and each is asking the student to use a different skill to complete the response. Asking students to do multiple responses in one part of an FRQ (e.g., "Describe TWO characteristics of…") will be minimized.

The responses to the FRQ's need are to be structured according to the task verb that guides the question. The following task verbs are commonly used in the free-response question:

Compare: Provide a description or explanation of similarities and/or differences.

Define: Provide a specific meaning for a word or concept.

Describe: Provide the relevant characteristics of a specified topic.

Explain: Provide information about how or why a relationship, process, pattern, position, or outcome occurs, using evidence and/or reasoning.

Identify: Indicate or provide information about a specified topic, without elaboration or explanation.

© 2019 The College Board

As of 2019, the AP Human Geography exam and curriculum addresses specific skills that AP Human Geography students should practice throughout the year. Exam questions will include these skills as part of the questions. The skills students should practice throughout the course and prepare to address on the exam are as follows:

1. **Concepts and Processes:** Analyze geographic theories, approaches, concepts, processes, or models in theoretical and applied contexts, 25–36% of multiple choice exam weight.

2. **Spatial Relationships**: Analyze geographic patterns, relationships, and outcomes in applied contexts, 16–25% of multiple choice exam weight.

3. **Data Analysis**: Analyze and interpret quantitative geographic data represented in maps, tables, charts, graphs, satellite images, and infographics, 13–20% of multiple choice exam weight.

4. **Source Analysis:** Analyze and interpret qualitative geographic information represented in maps, images (e.g., satellite, photographs, and cartoons), and landscapes, 13–20% of multiple choice exam weight.

5. **Scale Analysis:** Analyze geographic theories, approaches, concepts, processes, and models across geographic scales to explain spatial relationships, 13–20% of multiple choice exam weight.

The free response questions incorporate the following skills:

Concepts and Processes	23–29% exam weight
Spatial Relationships	33–43% exam weight
Data Analysis	10–19% exam weight
Visual Analysis	10–19% exam weight
Scale Analysis	10–14% exam weight

In addition to the skills, the AP Human Geography course is centered on the "big ideas:" (1) patterns and spatial organization, (2) impacts and interactions, and (3) spatial processes and societal change.

Types of exam items expect the students to describe characteristics and methods, identify patterns and processes, and explain cause and effect relationships within the context of the units of study. Ultimately, the course content is categorized under the concepts of the "big ideas," developed and investigated in greater depth using the skills to understand the spatial relationships of the data.

The following are the approximate percentages of the multiple-choice section that are devoted to each area:

I.	Geography: Its Nature and Perspectives	8–10%
II.	Population and Migration	12–17%
III.	Cultural Patterns and Processes	12–17%
IV.	Political Patterns and Processes	12–17%
V.	Agriculture and Rural Land Use Patterns and Processes	12–17%
VI.	Cities and Urban Land Use Patterns and Processes	12–17%
VII.	Industrialization and Economic Development Patterns and Processes	12–17%

The exam score is converted into The College Board AP Central's 5-point scale as follows:

5   Extremely well-qualified

4   Well qualified

3   Qualified

2   Possibly qualified

1   No recommendation

Strategies for Success in AP Human Geography

1. Thinking Geographically

Much of the content of this course deals with themes and issues that are integral to our world today. For example, population policies, political conflicts between and within countries, and the problems of suburban sprawl are all regular newsworthy items. The key is to think about current events in geographical terms. Students should always consider the spatial aspects of world events. For example, in a conflict between two countries, the geographical importance lies in understanding boundary disputes, the location of different ethnic groups, conflict over land and resources, and infrastructural considerations. This way of thinking should be imprinted throughout the course.

2. Using and Interpreting Graphs, Maps, and Charts

The textbook contains numerous graphics, especially maps. It is critical that students practice reading and interpreting these maps. Make sure that they understand the title, key, and scale and can describe what the map is showing. Specific graphics must be understood. For example, what does a population pyramid show? There will be graphs, maps, and charts on the Advanced Placement Human Geography examination, both in the multiple-choice section and the free-response questions. This guide includes activities and free-response questions that integrate graphs, maps, and charts so that students can practice reading and interpreting them.

3. Integrating the Content

In the high school social studies curriculum, we tend to think in compartments such as history, geography, economics, and politics. Within this course, we do the same thing and consider topics such as political geography, industry and development, and urbanization. It is imperative that students have a more holistic way of thinking before they go into the examination. For example, ethnicity and political geography overlap. Population is relevant to urbanization, and development incorporates material from culture, economics, population, and political topics in the course. Some of the free-response questions on the examination will require students to draw information from a number of different units and so they must integrate the content.

4. Knowledge and Use of Case Studies

In both sections of the examination, students will be required to answer questions that involve a specific knowledge and understanding of different places in the world. On the free-response section, they may have to exemplify a concept with a specific example. Thus, a working knowledge of case studies is essential. These may include conflicts in Southwest Asia, demographic changes in Europe and East Asia, ethnic and political conflict in the Caucasus, or the political boundaries of Africa. In each of these case studies, there are geographic issues that transcend specific chapters in the text. For example, students should be familiar with population, religious, ethnic, political, and economic aspects of regional case studies as appropriate.

5. A Broad Geographical Knowledge

More than any other geography course, Advanced Placement Human Geography requires students to think and write critically in the content area. This should not take away from the fact that they also need to have a working knowledge of world political geography. For example, they should be expected to have a pretty good idea of which countries colonized different parts of the developing world and the characteristics of different regions of the globe. Can students identify the major countries in each region or realm of the world? In the context of higher-level questions, the examination will still require this knowledge. For example, a map that accompanies a free-response question will often show political boundaries without showing the names of countries, and students will be expected to identify these countries correctly.

6. Knowledge and Use of Models

Models are integral to human geography, and students need to be familiar with them. These include but are not limited to the demographic and migration transition, models of industrial location and agricultural land use, development models, central place theory, and models of urban structure. Students should know the title, content, and author of the model together with the underlying assumptions. Where they deviate from reality, students need to be able to explain those differences. To what extent is the model useful in explaining spatial reality in that context? Students' knowledge of models in human geography will be tested on the examination. It is always possible that one of the free-response questions will focus on a specific model. More importantly, it is essential that students understand these are models and they may or may not completely represent the topic in any one place at any particular time.

7. Material from a Variety of Texts and Other Support Materials

This textbook covers most of the key concepts and content areas of the course. The correlation guide aligns every part of the Advanced Placement Human Geography outline to key issues throughout the text. The key vocabulary terms are highlighted and defined in the textbook and highlighted again in this guide. Together, they provide the necessary content for success in the course. At the same time, it must be realized that the examiners are not working from this text alone. Thus, it is the instructor's responsibility to make sure that students are exposed to some other materials and texts as part of the preparation for the examination. This guide has made every effort to contain a review of all the content and vocabulary that might be part of the Advanced Placement Human Geography examination, including material that is only briefly mentioned or not covered in Rubenstein's text.

8. Review and Exam Preparation

This guide is a comprehensive review and examination preparation manual. Students need to take the practice tests under exam conditions. The guide includes two multiple-choice examinations of 60 questions each, together with six free-response questions. On the multiple-choice section, they need to read the entire question and use a process of elimination. There is no penalty for guessing, so students should answer all questions on the multiple-choice portion.

On the free-response questions, students should read the question, underlining key terms, and then spend a few minutes writing down ideas and making an outline that will help them to answer it. If a question is organized A, B, and C, make sure their answer follows the same format. Introductory and concluding paragraphs are not necessary; students should get to the point quickly and be as succinct as possible. Recognize what the question is asking. One that asks a student to evaluate or analyze involves more and will be worth more points than one where the task is to list or describe. Use specific examples where asked to do so. Students should make sure they are responding to the command term in the prompt. If the statement requests you to discuss a topic, then the answer should provide a balanced review or any perspectives including facts, arguments, or supported opinions. The course preparation should practice the different types of directions and types of responses that address those terms. There are three free-response questions on the exam, each of which must be answered. Some questions will deal with content material specific to one unit, while others will require students to draw on material from more than one unit. It is always in the student's best interest to make connection from many different units, when possible, as geographic units and concepts are not "stand alone" but rather are interwoven.

On both sections of the examination, students should be cognizant of the time limit throughout. On the multiple-choice part of the exam, students should come back to questions where they are unsure. On the free-response questions, students should answer the question(s) about which they are most confident first, leaving what they consider to be the most difficult to last. It is imperative that students try to answer all the questions.

About the Author

Ann Linsley teaches IB/AP (*International Baccalaureate* and *Advanced Placement*) Geography and IB Environmental Science at Bellaire High School in the Houston Independent School District, where she has taught for the past 32 years. Ann earned an MS in GeoScience from Texas A&M University in 2006 under the guidance of Dr. Sarah Bednarz and Dr. Bob Bednarz. She also holds an MEd in Curriculum and Gifted & Talented instruction and a BA in Russian, from the University of Houston. Ann is a teacher consultant for the National Geographic Society, the Texas Alliance for Geographic Education, and the College Board. She is the recipient of several national and state awards, teacher of the year recognition, and honored with the opportunity to participate in national programs to extend her field work experiences sponsored by NOAA, NSF, NCGE, and NGS. Ann has worked with the College Board Geography program since its inception in 1998 as a reader, writer, consultant, and summer institute trainer. Ann was a *PolarTrec* teacher to McMurdo Station, Antarctica, participating in a human impact study of the region with a team from Texas A&M, Department of Geography. She is also a National Geographic Fellow and a participant in the NGS Arctic-Svalbard program.

To the Student

Preparing for the AP Human Geography Exam

I. Stay Organized and Keep Up with Current Events

You should take notes, not only on your teacher's lectures but also on reading assignments you are given. The use of study groups is a great way to make sure you understand the content. In our digital age, some students find it helpful to create a Google doc to share with their friends so that you can ask questions of each other and comment on questions that may arise. Every single unit you study is illustrated daily on the news. Get in the habit of looking at the world news and making connections with what you are learning in class.

II. Use AP Central's Website: http://www.apcentral.collegeboard.co

This site gives you valuable information about the exam, as well as sample multiple-choice and free-response questions. The more you are exposed to different types of questions, the better. You will also use this website to register to receive your scores after the exam.

III. APHG Multiple-Choice Questions

There will be 60 multiple-choice questions, each with five choices on your exam. You will have 60 minutes to answer all 60. The multiple-choice questions will emphasize the analysis of quantitative and qualitative sources. The questions will consist of five to eight sets of two to three questions with a quantitative or qualitative source. One or more of these question sets will include a paired set of sources. You should **answer those you know first**, then go back to the ones you are unsure of. **There is no penalty for guessing,** so you should try to answer all of the questions. This portion of the test consists of 50 percent of your score.

IV. APHG Free-Response Questions

There will be **three** free-response questions on your exam. You will have a task and two stimulus questions: (1) Describe, explain, and apply geographic data to a situation or scenario (no stimulus). (2) Describe, explain, and apply geographic data using data, image, or map (one quantitative or qualitative source). (3) Describe, explain, and apply geographic data using data, image, and/or map (two sources, qualitative and/or quantitative). Each free-response question will be worth 7 points (© 2019 The College Board). The questions are formatted A–G and ask you to respond according to the task term for one or two points each.

For example, if there is a question:
A. Define urbanization.

Your answer should be:
A. Urbanization is the process by which the population of cities grows, both in *numbers* and *percentage*.

Make sure that you **underline** all required parts of the prompt. Important words that are commonly used might ask that you **define** and **explain**, or **interpret** from information given. A common problem that occurs is that you might do one, such as define, and not the other, such as explain. You will be given a point for the definition but will not receive a point for the explanation, so it is important to answer all that is being asked of you. As with the multiple-choice section, **answer the free-response question that you know for sure, FIRST,** then go on to the other ones. **There is no penalty for attempting to answer a free-response question.** Try to bring in concepts from all units of APHG whenever possible.

V. Registering for the Exam

Beginning in the fall of 2019, students will register for AP exams in their classes. The teacher will receive a code that will be shared with the students. The students will log into the College Board registration site and enter the codes for the classes that they are participating in. See the school AP coordinator for any changes regarding registration.

The AP Human Geography exam fee is currently $93.

If for some reason you want to cancel your AP Human Geography score and have it permanently removed from your records, you should fill out a score cancellation form and send it to College Board.

VI. Using the AP Test Prep for AP Human Geography

The review material is in the order of the chapters in the textbook. However, the course does not have to be taught in the textbook chapter order or the order from the College Board AP guide. Each chapter addresses the AP topics applicable to the content of each chapter. Explanations of geographic content, connections, and application to real-world situations and the definition and application of geographic vocabulary are developed within each section of the chapter. Each section includes review questions. Each chapter has chapter review questions and practice free-response questions designed for that particular topic. Each chapter in the test prep also includes an application exercise to help understand how a geographer thinks in regard to this particular topic. After working through all of the chapters in collaboration with your teacher's instruction and other materials, you should complete the practice tests in a timed testing situation to simulate the actual exam and the pacing that you need to anticipate. For any quiz and chapter questions that you miss, you should go back into the test prep guide and the text material and determine the correct answer and read through the content information that supports the answer.

Chapter

1 This Is Geography

Why Is Geography a Science?

Learning Outcome 1.1.1: Summarize among geography's basic concepts.
Explain differences between early maps and contemporary maps.

Learning Outcome 1.1.2: Explain the development of the science of cartography.
Maps are a reference and a communication tool illustrating a spatial distribution on the Earth's surface.

Learning Outcome 1.1.3: Identify geography's principal contemporary analytic mapping tools.
Geographers today use the tools of Geographic Information Science (GIS). Data gathered by remote sensing and GPS to measure changes over time and the characteristics of places can be combined and analyzed using geographic information systems (GIS).

Learning Outcome 1.1.4: Explain the role of map scale and projection in reading maps.
Contemporary maps indicate scale in three ways. Four types of distortion can occur in the transfer of Earth's round surface to a flat map.

Learning Outcome 1.1.5: Explain how the geographic grid locates points on Earth's surface and helps to tell time.
The geographic grid determines exact locations while **thematic maps** illustrate the data that shape places.

Geography is the study of where things are found on the Earth's surface and the reasons for the locations. Human geographers focus on where people and activities are found and why are they found there, essentially the "why of where." This first chapter introduces the basic concepts that geographers use to answer these questions. The focus of questions that are the basis of the AP Human Geography course centers around maps and map analysis, components of places and characteristics that influence places, regional perspectives of places from local to global scales, the concept of scale, how space is used, and how ideas diffuse over time and space. Geography can be divided into two major fields—human geography and physical geography. Physical geography is the study of the physical features and processes on Earth's surface. The Advanced Placement Human Geography course cannot completely ignore physical geography because the two are integrally connected. For example, physical geography influences agricultural decisions, migration patterns, and housing choices. Human geography is the scientific study of the **location** of people and activities on Earth's surface. It is the study of **where** and **why** human activities are located where they are. Geographers look at the world from a **spatial perspective** and will study how people and objects vary across Earth's surface. They will also study the relationship or **spatial interaction** between people and objects, as well as the movement or **diffusion** of people and ideas.

The earliest geographers studied places mainly because of the necessities of trade routes and navigation. The maps made by Chinese, Greek, and North African scholars became the foundation of the art and science of mapmaking or **cartography**. Maps are a geographer's tool because maps function as a means of reference about what is located in a particular place or how to access places. A map is also a means of communicating about the make up of the land and the distribution of human activities. The ancient Greek scholar Eratosthenes invented the word geography during the third century B.C.; *geo* means "Earth" and *graphy* means "to write." He also accepted the findings of Aristotle and Plato that the planet was round. Ptolemy, known as the father of cartography, published numerous maps in his eight-volume *Guide to Geography*. After Ptolemy's time (A.D. 100–170), mapmaking became more like a form of artistic expression in Europe and little new exploration came about during this time. However, geographic inquiry continued in other parts of the world. In China, Pei Xiu (the father of Chinese cartography) produced a map of China that used a grid system and graduated scale. It is through the works of Muhammad al-Idrisi and later through the travels of Ibn Battuta that the Islamic world flourished in cartography. European explorers such as the Vikings, Bartolomeu Dias, Christopher Columbus, Vasco Nunez de Balboa, and Ferdinand Magellan mapped the world beyond their continent.

Geography is a discipline developed from description to explanation and analysis. The philosopher Immanuel Kant had placed geography within an overall framework of scientific knowledge by arguing for logical or physical classification. He wanted to know where something was located and why it was there. In the eighteenth century, Alexander von Humboldt and Carl Ritter argued for **environmental determinism**, the belief that the physical causes social development.

Later geographers argued that landscapes are the products of complex human–environment relationships. This is known as **cultural ecology**. The approach that the physical environment may limit certain human activities but also that people can adapt to their environment is called **possibilism**.

The **regional** (or **cultural landscape) studies** approach, which emphasizes the unique characteristics of each place, both human and physical, is a third approach to the study of geography. It was pioneered in the late-nineteenth and early-twentieth centuries by Paul Vidal de la Blache, Jean Brunhes, **Carl Sauer**, and Robert Piatt. While the **environmental determinist** approach has largely been abandoned by modern geographers, the human–environmental relationships and regional studies approaches remain integral to the scientific study of geography today.

Important technologies related to geography that have been developed since the 1970s include remote sensing, the **Global Positioning System (GPS)**, and Geographical Information Systems (GIS). **Remote sensing** is the process of acquiring data about Earth's surface from satellites. This could include the mapping of vegetation, winter ice, or changes in weather patterns or deforestation. A GPS device enables one to determine absolute location through an integrated network of satellites. It also allows geographers to determine distances between two points and is thus a valuable navigational tool. Data about places and location are recorded through geotagging when using electronic devices or digital cameras. GIS enables geographers to map, analyze, and process different pieces of information about a location. These **thematic layers** could include various physical features, transportation infrastructure, and population and settlement patterns and could be analyzed individually or together. Last, the exact location or **absolute location** of a place on Earth's surface can be pinpointed and gives us our global address. Through elaborate contemporary mapping using mashups, geographers can see the unique characteristics that are at each point on the grid. **Geographic Information Systems (GIS)** is a computer-based analysis tool. GIS is especially useful when relationships can be seen among the different layers. This is a more sophisticated and technological version of a thematic map such as a **choropleth map** (a color-coded map used to show the distribution of a geographic phenomena over space).

Scale

The level of detail and the amount of area depicted on a map depends on the scale of the map. The **scale** is the relationship of a feature's size on a map to its actual size on Earth. Scale is one of the most important concepts for human geographers because it can change one's perceptions of a place depending on which scale you are looking at it through. Scale is usually presented by cartographers as a fraction (1/24,000), a ratio (1:24,000), a written statement ("1-inch equals 1 mile"), or a **graphic scale** (equals 1 mile). In a **small-scale map**, the ratio between map units and ground units is small (such as 1:100,000), and since one map unit equals so many of the same units on the ground, these maps tend to cover large regions (such as a map of the United States). In a **large-scale map**, the ratio between map units and ground units is large (such as 1:5,000) and thus cover much smaller regions (such as a map of a city). Many people confuse these two scales; remember that a small-scale map shows a large area without much detail, where as a large-scale map shows a small area in great detail.

Projections

A map can be used as a **reference tool**, to learn where something is found and to navigate from one place to another. Maps can also be used as a **communication tool** to depict the location of human activities and physical features, as well as to explain their distribution. Globes are relatively impractical for these uses; thus, most maps are flat. The scientific method of transferring the Earth to a flat map is called a **projection** and inevitably involves some distortion. The things that are commonly distorted on maps usually involve one or more of the following: the **shape** of an area is distorted, the **distance** between two areas is incorrect, the **relative size** of an area appears larger or smaller than it really is, and the **direction** of a place relative to another can be misleading.

An **equal area projection** shows the relative size of an area even though the shapes are distorted. **Conformal maps** distort area but not shape. The uninterrupted **Robinson projection** allocates space to oceans but shows land areas much smaller than on interrupted maps of the same size. The **Mercator projection** minimizes the distortion of shape and direction but grossly distorts the area toward the poles, making high latitude places look much larger than they actually are. The interrupted **Goode Homolosine Projection**, often referred to as the "orange peel map," is good at mapping human phenomena across space.

Maps Are Used for Interpretation

The exact location or absolute location of a place on Earth's surface can be pinpointed on a standard grid or **coordinate system**. This universally accepted system of **latitude** and **longitude** consists of imaginary arcs on a globe. Lines of longitude or **meridians** are drawn between the North and South Poles according to a numbering system. 0° is the **prime meridian,** which passes through the Royal Observatory at Greenwich, Great Britain. The meridian on the opposite side of the globe is 180° longitude and is called the **International Date Line.** Lines of latitude or **parallels** are circles drawn around the globe parallel to the **equator**. The grid system is especially useful for determining location where there has been no human settlement.

Maps help interpret the arrangement and relationships of places and are used to illustrate spatial data. Different types of maps are used to display the distribution of data. Isolines connect places of the same value, whereas dot maps, graduated symbol maps, and choropleth maps use graduated size or shading to reflect the amount of data in a particular place. It is essential to be able to interpret this type of spatial data in addition to understanding how the data are derived.

Key Issues Revisited

1.1. Why Is Geography a Science?

- Geographers use maps to display the location of objects and to get information about places.

- Early geographers drew maps of the Earth based on exploration and observation.

- GIS and other contemporary technological tools help geographers to understand what they see on Earth's surface.

- The geographic grid system determines the location of a place and tells time, and thematic maps illustrate data that explain a phenomena in a place.

Review Questions

1.1.1. The most important tool to help geographer think spatially is a:
A. census.
B. map.
C. stick model.
D. satellite.
E. survey.

1.1.2. He invented the word *geography* and calculated the circumference of the Earth within .5 percent accuracy.
A. Pei Xiu
B. Ibn Battuta
C. Ptolemy
D. Eratosthenes
E. Columbus

1.1.3. What type of technology allows for analysis of Earth data acquired through satellite and other electronic information technologies?
A. GPS
B. GIS
C. Remote sensing
D. Landsat
E. Isopleth

1.1.4. Which of the following is not a factor of distortion on a map projection?
A. Direction
B. Relative size
C. Distance
D. Space
E. Shape

1.1.5 What happens to the time if you are traveling west and cross the 180° longitude?
A. You turn the clock ahead 24 hours.
B. You turn the clock back 24 hours.
C. You change the clock 1 hour backward.
D. You change the clock 1 hour forward.
E. The time does not change.

KEY ISSUE 2

Why Is Every Place Unique?

Learning Outcome 1.2.1: Identify the distinctive features of a place.
Location is the position something occupies on Earth. Geographers identify a place's location using place names, site, and situation.

Learning Outcome 1.2.2: Identify the three types of regions.
A **formal region** is an area within which everyone shares distinctive characteristics. A **functional region** is an area organized around a node. A **vernacular region** is an area that people believe exists.

Learning Outcome 1.2.3: Explain two geographic elements in defining culture.
Culture can refer to cultural values such as language and religion, or to material culture such as food, clothing, and shelter.

A **place** is the description of a specific point on Earth's surface; it includes the human and physical features that make it unique. When most people are going on vacation, this is what they subliminally think of: What is the place like? What will I do there? What will the weather be like? All these questions help explain a place's unique characteristics. Geographers identify the location of places on Earth in one of four ways—place-names, site, situation, and absolute location. All inhabited places on Earth's surface have been given place-names or **toponyms**. Place-names may tell us about historical origins, such as "Battle" in southern England which is named for the Battle of Hastings. They can also give us an indication of the physical environment such as Aberystwyth in Wales, which means "mouth of the River Ystwyth" or the city of Delta Junction at the Delta of the Tanana River in Alaska. Place-names may speak religion, such as Islamabad, Pakistan, and Christchurch, New Zealand or economics such as Gold Point, Nevada and Hershey, Pennsylvania. Place-names also change because of political turmoil. The city that was Leningrad in Russia during the Communist era has now been changed back to St. Petersburg.

Site refers to the specific physical characteristics of a place. Site factors such as hilltop, river, and island locations have been important in the historical origins of settlements. The site of Singapore, for example, is a small, swampy island near to the southern tip of the Malay Peninsula. Site characteristics can be modified to a certain extent by humans.

Situation or **relative location** describes a place's relationship relative to other places around it. Gibraltar's relative location near the Strait of Gibraltar, which is a major passageway between the Mediterranean and the Atlantic Ocean, has had strategic importance for centuries.

A **region** is generally defined as an area containing unifying cultural and/or physical characteristics. Regions are sometimes referred to as a "world within a world" because geographers are trying to categorize and make sense of a large area, thus they are looking for common characteristics found within each. The concept is controversial because geographers will debate what exactly makes a region. However, a region is important as a basic unit of geographic research and an area that can be examined geographically. Geographers have identified three types of regions: formal, functional, and vernacular.

A formal region is also called a **uniform region** or a **homogeneous region** because it has specific characteristics that are fairly uniform throughout that region. For example, South Korea is a political region, easily identified on a map and also with a very homogenous culture, Korean. Montana is an example of a formal region formed by legal delineated boundaries. The Rocky Mountains constitute a physical region stretching through the United States and Canada. North Africa and the Southwest Asia constitute a formal region characterized by a desert climate as well as an Arab/Islamic culture.

A functional region is also called a **nodal region** because it is defined by a social or economic function that occurs between a node or focal point and its surrounding areas. For example, the circulation area of the *New York Times* is a functional region and New York is the node. Television stations function as a nodal point and their broadcast reception area is the functional region.

A vernacular region or **perceptual region** is one that exists in people's minds such as the American "South." When individuals are asked to draw a boundary around this region, their boundary will probably be based on stereotypes they associate with the South such as climate, accent, cuisine, and religious practices such as Southern Baptist. It would be difficult to determine the precise boundary of the South. One's attachment to a region perceived as home is sometimes called a **sense of place**. Sometimes people can identify their perceptual region by envisioning or drawing a **mental map**. A mental map is an internal representation of a place on Earth's surface.

Geographers study why the customary ideas, beliefs, and values of a people produce a distinctive culture in a particular place. Geographers study culture to examine what people care about and what people take care of. Culture evolves out of language, religion, and ethnicity. Communication of cultural values and identification of certain words with particular meanings shape the culture of a group of people. The geographic study of religion examines the distribution of religious groups and the ways that various groups interact with their environment. Geographers look at ethnicity because that encompasses a group's language, religion, and values with common physical attributes. Food, clothing, and shelter encompass the material wealth of a culture. The world is divided into the developed and developing world to distinguish the ability to secure and maintain the elements of a material culture. These elements are also dependent on the role of the government and the economy as these can facilitate or hinder the access to elements of a material culture. The spatial association within a place and among places contribute to the unique culture and regional identification.

Key Issues Revisited

1.2. Why Is Every Place Unique?

- Every place in the world has a unique location on Earth's surface identified by name, site, and situation.

- Geographers identify regions as areas distinguished by a distinctive combination of cultural, economic, and environmental features which helps us to understand why every region and place is unique.

- Culture encompasses what people value, identify with, and can observe through association.

Review Questions

1.2.1. When giving directions to a person, if we say "my house is **located** past the firehouse," we are describing:
A. site.
B. distance.
C. situation.
D. toponym.
E. absolute location.

1.2.2. A mental map is a good way to represent what type of region?
A. Formal region
B. Functional region
C. Vernacular region
D. Economic region
E. Political region

1.2.3 The reason why each region on Earth is distinctive is because of the:
A. topography.
B. history.
C. people.
D. culture.
E. cartography.

KEY ISSUE 3

Why Are Different Places Similar?

Learning Outcome 1.3.1: Relate the geographic concept of scale to economic and culture change.
Globalization means that the scale of the world is shrinking in terms of economy and culture.

Learning Outcome 1.3.2: Compare the three properties of distribution.
Density is the frequency with which something occurs, concentration is the extent of spread, and pattern is the geometric arrangement.

Learning Outcome 1.3.3: Summarize geographic thought, with application to the geography of inequality.
Geographers respect cultural diversity and seek to understand the spatial elements of cultural inequality.

Learning Outcome 1.3.4: Analyze geographic approaches to important elements of cultural identity.
Spatial patterns vary according to gender, ethnicity, and sexuality.

Learning Outcome 1.3.5: Discuss geographic approaches to ethnicity and sexuality as important elements of cultural identity.
Gender, ethnicity, and sexual identification use and access space differently.

Learning Outcome 1.3.6: Describe the various ways that features can spread through diffusion.
Something originates at a hearth and diffuses through either relocation diffusion (physical movement) or expansion diffusion (additive processes).

Learning Outcome 1.3.7: Explain how places are connected through networks.
Electronic communications have removed many physical barriers to interaction for those with access to them.

Spatial interaction and interdependence have become increasingly important concepts in geography because of globalization. Globalization is the process through which the world is becoming interdependent on a **global scale** and events on a smaller scale are less important. Globalization produces a more uniform world at a global scale and an opposite response at a local scale of preserving unique and distinctive characteristics. Some might argue that through globalization, we are entering a monoculture, where everyone eats at McDonald's, wears the same brand of jeans, and speaks the same language. Globalization is creating a more homogeneous culture that is also causing an attempt to preserve distinctive cultural characteristics while **glocalization** is attempting to preserve the local through accommodating the global aspects.

Economic globalization has led to an increase in **transnational corporations** (also known as multinational corporations) that invest and operate in many countries. Modern communication and transportation systems have made it much easier to move economic assets around the world. Economically some places are more connected than others because they can supply specialized goods or services within their location. **Complementarity** is the degree to which one place can supply something that another place needs. The concept of **intervening opportunities** also helps explain connectivity. It is the idea that if one place has a demand for something and there are two potential suppliers, the closer supplier will represent an intervening opportunity because transportation costs will be less. Thus, **accessibility** is an important factor in costs and interaction between places. **Transferability** refers to the costs involved in moving goods from one place to another. There will generally be more interaction among things that are closer than those that are further away. This is Tobler's First Law of Geography or the **friction of distance**. Contact will diminish with increasing distance until it ultimately disappears. This is called **distance decay**.

Ideally, the multinational corporation will locate in a place that has good accessibility to markets and suppliers can complement the industry with needed materials and transferability of those materials and goods is funded through compatible market economies. However, the further away from a market or source of materials the cost will be affected by distance decay.

Space and Pattern

Distribution refers to the spatial arrangement of something across Earth's surface. The three main properties of distribution are density, concentration, and pattern. Density is the frequency with which something occurs in an area. The density of anything could be measured, but in the context of human geography, it is usually population. The way in which a feature is spread over an area is its **concentration.** Objects that are closer together are **clustered** and those that are further apart are

dispersed. Again, geographers usually use the concept of concentration in the context of population. **Pattern** is the geometric arrangement of objects, which could be regular or irregular. For example, geographers could describe the regular pattern of streets in American and Canadian cities as a grid pattern.

Geographers study the distribution of cultural traits and demographic data to study spatial patterns at different levels of scale. Distribution patterns of ethnicity are best examined at a local scale in order to analyze where and why certain clusters occur. The clustering of certain demographic characteristics can be correlated, and others will not show any correlation. For example, long life expectancy and higher income have a positive correlation and will be clustered together while a negative correlation exists between population increase and growth of average income.

Geographer's understanding of spatial distribution is rooted in an understanding of cultural diversity and a deep respect of all cultural groups. In the modern world, unequal access to electronic communications creates barriers to interaction, restricting connectivity and accessibility as well as increasing the friction of distance thus creating an isolation of a culture and a population. The global culture is centered on the hearths of North America, Europe, and Japan. Advanced technology, investment capital, and wealth make London, New York City, and Tokyo the pivot points of global economics and modern telecommunications. Places on the periphery of this modern "global core" experience an **uneven development** from lack of globalization.

The patterns of uneven development, discrimination, and the use of space as a result of the actions of ruling parties has led to the development of poststructuralist geography. This postmodern perspective examines the increasing gap in economic conditions from local to global scales, reasons for uneven development, inequality between and within countries, gender, ethnicity, and cultural identity patterns.

Spatial diffusion describes the way that phenomena, such as technological ideas, cultural innovations, disease, or economic goods, travel over space. Ideas, innovations, and cultural characteristics diffuse from their origins known as a **hearth. Relocation diffusion** or **migration diffusion** refers to the physical movement of people from one place to another. It will be discussed later in the context of migration.

Expansion diffusion is the spread of something in a snowballing process. There are three types of expansion diffusion. **Hierarchical diffusion** is the spread of an idea from one node of power and authority to another. For example, trends in music, fashion, and art are more likely to diffuse hierarchically from one key city to another (such as from New York to Los Angeles). **Contagious diffusion** is the rapid and widespread diffusion of something throughout a population because of proximity, such as a contagious disease like influenza. **Stimulus diffusion** is the spread of a principle rather than a specific characteristic, such as the certain features of an iPad that are now common on competitor's products.

As a result of globalization, there is now greater communication between distant places. **Time–space compression** describes the reduction in time that it takes to diffuse something to a distant place. However, technology may stimulate a time–space compression distance decay that causes a decrease in contact when the distance is far away and when alternatives for contact are present.

Geographers study the connections among cultural groups. The way that different cultural groups blend or resist affects the connections, which can occur with a broader, global world. When a group's cultural features are altered to resemble those of another group, the second group has **assimilated** into the first. However, when two cultural groups interact and changes happen within each cultural group, then the process of **acculturation** has occurred. If the two cultural groups blend to create a new culture, then they have developed a **syncretic culture**.

Key Issues Revisited

1.3. Why Are Different Places Similar?

- Geographers examine at all scales however are increasingly concerned with the global scale.

- Places display similarities because they are connected to each other and phenomena spread through relocation and expansion diffusion.

- Geographers study the interactions among people and human activities across space and identify the different processes by which people and ideas diffuse from one place to another over time.

Review Questions

1.3.1. Globalization means that the scale of the world is:
A. increasing.
B. not affected.
C. shrinking.
D. status quo.
E. the same.

1.3.2. The extent of a feature's spread over space is:
A. density.
B. distribution.
C. concentration.
D. area.
E. pattern.

1.3.3. The economic gap between the core and the periphery is known as:
A. poverty.
B. inequality.
C. uneven development.
D. acculturation.
E. distribution.

1.3.4 Which measurement is not part of the gender gap?
A. Economic participation and opportunity
B. Health and life expectancy
C. Total fertility rate
D. Political empowerment
E. Level of education attained

1.3.5. What do geographers study to explain why people occupy certain space and move across the landscape in specific patterns?
A. Cultural identity
B. Cultural density
C. Cultural orientation
D. Cultural isolation
E. Cultural diffusion

1.3.6. Which of the following does not result from an expansion process from one place to another?
A. Hierarchical diffusion
B. Stimulus diffusion
C. Contagious diffusion
D. Relocation diffusion
E. None results from expansion

1.3.7. The farther away someone is from another, the less likely the two are to interact is known as:
A. syncretic diffusion.
B. network.
C. space–time compression.
D. distance decay.
E. peripheral relationship.

KEY ISSUE 4

Why Are Some Human Actions Not Sustainable?

Learning Outcome 1.4.1: Describe the three pillars of sustainability.
Sustainability is the use of Earth's natural resources in ways that ensures their availability in the future. This is accomplished through a combination of environmental, economic, and social action.

Learning Outcome 1.4.2: Explain Earth's three abiotic physical systems.
Earth comprises three abiotic and one biotic physical systems: the atmosphere, hydrosphere and lithosphere are abiotic physical systems, whereas biosphere is a biotic physical system.

Learning Outcome 1.4.3: Explain how the biosphere interacts with Earth's abiotic systems.
An ecosystem comprises a group of living organisms in the biosphere and their interaction with the atmosphere, lithosphere, and hydrosphere.

Learning Outcome 1.4.4: Compare ecosystems in the Netherlands and South Africa.
The ecological modification of the Netherlands is more sustainable than that of South Africa.

Human geographers must focus on the relationship between the physical environment and the humans that live there. Most human geographers focus on the concept of sustainability, using Earth's resources (**both renewable** and **nonrenewable**) in ways that ensure their availability for future generations. The United Nations recognizes the need for **sustainable development** and has embraced the idea of bringing together the environment, the economy, and society.

According to the United Nations, sustainability is achieved through the cooperation of environmental, social, and economic sectors to meet the demands of future generations. Sustainability requires reducing the use of nonrenewable resources and limiting the use of renewable resources to the level that the environment can continue to provide these resources indefinitely. Sustainability can only be achieved by supporting the interrelationship among environmental protection, economic growth, and social equity. The key to sustaining the environment is **conservation**. Conservation calls for management of natural resources by using less today in order to provide for future generations. The need for society is to make conscientious choices in regard to consumption and waste of resources based on actual need and not over consumption. The social factor calls for a change in the resources used for food, shelter, and clothing. The economic factor of sustainability is determined by supply and demand in a market economy. The greater the supply, the lower the price; the greater the demand, the higher the price. Ultimately, the price of a resource depends on a society's technological ability to obtain it and to adapt to the needs of society.

The global economy will adjust with the market for natural resources and will allow resources to be more affordable to the majority of people in the world. Although all humans need food, shelter, and clothing, the choices consumers make will aid in sustainable development. If people choose recycled items, or clothes made of natural products, their choices might slow down the resource depletion that is currently happening due to consumerism around the globe.

The Earth is divided into four physical systems: atmosphere, hydrosphere, lithosphere, and the biosphere. The atmosphere includes the gaseous layer surrounding the Earth. The hydrosphere includes all of the fresh and salt water which makes up 78% of the planet. The lithosphere, which is the Earth's crust and a portion of the upper mantle, shapes the surface. The biosphere includes all the living organisms. The biosphere is a biotic system of all living organisms. The other three systems are classified as abiotic. Human geographers are interested in the operations of the **ecosystem,** namely, how all living organisms and the abiotic spheres (atmosphere, lithosphere, and hydrosphere) interact with one another. The biosphere is a source of food, clothing, and shelter, the atmosphere is the source of air that we breathe, the hydrosphere is the water that we need to live, and the lithosphere is the source of fuel, and it shapes the landscape.

Human geographers are concerned with the way in which cultural groups modify the environment around them. Cultural ecology is the study of human–environment relationships. There are two schools of thought that examine the role of the environment and the interaction with the human realm. Alexander von Humboldt and Carl Ritter followed the school of thought of environmental determinism and encouraged the adoption of scientific inquiry when analyzing the relationships between the physical environment and human actions. Other influential geographers applied the perspective of environmental determinism to explain that geography was the study of the influences of the natural environment on people. Further arguments by Ellsworth Huntington asserted that climate was a major determinant of the success or failure of a civilization.

Environmental determinism has been rejected by some in favor of possibilism. Possibilism argues that the physical environment may limit some human actions, but people have the ability to adjust to their environment. One of the best examples of possibilism is agricultural production and the influence of climate. People choose to plant the crops they grow in a given climate based on the amount that the crop will yield. Human geographers use the cultural ecology to understand the particular patterns and processes and whether they are sustainable.

Comparing ecosystems in the Netherlands and South Africa provide an investigation into the sustainability of the land after human modification of the land. Both areas involved modifying the environment to address their water concerns. In the case of the Netherlands, the reclamation of land from the seas to convert to productive farmland proved to be effective but now faces challenges from sea level rise. Cape Town, South Africa has created an unstable ecosystem from the needs to provide a water supply in a changing climatic environment. Once regarded as a leader in sustainable resource use, a two-year drought and inconsistent winter snow melt have left the city with an uncertain ability to provide for the water needs of the population.

Key Issues Revisited

1.4. Why Are Some Human Actions Not Sustainable?

- Sustainability combines environment, economic systems, and society.
- The abiotic systems of the Earth influence and interact with the biotic systems.
- The abiotic systems include the hydrosphere, atmosphere, and lithosphere while the biotic system includes the biosphere and all living elements.
- Human actions on Earth have, in many cases, led to most of the environmental degradation that we now see on Earth.

Review Questions

1.4.1. All living systems on Earth would be found in the:
A. lithosphere.
B. atmosphere.
C. hydrosphere.
D. biosphere.
E. climosphere.

1.4.2. Which of the following is NOT one of the physical systems of the planet?
A. Lithosphere
B. Atmosphere
C. Hydrosphere
D. Biosphere
E. Climosphere

1.4.3. The belief that the environment causes social development is known as:
A. psychology.
B. ecology.
C. environmental determinism.
D. possibilism.
E. sustainability.

1.4.4. A sustainable ecosystem:
A. uses all available surface waters to meet the demands for today's population.
B. creates a natural balance between the humans and the environment in a natural process.
C. adjust uses of elements in a physical environment today to ensure there is an environment that can be used in the future.
D. produces enough products to meet the demands of the modern society.
E. is one that can be modified as the environment changes in order to maintain its productivity.

Key Terms

Absolute location*
Accessibility
Alternative resources
Cartography
Choropleth map
Clustered*
Complementarity*
Concentration
Conformal maps
Conservation
Contagious diffusion*
Coordinate system
Cultural*
Cultural landscape*
Ecology
Density*
Diffusion*
Dispersed*
Distance decay*
Distribution
Environmental determinism*
Equal area projection
Expansion diffusion*
Formal region*
Friction of distance
Functional region*
Geographic Information Systems (GIS)*
Global Positioning System (GPS)
Globalization*
Globalizing forces
Goode Homolosine Projection
Hearth*
Hierarchical diffusion*
Homogeneous region
Intervening opportunities*
Large-scale map
Latitude
Location*
Longitude
Map*

Map as a communication tool
Map as a reference tool
Map projection
Mercator projection
Meridians
Migration diffusion*
Nodal region
Nonrenewable resource
Parallels
Pattern
Perceptual region*
Place
Possibilism*
Prime meridian
Region*
Relative location*
Relocation diffusion*
Remote sensing*
Renewable resource
Robinson projection
Scale*
Sense of place*
Site*
Situation*
Small-scale map
Soil depletion*
Space*
Spatial association*
Spatial diffusion*
Spatial interaction*
Spatial perspective*
Stimulus diffusion*
Sustainability*
Thematic map*
Time–space compression*
Toponyms*
Transferability
Transnational corporations*
Uniform region
Vernacular region*

* Term is in 2019 College Board Curriculum & Exam Description.

Think Like a Geographer Activities

Geographers examine spatial relationships. Are there connections with places that have unique phenomena occurring even if they are miles away from each other? Can you identify such a phenomenon and make a connection with other places it is occurring? Let's try.

Go to www.cdc.gov/dhdsp/maps/national_maps/ and look at the maps on this site dealing with heart disease and strokes among adults in America. Now search for maps showing fast food restaurants in the United States and obesity rates; explain if there appears to be a correlation. Do your maps look similar for these phenomena?

Quick Quiz

1.1. What is a geographer's most important tool for thinking spatially?
A. Remote sensing
B. Global positioning satellites
C. Globes
D. Mashups
E. Maps

1.2. A toponym is:
A. a physical characteristic of a place.
B. the location of a place in relationship to another place.
C. a name given to a place on Earth.
D. the characteristics that make a place distinct.
E. mathematical grid used to find a place.

1.3. Functional or nodal regions are now being less important because of:
A. redistricting.
B. redlining.
C. technology.
D. blockbusting.
E. culture.

1.4. Spatial association requires geographers to look at the distribution of phenomena:
A. on a national, state, and urban (local) scale.
B. only on a national scale.
C. only at a state scale.
D. at a global scale.
E. on a global and national scale only.

1.5. A transnational corporation:
A. conducts research.
B. operates factories.
C. sells products.
D. does business in many countries.
E. All of these are correct.

1.6. The pillars of sustainability include:
A. things that are non-tangible and are only hoped for.
B. creating laws with rigid consequences.
C. bringing together environmental protection, economic growth, and social equity.
D. education for all children.
E. equal access to clean water.

1.7. The school of thought that says that the physical environment may limit some actions but people can adjust to their environment is:
A. environmental determinism.
B. possibilism.
C. sustainable geography.
D. cultural ecology.
E. gaia hypothesis.

1.8. A topographic map shows:
A. the type of climate.
B. the different types of crops that are raised in an area.
C. the alteration to the landscape caused by humans.
D. the natural landscape as caused by natural and human processes.
E. the size of landmasses in relation to others.

1.9. A large-scale map would best illustrate:
A. connections among world cities.
B. highways connecting regions in a country.
C. farm to market roads connecting rural areas to the city.
D. freeway routes in a large city.
E. neighborhood streets in a suburb.

1.10. Which of the following is responsible for space–time compression?
A. Accommodation
B. Globalization
C. Regionalization
D. Syncretization
E. Modification

Free Response

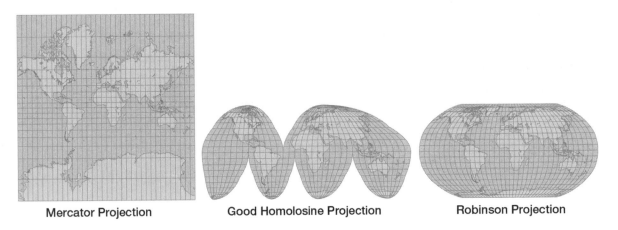

Figure 1-1 Projection

Transferring the locations on Earth's surface is called projection. The problem with projecting a round sphere to a flat plane is that it causes distortion.

1. Describe the four types of distortion using the maps above for reference.
2. Explain one reason for the use of each type of projection.

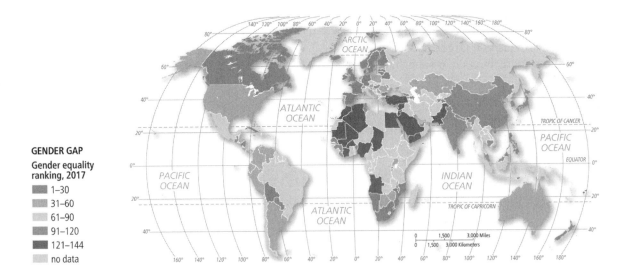

Question:
1. Identify one country in Africa and one country in Asia that have the lowest gender equality.
2. Using an example, explain one social reason for a low gender equality.
3. Using an example, explain one economic reason for a high gender equality.
4. Using an example, explain one political reason for a high gender equality.

On the Web

Websites that support this topic:

www.masteringgeography.com

www.nationalgeographic.com

www.worldatlas.com

www.google.com/earth/index.html

www.globalcitizen.org/en/content/whats-in-a-map-facts-half-truths-and-outright-lies/

www.youtube.com/watch?v=5SnR-e0S6Ic **Globalization 1 The Upside**

www.youtu.be/dldHalRY-hY **42 Amazing Maps**

TED Talks

TED Talks that support this topic:

Steven Johnson Tours the Ghost Map 1

www.ted.com/talks/lang/eng/steven_johnson_tours_the_ghost_map.html

Key Figures

Reference the following figures from Chapter 1 in your textbook in order to help you study and prepare for your exam.

Figure 1-2 Panama Region

Figure 1-16 Map Scale

Figure 1-17 Winkel Projection

Figure 1-18 Mercator Projection

Figure 1-19 Goode Homolosine Projection

Figure 1-20 Gall-Peters Projection

Figure 1-21 Geographic Grid

Figure 1-23 Isoline Map

Figure 1-24 Dot Distribution Map

Figure 1-25 Choropleth Map

Figure 1-26 Graduated Symbol Map

Figure 1-27 Cartogram

Figure 1-29 Changing Site of Boston

Figure 1-30 Situation of Gibraltar

Figure 1-32 Formal Region: Indigenous Peoples and Languages of Alaska

Figure 1-33 Function Regions: Florida TV Markets

Figure 1-35 Vernacular Region: The South

Figure 1-52 Gender Gap

Figure 1-53 Distribution by Gender: Female Income as a Percentage of Male Income by Country

Figure 1-59 Relocation Diffusion

Figure 1-60 Hierarchical Diffusion

Figure 1-63 Space-Time Compression

Figure 1-68 Three Pillars of Sustainability

Figure 1-70 Climate Regions

Figure 1-78 Time Zones

AP® Human Geography Outline of Thinking Geographically

Unit 1: Thinking Geographically

Topic	APHG Topic No. Title	Suggested Skills	Enduring Understandings	Learning Objective	Big Ideas
1.1.1; 1.2.1; 1.2.3	1.4: Spatial Concepts	3.B: Describe spatial patterns presented in maps and in quantitative and geospatial data.	PSO-1: Geographers analyze relationships among and between places to reveal important spatial patterns	PSO-1.A: Define major geographic concepts that illustrate spatial relationships	BI-1 Patterns and spatial organization
1.1.2; 1.1.4; 1.1.5	1.1: Introduction to Maps	3.A: Identify the different types of data presented in maps and in quantitative and geospatial data.	IMP-1: Geographers use maps and data to depict relationships or time, space, and scale	IMP-1A: Identify types of maps, the types of information presented in maps, and different kinds of spatial patterns and relationships portrayed in maps	BI-2 Impacts and Interactions
1.1.3	1.2: Geographic Data	3.A: Identify the different types of data presented in maps and in quantitative and geospatial data.	IMP-1: Geographers use maps and data to depict relationships or time, space, and scale	IMP-1.B: Identify different methods of geographic data collection	BI-2 Impacts and Interactions
1.2.2	1.7: Regional Analysis	1.A: Describe geographic concepts, processes, models, and theories.	SPS-1: Geographers analyze complex issues and relationships with a distinctively spatial perspective	SPS-1.A: Describe different ways that geographers define regions	BI-3 Spatial Processes and Societal Change
1.3.1; 1.3.2	1.6: Scales of Analysis	5.A: Identify the scales of analysis presented by maps in quantitative and geospatial data, images, and landscapes.	PSO-1: Geographers analyze relationships among and between places to reveal important spatial patterns	PSO-1.C: Define scales of analysis used by geographers	BI-1 Patterns and spatial organization

1.3.3	1.6: Scales of Analysis	5.A: Identify the scales of analysis presented by maps in quantitative and geospatial data, images, and landscapes.	PSO-1: Geographers analyze relationships among and between places to reveal important spatial patterns	PSO-1.D: Explain what scales of analysis reveal	BI-1 Patterns and spatial organization
1.3.4; 1.3.5	1.3: The Power of Geographic Data	3.B: Describe spatial patterns presented in maps and in quantitative and geospatial data.	IMP-1: Geographers use maps and data to depict relationships of time, space, and scale	IMP-1.C: Explain the geographical effects of decisions made using geographical information	BI-2 Impacts and Interactions
1.3.6; 1.3.7	1.4: Spatial Concepts	3.B: Describe spatial patterns presented in maps and in quantitative and geospatial data.	PSO-1: Geographers analyze relationships among and between places to reveal important spatial patterns	PSO-1.A: Define major geographic concepts that illustrate spatial relationships	BI-1 Patterns and spatial organization
1.4.1; 1.4.2; 1.4.3; 1.4.4	1.5: Human Environmental Interaction	1.B: Explain geographic concepts, processes, models, and theories.	PSO-1: Geographers analyze relationships among and between places to reveal important spatial patterns	PSO-1.B: Explain how major geographic concepts illustrate spatial relationships	BI-1 Patterns and spatial organization

Source: College Board AP® Human Geography Curriculum Framework, 2019

FRQ's From College Board

2003 FRQ #2
2009 FRQ #1

Chapter

2 Population & Health

Where Are People Distributed?

This chapter describes where the world's population is distributed, the spatial distribution of livable areas of the Earth's surface, and where population is growing. The chapter explains why population is growing at different rates in different regions. Factors influencing population growth, the role of gender, health, and an aging population are linked to factors of development and differ at local and national levels of scale. This chapter discusses the extent to which certain regions of the world may be facing population challenges in the future.

> **Learning Outcome 2.1.1: Describe the distribution of the world's population.**
> The world's population can be divided into seven portions of 1 billion each.
>
> **Learning Outcome 2.1.2: Contrast regions of high and low population concentrations.**
> Two-thirds of the world's people live in four clusters—East Asia, South Asia, Europe, and Southeast Asia.
>
> **Learning Outcome 2.1.3: Compare different approaches to measuring density.**
> Arithmetic density is used to describe where people live in the world. Physiological density compares population to resources. Agricultural density measures economic efficiency of food production.

The relationship between the World's population and its ability to sustain a growing population is the basis of understanding the carrying capacity of the planet and predicting for the future needs of the population. The study of population geography, or **demography**, is very important because there are more than 7.2 billion people alive today, the growth of the world's population has been most rapid in the last century, and the fastest growth today is in the developing world. Population-related issues are key to other chapters, especially development, agriculture, and urbanization.

The global scale of world population is generalized. The analysis of population patterns at different scales—including continental, national, state, provincial, and local—will reveal different trends and patterns. Two-thirds of the world's population is clustered in four regions—East Asia, South Asia, Europe, and Southeast Asia. The clustering of the world's population can be shown on a **cartogram**, which depicts the size of countries according to population rather than land area (Figure 2-5 in your textbook). Approximately two-thirds of the world's population lives within 500 kilometers of an ocean. China and India each have over a billion people and together hold over one-third of the world's population. The largest percentages of people in Asia live in rural areas, whereas three-quarters of all Europeans live in towns and cities. The harsh physical environments of Earth's surface, including deserts, tropical rainforests, mountains, and polar regions, are sparsely populated. The portion of the Earth's surface occupied by permanent human settlement is called the **ecumene**, and uninhabited area the **nonecumene**.

Arithmetic density (also called **population density**) is a misleading measure of the distribution of people because it is the total number of people divided by the total land area. For example, to say that the arithmetic population density of Egypt is 84 people per square kilometer hides the fact that the vast majority of that country's population lives in the delta and valley of the Nile River, and much of the country is virtually uninhabited.

Physiological density is a more useful measure of population because it is the number of people supported by a unit area of arable land or the ecumene. The physiological population density of Egypt is 3,350 people per square kilometer, which is a better measurement of the pressure on agricultural land in that country.

Agricultural density is the ratio of the number of farmers to the amount of agricultural land. Countries like Canada and the United States have much lower agricultural densities than less-developed countries like India and Bangladesh. In more-developed countries, technology related to agriculture allows a few farmers to work huge area of land and feed many people. This is an indicator of economic development because farmers can afford and have access to large farm equipment and extensive farmland to cultivate. Thus, agricultural density and physiological density are good measures of the relationship between population and resources, together with the level of development in a country.

Key Issues Revisited

2.1. Where Are People Distributed?

- The world's population is concentrated in four regions.

- People tend to avoid places that they consider to be too wet, too dry, too cold, or too mountainous.

- Population density and distribution can be described in arithmetic, physiological, and agricultural perspectives.

Review Questions

2.1.1. The study of populations is:
A. physiography.
B. democracy.
C. demography.
D. ethnography.
E. biology.

2.1.2. Most of the world's population is clustered into these four areas:
A. East Asia, South Asia, Europe, and Southeast Asia
B. Europe, East Asia, South Asia, and Africa
C. East Asia, South Asia, Southeast Asia, and Africa
D. South Asia, Southeast Asia, Europe, and Africa
E. South Asia, Southeast Asia, East Asia, and Europe

2.1.3. Which measurement connects population density and level of development within a country?
A. Agricultural density
B. Physiological density
C. Arithmetic density
D. Ecumene
E. Non-ecumene

Why Is Population Increasing?

Learning Outcome 2.2.1: Summarize historical and current rates of population increase.
The **natural increase rate (NIR)** is the percentage by which a population grows in a year: (CBR–CDR)/1,000.

Learning Outcome 2.2.2: Compare global patterns of births and deaths.
Population increases in places where more people are born than die, and it declines in places where deaths outnumber births.

Learning Outcome 2.2.3: Explain the stages of the demographic transition model.
The demographic transition is a process of change in a society's population from high crude birth and death rates to a condition of low crude birth and death rates and a higher total population. A society moves through demographic transition as development status changes.

The crude birth rate, crude death rate, and natural increase rate are used to measure population change in a country. The **crude birth rate (CBR)** or **natality rate** and **crude death rate (CDR)** are statistical terms that refer to the total number of live births and deaths, respectively, per thousand people in a country. Where the CBR is higher than the CDR, natural increase, measured by the natural increase rate (NIR), occurs. This does not account for migration. If the CDR is about the same as the CBR, a country has **zero population growth (ZPG)**. If the CDR is higher than the CBR, there is a **negative NIR**. The **demographic equation** is the global difference between births and deaths: (CBR–CDR)/1,000 = NIR. See the maps in Figures 2-19 and 2-20 and compare the mortality rates among the countries.

Currently, the world rate of natural increase is 1.07 percent which means that the world's population is growing each year by 1.07 percent. It would take the world 65 years to double its population given this rate of growth; this is called **doubling time**. During the 1960s and 1970s, the world's doubling time was about 35 years because the NIR was 2.2 percent.

There are major regional differences in rates of population growth. The NIR exceeds 2 percent in many countries in sub-Saharan Africa. Most of the world's population growth is now in developing countries, while the more-developed regions are experiencing the lowest (in some cases, negative) growth rates. For example, Germany has a NIR of – 0.2 percent.

The highest crude birth rates are in Africa and the lowest are in Europe and North America. The **total fertility rate (TFR)** is used by demographers to measure the number of births in a country. The TFR is the average number of children a woman will have during her childbearing years (ages 15 through 49). In some cases, like in Angola, the TFR exceeds six. China, the most populous country in the world, implemented government restrictions to lower its population growth rates. However, the country ended its "One-Child Only" policy in 2016. India will soon surpass China as the most populous country in the world, as it does not have any government-imposed fertility restrictions.

The **infant mortality rate (IMR)** is the annual number of infant deaths under one year of age, compared with total live births, and is usually expressed as number of deaths per 1,000 births. IMR is a measure of a country's level of health care, and the highest rates are in less developed countries. The other useful measure of mortality is **life expectancy**. This is the number of years a newborn infant can expect to live at current mortality levels. Life expectancy rates are sometimes twice as high in developed countries than in developing countries. For instance, the life expectancy in Sierra Leone is only 50.1 years, whereas in Japan it is 83.7 years.

The **demographic transition model** explains changes in the natural increase rate as a function of economic development. It illustrates the change in birth and death rates in relation to economic development of a country. Proposed in 1929, the model examined the change in the natural increase rate of developed countries over a 200 years period of time. The model is a process with four stages, and every country is in stage 2–4 today. However, in a postindustrial world, an emerging fifth stage has developed as populations decline with predominate old-age mortality. Stage 1 of the demographic transition is one of high birth rates and death rates and consequently very low growth. Most of human history was spent in stage 1, but no countries remain in that stage today. Stage 2 is one of high growth or **demographic momentum** because death rates decline and birth rates remain high. Demographic momentum will be sustained because of a relatively young population. The demographic transition assumes that countries enter stage 2 because they go through an **industrial revolution**. Technologies associated with industrial production helped countries to produce more food and improve sanitation and health. Western European countries and North America entered stage 2 after 1750. Countries in Latin America, Asia, and Africa have experienced stage 2 much more recently, without experiencing an industrial revolution. The rapid increase in population associated with stage 2 is often referred to as a **population explosion**. Developing countries have moved into stage 2 because of a global medical revolution (**epidemiological transition**), the diffusion of medical technologies to less developed countries (LDCs). This infusion of global aid includes providing better access to safe water, food security, and medical practitioners. The sudden decline in death rates that comes from technological innovations causes a decline in infant mortalities, an expansion of life expectancies, and, ultimately, a decline in crude birth rates.

Countries will move from stage 2 to stage 3 when their crude birth rates drop sharply as a result of changes in social and economic patterns, as well as government policies that encourage people to have fewer children. The demographic transition assumes that people in stage 3 are more likely to live in an urban and industrial world with few children. Chile is in stage 3 of the demographic transition. The drop in birth rates that comes with changes in social customs has yet to be achieved in many countries.

Countries will reach stage 4 of the demographic transition when their birth rates continue to decline and the natural increase rate drops to zero. In stage 4, death rates fluctuate and exceed birth rates; however, the mortality is old-age mortality, reflective of highly developed societies. This is true of countries in Europe, together with Canada, Australia, and Japan. The demographic transition assumes that this occurs because of more changes in social customs including the education of more women and expectations of working in all sectors, thus contributing to the family income.

Some countries, primarily in Western and Northern Europe, are now experiencing a population decline. With a very low CBR and an increasing CDR, the result is a negative NIR. These countries will have entered a predicted stage 5 of the demographic transition model. They have a growing or high old-age dependency ratio, which means that there are fewer working-age people (15 to 64) than there are older people who depend on pensions, health care, and other government support.

Key Issues Revisited

2.2. Why Is Population Increasing?

- Most of the world's natural increase is in the less-developed countries of Africa, Asia, and Latin America.

- Most European and North American countries now have low population growth rates, and some are experiencing population decline.

- The difference in NIRs between MDCs and LDCs is mainly due to differences in CBRs rather than CDRs.

- The crude birth rate and crude death rate are the primary measures of population change in a society.

- Countries pass through the four stages of the demographic transition as they experience increased development and improved health care.

- The demographic transition shows the change in a country's population. According to this model, a country will move from a situation of high birth and death rates, with little population growth, to one of low birth and death rates, with low population growth.

Review Questions

2.2.1. With a NIR of 1.07 percent, the world's population would double in approximately _____.
A. 35 years
B. 87 years
C. 65 years
D. 7 years
E. 110 years

2.2.2. The region with the highest TFR is:
A. Europe.
B. North Africa.
C. Sub-Saharan Africa.
D. India.
E. China.

2.2.3. In which stage of demographic transition is the total population of a country going to be much higher, even though birth and death rates are low?
A. Stage 1
B. Stage 2
C. Stage 3
D. Stage 4
E. Stage 5

KEY ISSUE 3

Why Does Health Vary by Region?

Learning Outcome 2.3.1: Describe differences in health-care services among countries.
Health care varies widely around the world because developing countries generally lack resources to provide the same level of health care as developed countries.

Learning Outcome 2.3.2: Explain reasons for risks to baby girls and mothers.
Health risks for females are especially acute at childbirth for both the mother and the baby.

Learning Outcome 2.3.3: Relate the demographic transition to the distribution of age groups.
A country's stage of the demographic transition determines the percentage of people in different age groups. The percentage of different age groups helps understand a country's health challenges.

Learning Outcome 2.3.4: Explain four stages in the epidemiologic transition.
Stage 1 is characterized by pestilence and famine, stage 2 by pandemics, and stages 3 and 4 by degenerative diseases.

A country's level of development is directly connected to the health-care services that are available to the population. Developed countries are able to provide advanced health care from cradle-to-grave while developing countries spend below $100 per capita on very limited health-care costs.

The role of females in the population of a country is directly tied to the development levels of a country. The age-sex distribution (numbers of males to females in each age group) is tied to cultural traditions and economic development. China and India have a cultural history of gender-based selection resulting in the "missing" of 117 million females over the past several decades. At the same time, the development of a country determines the access to health care during prenatal and infant delivery times. The cases of maternal death in developed countries are one-tenth the rate in developing countries with the highest maternal mortality in Sierra Leone at 1,360 per 100,000 births. The lowest is in Finland and Iceland, with 3 per 100,000 births; however, the United States experiences the highest maternal mortality rates of all the developed countries.

The **age-sex distribution (ratio)** of a country's population can be shown on a population pyramid. It will show the distribution of a country's population between males and females of various ages. The country's **sex ratio** is the number of males per 100 females. A population pyramid will normally show the percentage of the total population in five-year cohorts, with the youngest group at the base of the pyramid and the oldest group at the top. Males are usually shown on the left and females on the right. Each age-sex group is called a population **cohort**. Population pyramids can tell us much about the population history of a country. A pyramid with a wide base shows a rapidly growing country with a large proportion of young people and is typical of a less-developed county. A pyramid that is more rectangular depicts a country with a relatively even number of young, middle-aged, and older people and is typical of a more-developed country. **Population pyramids** are also useful tools to analyze and predict future population growth. Such a usage is referred to as **population projection**.

The **dependency ratio** is the percentage of people in a population who are either older (over 65) or younger (0–14), unable to work, and thus must be supported by others. A high dependency ratio of young children is reflective of a developing economy that will have even greater pressure when the large number of children reach working age and try to secure employment. On the other hand, a high dependency ratio of an older population is reflective of a **"graying" population** that is a developed economy. Society and government tend to favor providing adequate health care, social services, pensions, and attention to the needs of an aging population. As a result of the advanced development of some countries, there is a narrowing ratio of working age to elderly dependent age populations, particularly in Japan and parts of Europe.

Medical researchers have identified an **epidemiologic transition** that focuses on the causes of death in each stage of the demographic transition. **Epidemiology** is the branch of medicine that is concerned with disease. In stage 1 of the epidemiologic transition, infectious and parasitic diseases were the main causes of death. These include the Black Plague and cholera **pandemics**. A pandemic occurs over a very wide geographic area, unlike an **epidemic** which is more localized. These causes of death were most common for people of countries in stage 1 and the early part of stage 2 of the demographic transition.

Stage 3 of the epidemiologic transition is associated with degenerative and human-created diseases such as heart diseases and cancer. As LDCs have moved from stage 2 to stage 3 of the demographic transition, the incidence of infectious diseases has declined. Behavior-related diseases are more typical of countries in stage 4 of the demographic transition.

Key Issues Revisited

2.3. Why Does Health Vary by Region?

- Birth rates have declined in nearly all countries through family planning and improved economic conditions.

- The dependency ratio impacts the focus of health care to concentrate on the needs of the elderly or on the needs of children.

- The development level of a country influences the level of health care.

- The epidemiologic transition has four stages of diseases affecting the demographics and corresponds to the demographic transition as a country progressively develops.

Review Questions

2.3.1. In developing countries, improved medical care is more a factor of _____.
A. available facilities
B. government funding of free health care
C. ability to pay tax supported health care
D. environmental effects on health
E. cultural fear of modern medicine

2.3.2. In which region are maternal mortality and infant mortality rates the highest?
A. Northern Europe
B. Sub-Saharan Africa
C. North America
D. East Asia
E. South America

2.3.3. Which country would be considered a "graying" population?
A. India
B. United States
C. Japan
D. Peru
E. Saudi Arabia

2.3.4. Why is there a low incidence of cancer in sub-Saharan Africa and South Asia?
A. They have a low life expectancy and do not reach the ages when degenerative diseases occur.
B. They have a natural resistance to developing cancers.
C. They have poor medical facilities to diagnose cancers.
D. They lack the environmental factors that cause cancers.
E. Government funding of medical care includes preventative medicines.

KEY ISSUE 4

Why Might Population Change in the Future?

Learning Outcome 2.4.1: Assess a possible stage 5 of the demographic transition.
Education, family planning, improvements in health care, and economic empowerment of women lead to a reduction in birth rates in developing countries and improved development levels.

Learning Outcome 2.4.2: Describe two reasons for declining birth rates.
Local economic conditions and family planning are the reasons for declining crude birth rates since 1990.

Learning Outcome 2.4.3: List reasons for possible stage 5 of the epidemiologic transition.
Stage 5 of the epidemiologic transition could be caused by a reemergence of infectious and parasitic diseases as a result of evolution, poverty, and globalization.

Learning Outcome 2.4.4: Explain arguments for and against Malthus's theory.
In 1798, Malthus argued that population would grow more rapidly than food resources. Recent experiences show that the population has not grown as rapidly as Malthus predicted.

Many demographers agree that some parts of the world are **overpopulated**, where a country can no longer sustainably support its population because it has reached its carrying capacity. **Carrying capacity** refers to the number of people that a given area can support from the natural environment and from human actions to modify the environment through agriculture, industry, and extraction of raw materials.

The future of the size of the world's population will be determined by a mix of increased development, implementation of government policies, and available access to food supplies. Stage 5 of the demographic transition results in a decline in the NIR when the CDR exceeds the CBR. This mortality rate comes from an older population that has experienced a long-life expectancy and benefited from the highest degree of medical care. As developing countries reach developed status and the populations benefit from a better food supply, better resources, and stable governments, they too will experience the longest life expectancies, eventually shifting the dependency ratio and contributing to the aged mortality numbers.

The CBR has declined rapidly since 1990 except in some countries in sub-Saharan Africa. This has occurred partly as a result of economic development, which has resulted in more money for education and health care. Birth rates have also been lowered because of diffusion of modern contraceptives. Some countries, such as Bangladesh, have reduced their birth rates with this practice and without economic development. There is opposition to birth control programs from some countries for religious, cultural, and political reasons. A decrease in the crude birth rate accompanied with improved access to education has led to an improvement in the quality of life for many. With more education and job skills, women can contribute to the economic well-being of the family, leading to an improvement in the availability of food, access to medical care, and an overall improved quality of life.

Some medical researchers argue that the world is moving into stage 5 of the epidemiologic transition, characterized by a reemergence of infectious and parasitic diseases. This could be for several reasons, including the evolution of infectious disease microbes, poverty, and improved travel. Potential pandemic diseases that are reemerging include a drug-resistant tuberculosis and an insecticide-resistant malaria-carrying mosquito. However, AIDS is the most lethal epidemic of recent years, especially in sub-Saharan Africa, where there were more than 26 million people infected with HIV in 2017. Thirty-five million people have died of AIDS since the 1980s and another 37 million people are HIV positive today. The emergence of this stage 5 epidemiologic transition is ultimately blamed on evolution, poverty, and increased globalization. The most recent example of a pandemic disease that can spread rapidly through relocation diffusion and global connectivity is Ebola, which impacted West Africa in 2015.

One of the most famous models to explain changes in population over time was developed by **Thomas Malthus**. Malthus was an English economist and demographer who published *Essay on the Principle of Population* in 1798. He argued that the world's population was growing geometrically (exponentially) but food supplies were only growing arithmetically (see Figure 2-34 in your textbook).

According to Malthus, this would lead to "negative checks" consisting of starvation and disease because of a lack of food. The only way to avoid this would be for populations to lower crude birth rates through "moral restraints."

Malthus's theory is still potentially relevant today because of rapid population growth in some LDCs. **Neo-Malthusians** argue that the food supply, fuel, agricultural land, and other resources will be depleted by an unsustainable population, particularly in developing areas. Malthus had his critics, too. The Marxist theorist Friedrich Engels believed that the world has enough resources to eliminate hunger and poverty if they are more equally shared. Contemporary critics include Julian Simon and Esther Boserup, who argue that larger populations can actually stimulate economic growth. Malthus did not foresee the development of new agricultural technologies or the human ability to reduce population growth rates.

Key Issues Revisited

2.4. Why Might Population Change in the Future?

- Neo-Malthusians argue that population is depleting resources, food supplies, and available land.

- An emerging demographic transition stage 5 will result in a population decline in some of the most developed countries.

- An epidemiologic transition stage 5 is emerging as a result of changing infectious disease microbes, endemic poverty, and global connections.

- Birth rates have declined due to women having access to education, family planning, health care, and economic empowerment.

Review Questions

2.4.1. Stage 5 of demographic transition would be characterized by ____.
A. a low CBR and increasing CDR, resulting in a negative NIR
B. a high CDR and high CBR, resulting in an unchanging NIR
C. a low CBR and a low CDR, resulting in an unchanging NIR
D. a high TFR and a high CDR, resulting in a negative NIR
E. a low TFR and a low CBR, resulting in a positive NIR

2.4.2. Which region has experienced a significant decline in the crude birth rate between 1990 and 2015 due to education and health-care programs for women?
A. Mexico and Central America
B. Australia and Oceania
C. Southwest Asia
D. Central Africa
E. Eastern Europe

2.4.3. Most of the new pandemic diseases are spread through _____.
A. stimulus diffusion
B. relocation diffusion
C. hierarchical diffusion
D. global diffusion
E. environmental diffusion

2.4.4. What is overpopulation?
A. It is the relationship between population and a region's level of resources.
B. It is an overcrowded populated area.
C. Overpopulation is when carrying capacity is exceeded.
D. Overpopulation is when the resources are depleted.
E. Overpopulation occurs when poverty and hunger result from economic inequality.

Key Terms

Age-sex distribution (ratio)*	**Infant mortality rate (IMR)***
Agricultural density*	**Life expectancy***
Arithmetic density*	**Medical revolution***
Carrying capacity*	**Natality rate**
Cartogram	**Natural increase rate (NIR)***
Cohort	**Neo-Malthusian**
Crude birth rate (CBR)*	**Non-ecumene**
Crude death rate (CDR)*	**Overpopulated**
Demographic equation	**Pandemic**
Demographic momentum	**Physiological density***
Demographic transition model*	**Population density***
Demography*	**Population distribution***
Dependency ratio*	**Population explosion**
Doubling time*	**Population projection**
Ecumene	**Population pyramid***
Epidemic	**Sex ratio***
Epidemiologic transition*	**Thomas Malthus***
Epidemiology	**Total fertility rate (TFR)**
Graying population	**Zero population growth (ZPG)**
Industrial Revolution*	

* Term is in 2019 College Board Curriculum & Exam Description.

Think Like a Geographer Activities

Go to www.worldmapper.org/ and look at world cartograms.
Why do geographers display population-related issues using cartograms?

Go to www.populationpyramid.net/ and look at the population pyramids for Congo, Kuwait, the Russian Federation, and the United States. What similarities or differences do you see? What might account for these?

Quick Quiz Matching

2.1. Total fertility rate	A. Males per 100 females
2.2. Dependency ratio	B. Average number of children that women have
2.3. Infant mortality	C. People who are too old or too young to work
2.4. Natural increase rate	D. Number of deaths compared to births
2.5. Sex ratio	E. Percentage by which population grows annually

2.6. A population pyramid that looks like a column with no growth at the bottom would most likely describe a country in which stage of demographic development?
A. Stage 1
B. Stage 2
C. Stage 3
D. Stage 4
E. Stage 5

2.7. Maternal mortality rate is higher _____.
A. when access to prenatal health care is insufficient
B. with multiple births
C. in developed countries
D. in areas that lack industrial development
E. northern latitudes

2.8. By 2050, which issue will most likely concern the Japanese government?
A. Crude birth rates
B. Infant mortality rates
C. Radiation from nuclear power plants
D. Elderly support ratio
E. Lack of child-care facilities

2.9. What caused stage 2 of the demographic transition model to occur in Africa?
A. Neolithic Revolution
B. Medical Revolution
C. Industrial Revolution
D. Second Agricultural Revolution
E. Genetically Modified Crops

2.10. Which country has a negative NIR?
A. Russia
B. Angola
C. Guatemala
D. United States
E. China

2.11. Which area of the United States has the lowest number of AIDS cases?
A. California
B. Florida
C. Northeast
D. Texas
E. Montana

Changing Population Pyramids

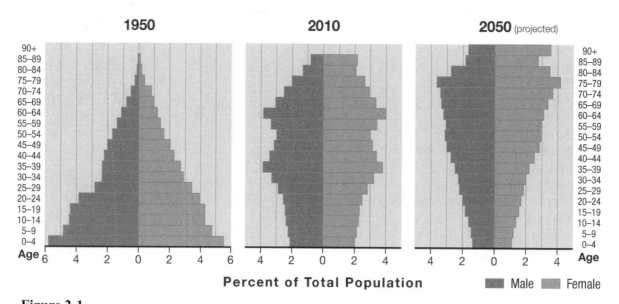

Figure 2-1

Use Figure 2-1 to answer the following questions.

1. With reference to the population structure of this country, identify the challenges for each of the following in 1950:
   a. Economic sectors
   b. Social support
   c. Health and education

2. In 2010, discuss the economic challenges facing this country due to the changing nature of the population.

3. In 2050, the population structure of this country is significantly different from 100 years prior. Explain the impact of an aging population on the following:
   a. Economic sectors
   b. Government infrastructure
   c. Health and education

On the Web

www.prb.org/ **Population Reference Bureau**
www.masteringgeography.com
www.worldpopulationatlas.org
www.populationpyramid.net
www.data.worldbank.org
www.cis.org **Center for Immigration Studies**
www.ameristat.org/ **Population Reference Bureau/AmeriStat**
www.census.gov **United States Census Bureau**
www.gapminder.org
www.iflscience.com/health-and-medicine/1-reason-people-die-early-your-country
www.time.com/5523805/china-aging-population-working-age/
www.youtu.be/r6eTr4ldDYg **IF THE WORLD WERE 100 PEOPLE UPDATED**

www.youtu.be/2LyzBoHo5EI **Why the world population won't exceed 11 billion | Hans Rosling |**
www.youtu.be/-UbmG8gtBPM **OVERPOPULATED - BBC Documentary**
www.youtu.be/-1eHfNYgOP4 **World in the balance - The people's paradox NOVA**

TED Talks

Hans Rosling shows the best stats you've ever seen; Development:
www.ted.com/talks/hans_rosling_shows_the_best_stats_you_ve_ever_seen.html

Hans Rosling's new insights on poverty; Development:
www.ted.com/talks/hans_rosling_reveals_new_insights_on_poverty.html

Hans Rosling on global population growth; Population and Development:
www.ted.com/talks/hans_rosling_on_global_population_growth.html

Hans Rosling: Asia's rise how and when; Political and Development:
www.ted.com/talks/hans_rosling_asia_s_rise_how_and_when.html

Hans Rosling: Insights on HIV; Development:
www.ted.com/talks/hans_rosling_the_truth_about_hiv.html

Key Figures

Figure 2-2 World Population Portions

Figure 2-4 World Population Distribution

Figure 2-5 World Cartogram

Figure 2-6 Ecumene

Figure 2-8 Arithmetic Density, 2018

Figure 2-9 Physiological Density, 2018

Figure 2-10 Agricultural Density, 2018

Figure 2-12 Natural Increase Rate, 2018

Figure 2-16 World Population Growth 1950–2017

Figure 2-17 Crude Birth Rate (CBR), 2018

Figure 2-18 Total Fertility Rate (TFR), 2018

Figure 2-19 Infant Mortality Rate (IMR), 2018

Figure 2-20 Crude Death Rate (CDR), 2018

Figure 2-21 Demographic Transition Model

Figure 2-23 Demographic Transition Stage 2: The Gambia

Figure 2-25 Demographic Transition Stage 3: Mexico

Figure 2-27 Demographic Transition Stage 4: Denmark

Figure 2-30 Health-care Expenditure

Figure 2-33 Maternal Mortality Rate, 2015

Figure 2-37 Life Expectancy at Birth, 2018

Figure 2-39 Potential Support Ratio

Figure 2-40 Population Under Age 15, 2018

Figure 2-44 Stage 3 Disease: Male Cancer, 2018

Figure 2-45 Stage 4 Disease: Opioids, 2016

Figure 2-46 Future Population Estimates

Figure 2-53 Women using Family Planning, 2017

Figure 2-57 Percent of Population Diagnosed as HIV-positive, 2016

Figure 2-59 Malthus's Theory

AP® Human Geography Outline of Population

Unit 2: Population and Migration Patterns and Processes

Topic	APHG Topic No. Title	Suggested Skills	Enduring Understandings	Learning Objective	Big Ideas
2.1.1	2.2: Consequences of Population Distribution	3.A: Identify the different types of data presented in maps and in quantitative and geospatial data.	PSO-2: Understanding where and how people live is essential to understanding global cultural, political, and economic patterns.	PSO-2.D: Explain how population distribution and density affect society and the environment.	BI-1 Patterns and Spatial Organization
2.1.2	2.1: Population Distribution	3.A: Identify the different types of data presented in maps and in quantitative and geospatial data.	PSO-2: Understanding where and how people live is essential to understanding global cultural, political, and economic patterns.	PSO-2.A: Identify the factors that influence the distribution of human populations at different scales.	BI-1 Patterns and Spatial Organization
2.1.3	2.1: Population Distribution	3.A: Identify the different types of data presented in maps and in quantitative and geospatial data.	PSO-2: Understanding where and how people live is essential to understanding global cultural, political, and economic patterns.	PSO-2.B: Define methods geographers use to calculate population density. PSO-2.C: Explain the differences among and the impact of methods used to calculate population density. PSO-2.D: Explain how population distribution and density affect society and the environment.	BI-1 Patterns and Spatial Organization
2.2.1; 2.2.2; 2.3.1; 2.3.2	2.4: Population Dynamics	3.C: Explain patterns and trends in maps and in quantitative and geospatial data to draw conclusions.	IMP-2: Changes in population are due to mortality, fertility, and migration, which are influenced by the interplay of environmental, economic, cultural, and political factors.	IMP-2.A: Explain factors that account for contemporary and historical trends in population growth and decline.	BI-2 Impacts and Interactions

2.2.3	2.5: The Demographic Transition Model	3.B: Describe spatial patterns presented in maps and in quantitative and geospatial data.	IMP-2: Changes in population are due to mortality, fertility, and migration, which are influenced by the interplay of environmental, economic, cultural, and political factors.	IMP-2.B: Explain theories of population growth and decline.	BI-2 Impacts and Interactions
2.3.3	2.7: Population Policies 2.3: Population Composition	3.B: Describe spatial patterns presented in maps and in quantitative and geospatial data. 3.A: Identify the different types of data presented in maps and in quantitative and geospatial data.	SPS-2: Changes in population have long- and short-term effects on a place's economy, culture, and politics. PSO-2: Understanding where and how people live is essential to understanding global cultural, political, and economic patterns.	SPS-2.C: Explain the causes and consequences of an aging population. PSO-2.F: Explain ways that geographers depict and analyze population composition.	BI-3 Spatial Processes and Societal Change BI-1 Patterns and Spatial Organization
2.3.4	2.4: Population Dynamics	3.C: Explain patterns and trends in maps and in quantitative and geospatial data to draw conclusions.	IMP-2: Changes in population are due to mortality, fertility, and migration, which are influenced by the interplay of environmental, economic, cultural, and political factors.	IMP-2.B: Explain theories of population growth and decline.	BI-2 Impacts and Interactions
2.4.1	2.7: Population Policies	2.C: Explain a likely outcome in a geographic scenario using geographic concepts, processes, models, or theories.	SPS-2: Changes in population have long- and short-term effects on a place's economy, culture, and politics.	SPS-2.A: Explain the intent and effects of various population and immigration policies on population size and composition.	BI-3 Spatial Processes and Societal Change

2.4.2	2.8: Female and Demographic Change	3.B: Describe spatial patterns presented in maps and in quantitative and geospatial data.	SPS-2: Changes in population have long- and short-term effects on a place's economy, culture, and politics.	SPS-2.B: Explain how the changing roles of females have demographic consequences in different parts of the world.	BI-3 Spatial Processes and Societal Change
2.4.3; 2.4.4	2.4: Population Dynamics	3.B: Describe spatial patterns presented in maps and in quantitative and geospatial data.	IMP-2: Changes in population are due to mortality, fertility, and migration, which are influenced by the interplay of environmental, economic, cultural, and political factors.	IMP-2.B: Explain theories of population growth and decline.	BI-2 Impacts and Interactions

Source: College Board AP Human Geography Course Description, effective Fall 2019

FRQ's From College Board

2003 FRQ#3
2004 FRQ #3
2008 FRQ #3
2010 FRQ #3
2011 FRQ #2
2013 FRQ #2
2019 FRQ #2 set 1

Chapter

3 Migration

Where Are Migrants Distributed?

The focus of this chapter is on migration. Relocation diffusion occurs with migration. It examines the causes for why people move permanently or migrate, both interregional and internationally, and the potential consequences. Major migration patterns of today and historical periods of the past are considered.

Learning Outcome 3.1.1: Describe the relationship between the migration transition and the demographic transition.

International migration is primarily a phenomenon of countries in stage 2 of demographic transition, whereas internal migration is more important in stages 3 and 4.

Learning Outcome 3.1.2: Recognize the principal streams of international and internal migration.

Migration can be international (between countries, either voluntary or forced) or internal (within a country, either interregional or intraregional).

Learning Outcome 3.1.3: Explain the difference between emigration and immigration.

The flow of migration is a process of connections. **Emigration** is migration from a place while **immigration** is migration to a place. The difference in the number of immigrants and emigrants is the **net migration** to a place.

Learning Outcome 3.1.4: Describe the changing places of origin of U.S. immigrants.

The United States has had three main eras of immigration. The principal source of immigrants has shifted from Europe during the first two eras to Latin America and Asia during the third (current) era since the 1950s.

Migration is the movement of a person from one place to another. It can include movement at many different scales, such as short-term, repetitive, or cyclical movements called **circulation**, or **intercontinental migration**, which is from one continent to another.

E. G. Ravenstein, a nineteenth-century geographer, identified 11 laws of migration, which can be roughly organized into three main elements: the reasons migrants move, the distance they move, and the major characteristics of migration. Migration is a specific type of relocation diffusion and is a form of **mobility,** a more general term dealing with all types of movement. Today's immigrants to the United States are clustered in California, New York, Florida, and Texas. New immigrants often move to places where family members and friends from their home country have already migrated. This is called **chain migration**.

The demographer Wilbur Zelinsky has identified a **migration transition**, which associates changes in the migration pattern in a society with different stages of the demographic transition. According to the migration transition, international migration usually occurs when countries are in stage 2 of the demographic transition. For example, international migrants moved from Western Europe to the United States as a result of the technological changes related to the Industrial Revolution. Internal migration becomes more important when countries are in stages 3 and 4 of the demographic transition. According to migration transition theory, people generally move from cities to suburbs during these stages. Zelinsky theorizes that countries in stages 3 and 4 of the demographic transition are the destinations of international migrants leaving stage 2 counties because of economic push and pull factors.

At a global scale, people generally migrate from the developing to the developed world. The three largest flows are from Asia to Europe and North America and from Latin America.

More than most other countries, the United States is a land of immigrants. About 75 million people migrated to the United States between 1820 and 2015. There have been three major eras of immigration to the United States. The first era was the original settlement of colonies in the 1600s and

1700s. There were three peaks of migration between the mid-1800s and the 1920s during the second era of immigration. The first peak of immigration during the 1840s and 1850s consisted of people largely from Western Europe. The second peak during the late 1800s included migrants from Western Europe, especially Germany, Ireland, and Scandinavia. The third peak in the early years of the 1900s brought in migrants largely from Southern and Eastern Europe who came to work in the factories of the Industrial Revolution. All three eras have involved people coming to the United States from countries that were at stage 2 of the demographic transition.

Recent immigration to the United States has been from less-developed regions. Asia and Latin America make up over three-fourths of the migrants to the United States. The four leading sources of U.S. immigrants from Asia are China, India, Vietnam, and the Philippines. In the 1980s, Mexico became the leading source of immigrants to the United States. Although the pattern of immigration to the United States has changed, the reason for immigration remains essentially the same. People are pushed from their homeland by economic and political conditions and are attracted to the economic and social potential of life in the United States. Emigration is movement *from* a location whereas immigration is movement *to* a location. The difference between the number of immigrants and the number of emigrants is the net migration.

Key Issues Revisited

3.1. Where Are Migrants Distributed?

- Migration is a permanent relocation. At a global scale, the largest flows of migrants are from Asia to Europe and from Asia and Latin America to the United States.

- Migration can be international (voluntary or forced) or internal (interregional or intraregional).

- The United States has experienced three major periods of migration since the 1860s.

  As of 2017, the major contributor of migrants to the United States remains Mexico with 25.3%, with India and China following with 6% each. (www.migrationpolicy.org)

Review Questions

3.1.1. A country experiencing high international immigration and intraregional migration from cities to suburbs would typically be experiencing:
A. high NIR, high CBR, and falling CDR.
B. fluctuating CBR and CDR and no NIR.
C. low NIR, low CBR, and low CDR.
D. rising CBR, with declining CDR.
E. low NIR, high CDR, and high CBR.

3.1.2 A permanent move from one country to another is:
A. interregional migration.
B. internal migration.
C. intraregional migration.
D. tourist migration.
E. international migration.

3.1.3. Currently, where is the largest flow of international migrants from?
A. South and East Asia
B. West and North Africa
C. South America
D. Central Asia

3.1.4. Which European country was the source of the largest flow of migrants to the United States between the 1800s and 1900s?
A. France
B. England
C. Ireland
D. Germany
E. Italy

KEY ISSUE 2

Where Do People Migrate Within Countries?

Learning Outcome 3.2.1: Describe migration patterns among U.S. regions.

Migration within the United States has primarily occurred from east to west, at varying rates. Recently, interregional migration has also occurred from north to south.

Learning Outcome 3.2.2: Compare interregional migration in several large countries.

The world's two largest countries have distinctive patterns of interregional migration. These patterns derive unequal distribution of population within these countries. China and Brazil also have unequal distribution of their population. Chinese have been migrating from the rural interior to the large coastal cities. Brazilians have been encouraged to move from the large coastal cities to the interior.

Learning Outcome 3.2.3: Describe three types of intraregional migration.

Three intraregional migration patterns are from rural to urban, from urban to suburban, and from urban to rural areas.

Historically, the most significant migration trend has been **interregional migration** westward in the United States to obtain cheap, open land and potential wealth. The population center of the United States has moved westward and more recently southward into southern Missouri. In the 1960s and 1970s, large numbers of white, middle-class Americans moved from the older northeastern and midwestern states to the south and the west coast. New availability of lower-cost alternative energy sources and price pressure from imported steel led to the collapse of the northern industrial states dependent on coal and iron production in the 1960s and 1970s. The **Cotton Belt**, named for the extensive production of cotton and textiles in the south until the 1950s, soon became known as the **Sun Belt**, a land of opportunity, as the northern migrants moved south seeking new opportunities. The migration of African Americans followed a different pattern, from the rural south to large cities in the north. Interregional migration in the United States has not been as significant in the first decade of the twenty-first century largely because of a narrowing of regional differences in employment opportunities.

Interregional migration has also been important in other countries. In the world's largest countries, internal migration continues for economic purposes and from rural to urban areas. Canada has experienced a measurable east–west migration. For much of the same reasons that the United States has experienced a north–south and western migration, economic opportunity has pulled populations in Canada to the western provinces of Alberta and British Columbia. Interregional migration in Russia is a counter-migration from the times of Soviet-controlled industrial development. Regional migration from the east into the European western areas of Russia and to the cities has been the largest migration since 1990. China's internal migration is from the interior rural areas to the large urban areas of the eastern coast pulled by the opportunity for factory jobs. Brazil is also experiencing spatial migration similar to that of China and Russia. In Brazil, migration is pulled from the large cities along the coast into developing cities of the interior seeking jobs in new industries accessing Brazil's natural resources. A new trend in North America and Western Europe has been **counter-urbanization**, from urban to rural areas for lifestyle preferences especially now that modern technology allows people to work more easily from their homes.

Migration from rural to urban areas has been very important in LDCs. Worldwide, more than 20 million people are estimated to migrate each year from rural to urban areas. People seek economic opportunities with this type of migration and, especially in LDCs, are pushed because of failed agricultural systems.

Key Issues Revisited

3.2. Where Do People Migrate Within Countries?

- There is both interregional and intraregional migration within a country.

- Historically, interregional migration was important in settling the frontier of large countries such as the United States, Russia, and Brazil.

- The most important intraregional trends are from rural to urban areas within LDCs and from cities to suburbs within MDCs.

Review Questions

3.2.1. The "center of population gravity" in the United States has been moving:
A. eastward.
B. north.
C. northeast.
D. westward.
E. southeast.

3.2.2. The government of Brazil encouraged interregional migration by:
A. punishing those who refused to move.
B. cleaning out the Favelas.
C. moving the capital.
D. building a transcontinental railroad.
E. setting up a quota system.

3.2.3. Since 2010, the pattern of intraregional migration in the United States has increased to be more:
A. rural to urban.
B. suburban to cities.
C. cities to suburban.
D. suburban to rural.
E. south to north due to climate change.

KEY ISSUE 3

Why Do People Migrate?

Learning Outcome 3.3.1: Explain cultural reasons for migrating.
People migrate because of a combination of push and pull factors. These factors may be political, environmental, and economic. Most people migrate for economic push and pull reasons.

Learning Outcome 3.3.2: Explain environmental reasons for migrating.
Migration for environmental reasons to be push factors caused by environmental hazards; however, a greater sense of connectivity is stimulating environmental pull factors in more developed countries.

Learning Outcome 3.3.3: Identify economic reasons for international migration.
Economic pull factors are the major reason for migration. People emigrate from areas of few job opportunities in developing countries to places with greater economic prospects particularly in jobs that are not desired by local populations.

Learning Outcome 3.3.4: Describe the demographic characteristics of immigrants to the United States.
The demographic make up of international migrants has shifted from males to females and children since the late 1800s.

People generally migrate because of push and pull factors. **Push factors** include anything that would cause someone to leave their present location, such as the violation of a person's **activity space**. **Pull factors** induce people to move to a new location. Four major kinds of push and pull factors can be identified. These are economic, political, cultural, and environmental. Economic factors that can lead to migration include job opportunities, cycles of economic growth and recession, and cost of living. The United States and Canada have been important destinations for economic migrants lured by economic pull factors. **Place utility** is where a place may offer economic incentives in an effort to attract people to their town or city.

Armed conflict and the policies of oppressive regimes have been important political push factors in forcing out those who become refugees. A **refugee**, according to the United Nations, is a person who, "owing to well-founded fear of being persecuted for reasons of race, religion, nationality, membership in a particular social group, or political opinion, is outside the country of his nationality and is unable to, or owing to such fear is unwilling to, avail himself of the protection of that country." In 2015, 244 million people, or 3.3 percent of the world's population, have migrated outside of their country of origin; however, 65.3 million people have been forcibly displaced and 21.3 million are considered refugees. According to the UNHCR in 2015, 54 percent of all refugees come from three countries: 4.9 million from Syria, 2.2 million from Afghanistan, and 1.1 million from Somalia. There are also a significant number of **internally displaced people (IDP)** who are forced to migrate but are still within their national borders. The last type of forced migrant is an **asylum seeker**, a person who migrates to another country hoping to be recognized as a refugee. There are also political pull factors such as the promise of political freedom. It has been this factor that has lured so many people from the communist countries of Eastern Europe to Western Europe in the second half of the twentieth century.

Cultural factors can encourage people to move to places where they will be more at home culturally. A good example of a cultural pull factor is the relocation of Jews to the newly formed state of Israel after the Second World War. Israel is the ancestral hearth of Jewish culture and it serves as a place where Jewish people can reestablish social ties and create a sense of political unity.

Environmental pull and push factors are largely related to physical geography. People will be pulled toward physically attractive regions such as the Rocky Mountains and the Mediterranean coast of southern Europe. People are also pushed from places by floods and droughts. The flooding in New Orleans and other Gulf Coast communities in 2005 following Hurricane Katrina caused around 1,400 deaths and forced several hundred thousand people from their homes. Indeed, many people are forced to move by water-related disasters because they live in vulnerable areas, such as a floodplain.

Migrants do not always go to their intended destination because of an **intervening obstacle**, which is an environmental or cultural feature that hinders migration, in particular, a long or expensive passage over water or land. Sometimes, a migrant will stop and stay at a place en route to their intended destination because of an **intervening opportunity**, which is an environmental or cultural feature that favors migration.

According to E. G. Ravenstein, most migrants move only a short distance and within a country. **Internal migration** is permanent movement within a country. One of Ravenstein's laws states that long-distance migrants to other countries usually relocate to major economic and urban centers. The permanent migration from one country to another is **international migration**, and it can be voluntary or forced. **Voluntary migration** is when someone chooses to leave a place as a result of push or pull factors. **Forced migration** is when someone is moved from their home without any choice.

Key Issues Revisited

3.3. Why Do People Migrate?

- Push factors include emigration from a location for political, economic, and environmental reasons.
- Pull factors include immigration for political, economic, and environmental factors.
- We can distinguish between international and internal migration.

Review Questions

3.3.1. The largest number of internally displaced persons is in:
A. Northern Europe.
B. South America.
C. Middle East/West Asia.
D. Africa.
E. Southern Europe.

3.3.2. Where is coastal flooding a significant push factor for migration?
A. U.S. West Coast
B. West coast of South America
C. Gulf Coast of the United States
D. U.S. East Coast
E. Hawaiian Islands

3.3.3. The largest flow of remittances from immigrants in the United States goes to destinations in:
A. India.
B. China.
C. Latin America.
D. West Africa.
E. Eastern Europe.

3.3.4. According to E. G. Ravenstein, the most common reason people migrate is for:
A. political reasons.
B. environmental reasons.
C. war.
D. authoritarian reasons.
E. economic reasons.

KEY ISSUE 4

Why Do Migrants Face Challenges?

Learning Outcome 3.4.1: Explain how governments control who can immigrate into a country.

Immigration is tightly controlled by most countries and government policies are the major obstacle.

Learning Outcome 3.4.2: Explain the role of quotas in U.S. immigration policies.

Since the Quota Act of 1921 and the National Origins Act of 1924, limitations on the number of people can immigrate to the U.S. are legally restricted.

Learning Outcome 3.4.3: Summarize the diversity of conditions along the U.S.–Mexico border.

The border region is a rural, sparse area with only a few urban areas on the border with California and Texas.

Learning Outcome 3.4.4: Describe patterns of immigration in Europe and issues resulting from the patterns.

Immigrants in the wealthiest countries of western and northern Europe seek low-skill jobs that local residents won't accept. In the large cities, these immigrants provide essential services to the operation of the society.

The United States uses a quota system to limit the number of foreign citizens who can migrate permanently to the country. **Quotas** are maximum limits on the number of people who can immigrate to the United States from one country during a one-year period. Initial quota laws were designed to allow more Europeans to come to the United States, rather than Asians. Quotas for individual countries were eliminated in 1968 and replaced with hemisphere quotas. In 1978, the hemisphere quotas were replaced by a global quota, which was set at 700,000 in 1990. The majority of legal immigration today is chain migration. Some preference is also given to skilled workers, which leads to **brain drain**, the emigration of talented and well-educated people. According to the World Bank in 2012, 8 out of 10 Haitians with a college degree lived abroad.

There have been increasing numbers of illegal, **unauthorized**, or **undocumented immigrants** to the United States. In 2010, the Urban Institute estimated that there might have been as many as 11.3 million undocumented immigrants, including about 58 percent from Mexico. It is a controversial topic because although undocumented immigrants take jobs that few others want, most Americans would also like more effective border control. Thus, some favor **amnesty** for illegal immigrants, whereas others believe that they should be deported.

The United States has generally regarded emigrants from Cuba as political refugees since Castro's 1959 revolution. Economic and political refugees from Haiti have not been quite as welcome in the United States. Vietnamese boat people were regarded as political refugees after the Vietnam War, when thousands fled the war-ravaged country. Vietnam remains an important source of immigrants to the United States today but largely because of the pull of economic opportunity rather than the push of political persecution.

Immigrants often face opposition from some citizens of host countries because they are often culturally, ethnically, and religiously different. For example, there have been open ethnic and racial conflicts between citizens and migrants in Western Europe and Australia in the first decade of the twenty-first century. Europe allows temporary **guest workers** to legally work for at least minimum wages in their countries. They serve the same purpose as the vast majority of illegal immigrants in the United States. Guest workers to wealthy European countries were intended to be part of a circular migration. However, many have remained permanently in Europe. Anti-immigration opposition has escalated in Europe in recent years from nationalist organizations that fear a loss of their cultural identification and traditions. These feelings have been further compounded with recent terrorist attacks in France and Belgium led by immigrants or children of immigrants in Europe.

Key Issues Revisited

3.4. Why Do Migrants Face Challenges?

- Migrants have difficulty getting permission to enter other countries and often face hostility from local citizens once they arrive.

- Immigration laws restrict the number who can legally enter the United States.

- Americans and Europeans are divided on attitudes toward immigrants.

Review Questions

3.4.1. The major obstacle faced by most immigrants comes from:
A. nationalist movements.
B. global recession and depression.
C. transportation and access.
D. political restrictions.
E. terrorist actions.

3.4.2. Congressional preferences for people wishing to immigrate to the United States include all of these EXCEPT:
A. family reunification.
B. skilled workers.
C. ethnic diversification.
D. refugees.
E. professionals.

3.4.3. In border areas, many localities have passed resolutions to help unauthorized immigrants in a movement known as:
A. sanctuary city.
B. civil disobedience.
C. federalism.
D. egalitarianism.
E. amnesty.

3.4.4. Why was immigration to Europe initially welcomed?
A. Europe is in stage 5 and was experiencing a decline in population.
B. Europe needs low-skill workers to work in industrial areas.
C. European countries prefer very diverse cultural influences.
D. Many countries needed to replace emigrants who had left for other places.
E. Cities and towns have lost population and feared the development of ghost towns.

Key Terms

Activity space

Amnesty

Asylum seeker*

Brain drain

Chain migration*

Circulation*

Cotton Belt

Counter-urbanization

Emigration*

Forced migration*

Guest workers*

Immigration*

Intercontinental migration

Internally displaced people (IDP)*

Internal migration*

International migration

Interregional migration

Intervening obstacle*

Intervening opportunity*

Intraregional migration

Migration*

Migration transition

Mobility

Net migration

Place utility

Pull factors*

Push factors*

Quotas

Refugees*

Remittances

Rust Belt

Sun Belt

Step migration*

Time-contract workers

Transhumance*

Unauthorized immigrants

Undocumented immigration

Voluntary migration*

* Term is in 2019 College Board Curriculum & Exam Description.

Think Like a Geographer Activities

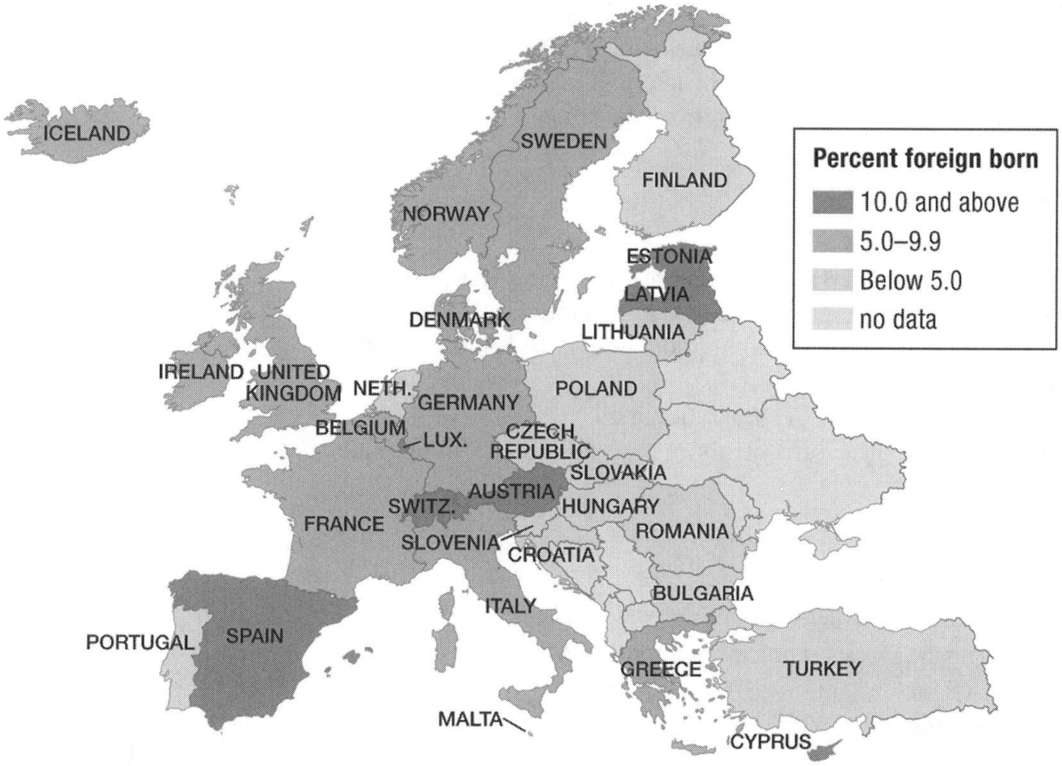

Figure 3-1 Percentage of Immigrants in Europe

Use Figure 3-1 to answer the following questions.

1. What are some social/cultural centrifugal factors in countries like Spain, Estonia, or Latvia as a result of a foreign born population?
2. Describe potential actions by the government to manage social/cultural differences between the native and foreign-born population.

Quick Quiz Matching

3.1. Net migration
3.2. Asylum seeker
3.3. Internally displaced person
3.4. Pull factor
3.5. Refugees
3.6. Chain migration
3.7. Intervening obstacle
3.8. Migration transition

A. Change in migration due to social/economic changes
B. Forced to migrate within their country for political reasons
C. Hope of economic opportunity
D. An ocean, a desert
E. Difference between in-migration and out-migration
F. Migrant to another country hoping to be called a refugee
G. Forced to migrate across country borders
H. Migrating to join family members

Free Response Question

Countries with large land areas have distinctive patterns of interregional migration.

1. Identify two countries that experience interregional migration.
2. Discuss two push and two pull factors for interregional migration in an identified region of a country.
3. Discuss one result of interregional migration occurring in both countries.

On the Web

www.masteringgeography.com
www.nationmaster.com/country-info/stats/People/Migration/Net-migration-rate
www.unstats.un.org/unsd/demographic/sconcerns/migration/
www.oecd.org/migration/internationalmigrationoutlook2011.htm
www.web.worldbank.org
www.forbes.com/special-report/2011/migration.html
www.migrationpolicy.org/article/frequently-requested-statistics-immigrants-and-immigration-united-
    states#Now

Key Figures

Figure 3-3 Destination of International Immigrants by U.S. State, 2016

Table 3-1 Comparing the Demographic Transition and Migration Transition

Figure 3-5 Global Migration Patterns, 2017

Figure 3-9 Migrants 1990–2017

Figure 3-10 Largest Country-to-Country Migration Flows, 1990–2017

Figure 3-11 Net Migration, European Union, 2017

Figure 3-13 Two Centuries of Immigration to the United States

Figure 3-14 Changing Center of U.S. Population

Figure 3-16 Interregional Migration in the United States

Figure 3-17 Interregional Migration: China

Figure 3-18 Interregional Migration: Brazil

Figure 3-20 Interregional Migration: Canada

Figure 3-23 Interregional Migration: Russia

Figure 3-31 Refugees and IDPS, 2017

Figure 3-32 Refugees from Syria 2011–2018

Figure 3-34 Migration from New Orleans After Hurricane Katrina

Figure 3-36 Emigration from Puerto Rico After Hurricane Maria

Figure 3-38 Migration to and from India, 2017

Figure 3-41 Flow of Remittances, 2016

Figure 3-44 Female Immigrants as a Percentage of All Immigrants

Figure 3-47 Immigration Policies as of 2015

Figure 3-48 Unauthorized Immigrants in the United States

Figure 3-59 Immigration in Europe, 2017

AP® Human Geography Outline of Migration

Unit 2: Population and Migration Patterns and Processes

Topic	APHG Topic No. Title	Suggested Skills	Enduring Understandings	Learning Objective	Big Ideas
3.1.1; 3.1.3; 3.1.4	2.12: Effects of Migration	2.B: Explain spatial relationships in a specified context or region of the world, using geographic concepts, processes, models, or theories.	IMP-2: Changes in population are due to mortality, fertility, and migration, which are influenced by the interplay of environmental, economic, cultural, and political factors.	IMP-2.E: Explain historical and contemporary geographic effects of migration.	BI-2: Impacts and Interactions
3.1.2; 3.2.1; 3.2.2; 3.2.3	2.11: Forced and Voluntary Migration	1.D: Describe a relevant geographic concept, process, model, or theory in a specified context.	IMP-2: Changes in population are due to mortality, fertility, and migration, which are influenced by the interplay of environmental, economic, cultural, and political factors.	IMP-2.D: Describe types of forced and voluntary migration.	BI-2: Impacts and Interactions
3.3.1	2.10: Causes of Migration	2.B: Explain spatial relationships in a specified context or region of the world, using geographic concepts, processes, models, or theories.	IMP-2: Changes in population are due to mortality, fertility, and migration, which are influenced by the interplay of environmental, economic, cultural, and political factors.	IMP-2.C: Explain how different causal factors encourage migration.	BI-2: Impacts and Interactions
3.3.2	2.10: Causes of Migration	2.B: Explain spatial relationships in a specified context or region of the world, using geographic concepts, processes, models, or theories.	IMP-2: Changes in population are due to mortality, fertility, and migration, which are influenced by the interplay of environmental, economic, cultural, and political factors.	IMP-2.C: Explain how different causal factors encourage migration.	BI-2: Impacts and Interactions

3.3.3	2.10: Causes of Migration	2.B: Explain spatial relationships in a specified context or region of the world, using geographic concepts, processes, models, or theories.	IMP-2: Changes in population are due to mortality, fertility, and migration, which are influenced by the interplay of environmental, economic, cultural, and political factors.	IMP-2.C: Explain how different causal factors encourage migration.	BI-2: Impacts and Interactions
3.3.4	2.10: Causes of Migration	2.B: Explain spatial relationships in a specified context or region of the world, using geographic concepts, processes, models, or theories.	IMP-2: Changes in population are due to mortality, fertility, and migration, which are influenced by the interplay of environmental, economic, cultural, and political factors.	IMP-2.D: Describe types of forced and voluntary migration.	BI-2: Impacts and Interactions
3.4.1	2.12: Effects of Migration	2.B: Explain spatial relationships in a specified context or region of the world, using geographic concepts, processes, models, or theories.	IMP-2: Changes in population are due to mortality, fertility, and migration, which are influenced by the interplay of environmental, economic, cultural, and political factors.	IMP-2.E: Explain historical and contemporary geographic effects of migration.	BI-2: Impacts and Interactions
3.4.2; 3.4.5; 3.4.4	2.12: Effects of Migration	2.B: Explain spatial relationships in a specified context or region of the world, using geographic concepts, processes, models, or theories.	IMP-2: Changes in population are due to mortality, fertility, and migration, which are influenced by the interplay of environmental, economic, cultural, and political factors.	IMP-2.E: Explain historical and contemporary geographic effects of migration.	BI-2: Impacts and Interactions

FRQ's From College Board

2003 FRQ #3
2005 FRQ #2
2006 FRQ #1
2008 FRQ #2
2012 FRQ #3

Chapter
4 Culture & Social Media

Where Are Cultural Groups Distributed?

Rubenstein defines culture as the body of customary beliefs, social forms, and material traits that together constitute a group of people's distinct tradition. Culture can be distinguished from habit and custom. A **habit** is a repetitive act that an individual performs, and a **custom** is a repetitive act of a group. Culture combines three things—values, material artifacts, and political institutions. This chapter deals with the material artifacts of culture or **material culture**, which includes the **cultural landscape** or the **built environment** of visible objects that a group possesses and leaves behind for the future. In human geography, culture is based on the two basic categories, folk and popular culture, their origins, diffusion, and spatial distribution. Popular culture has a more widespread distribution than folk culture, and its globalization causes problems that are addressed here.

Learning Outcome 4.1.1: Outline concepts of folk and popular culture.
Folk culture is traditionally practiced primarily by small, homogeneous groups living in isolated rural areas. Pop culture is found in large, heterogeneous societies that share certain habits despite differences in other personal characteristics.

Learning Outcome 4.1.2: Compare processes of origin, diffusion, and distribution of folk and popular culture.
Folk culture originates from unknown sources at a time not identifiable and developing in multiple isolated areas. Popular culture's origins and diffusion patterns are identifiable and reflective in a globally connected population.

Learning Outcome 4.1.3: Trace the origin and diffusion of social media.
Electronic media helps diffuse popular culture around the world to be viewed by anyone that has access to it.

Folk culture refers to the cultural practices of small, homogeneous groups living in traditional societies. Folk cultures are usually isolated and rural, with subsistence economies. Distinctive architecture and other material artifacts such as tools, musical instruments, and clothing contribute to the uniqueness of folk cultures. Nonmaterial aspects of folk culture include songs **(folk songs)**, stories **(folklore)**, and belief systems. Folk cultures originate in multiple **hearths** because of their isolation.

Popular culture refers to the cultural practices of large, heterogeneous societies that share many habits and characteristics. The elements of popular culture look similar in different places and result in a relatively uniform landscape. Artifacts include music, food, entertainment, fashion, recreation, and various forms of art. Popular culture is diffused through global connections and increased media to more remote parts of the world.

Folk culture diffuses slowly, on a small scale, usually through **relocation diffusion**. The Amish culture in the United States is a good example of the diffusion of a folk culture. Popular culture is easily diffused around the world, largely through **hierarchical diffusion**. The distribution of popular culture is dependent on access to the content and is limited by the ability to afford the access. Electronic media is the predominate form of distribution of popular culture in the twenty-first century. Smart cell phones and social media platforms facilitate the distribution of popular culture; however, it is not globally uniform due to lack of access to electronic media in less developed regions. The challenge of accessing folk cultures is the result of environmental factors and limited interaction with others.

Culture develops out of a hearth and is diffused through hierarchical or relocation diffusion, resulting in a global distribution of pop culture or the isolation of folk cultures at a smaller scale.

Key Issues Revisited

4.1. Where Are Cultural Groups Distributed?

- As a result of distinctive processes of origin and diffusion, folk and popular cultures have different distribution patterns.

- Folk culture is more likely to have an anonymous origin, diffuse slowly through relocation of members, and have limited spatial distribution.

- Popular culture is more likely to be invented and diffused rapidly with the use of modern communications through hierarchical diffusion reaching a widespread spatial distribution.

Review Questions

4.1.1. All of the following are components of culture EXCEPT:
A. ethnicity and governments.
B. language and religion.
C. customs and habits.
D. landscapes.
E. migration destinations.

4.1.2. Folk culture is primary spread through:
A. TV.
B. radio stations.
C. the Internet.
D. social media.
E. relocation.

4.1.3. What limits the global distribution of popular culture?
A. Inefficient airline access into less populated areas of the world
B. Lack of access to electronic media
C. Inability to understand other languages
D. Immigration restrictions
E. Social media networks are only in English

KEY ISSUE 2

Where Are Leisure & Material Culture Distributed?

Learning Outcome 4.2.1: Compare differences in geographic dimensions of folk and popular music.

Popular music has wide global distribution because of connections among artists and styles.

Learning Outcome 4.2.2: Describe how sports have been transformed from folk to popular culture.

Sports that originated as isolated folk customs have been organized into popular culture with global distribution.

Learning Outcome 4.2.3: Compare reasons for distribution of clothing styles in folk and popular culture.

Folk clothing is more likely to respond to environmental conditions and cultural values, whereas clothing styles vary more in time than in place.

Learning Outcome 4.2.4: Identify reasons for folk and popular food preferences.

Folk food culture is especially strongly embedded in environmental conditions. Popular food culture can display some regional variations.

Learning Outcome 4.2.5: Analyze factors that influence patterns of folk housing.

Folk housing styles, like other folk material culture, respond to environmental and cultural factors.

This section provides the reader with a series of examples applying the concept of folk and popular cultures in the real world. Additionally, each of these topics addresses the challenges to global diffusion.

Many different groups who are living in relative isolation practice folk cultures. They are especially susceptible to the various ways in which the physical environment can limit their activities and diffusion because of their low level of technology. Thus, their cultural identity and landscapes will be very diverse. For example, there are many different types of Himalayan art in a relatively small geographic area because of the harsh physical environment and limited interaction. Folk music and festivals generally tell stories about life in a particular place unique to that cultural group. This is explained in the text in regard to folk music of the Vietnamese. In contrast, popular music is the writing of a single artist conveying a message for entertainment purposes.

The globalization of soccer is an example of the transformation and diffusion of an English folk culture to a popular culture. Many Olympic sports and large regional sports are moving from folk culture to popular culture sports as people from these sports origins migrate to other places in the world.

Cultural traits such as food, clothing, and housing are influenced by physical geography, including agricultural practices and climatic conditions. Globalization has created an interconnected world that has allowed for diffusion of contemporary fashion styles. The same evolving global culture that influences clothing styles is also responsible for the diffusion of a popular food culture. Food preferences are influenced by local cultural traditions, which are based on what can be raised in a particular environment. Through relocation and contagious diffusion, traditional folk foods are now part of a diverse and fusion global diet. The unique agricultural products that are characteristic of a certain area contribute to the sense of place that has developed over the years and to the culture of the people. Restrictions on certain behaviors, like the consumption of particular foods, can also be imposed by social customs. This is called a **taboo**.

Housing provides another good example of the diversity of folk culture that results from the interaction of cultural and physical geography. The resultant landscapes exemplify distinctive and unique senses of place. Folk cultural traits, such as housing (**folk housing** or **indigenous architecture**), are especially responsive to the environment because of their low level of technology and utilization of available resources. In contrast, housing styles in the United States have for several decades reflected a mass production, convenience-oriented preference known as a neo-eclectic style.

Key Issues Revisited

4.2. Where Are Leisure and Material Culture Distributed?

- The physical environment, religion, and cultural values cause regional variations in cultural customs and habits.

- Popular preferences in food, clothing, and shelter vary more in time than in place. However, regional variations continue to persist.

Review Questions

4.2.1. All of the following are examples of folk music EXCEPT:
A. songs that deal with agriculture.
B. songs that deal with birth.
C. songs that deal with death.
D. songs that are made for the sole purpose of sales.
E. songs that deal with harvests.

4.2.2. How did sports like soccer, lacrosse, hockey, and baseball become global sports?
A. Hierarchical diffusion
B. Relocation diffusion
C. Stimulus diffusion
D. Contagious diffusion
E. Globalization

4.2.3. Which item of clothing has been restricted in some European countries?
A. Blue jeans
B. Burqa
C. Poncho
D. Dashikini
E. Beret

4.2.4. A restriction on a behavior imposed by religious law of social custom is a:
A. civil law.
B. prohibition.
C. constitutional law.
D. taboo.
E. tolerant.

4.2.5 Recently constructed housing in the United States reflects popular culture because:
A. they are constructed of materials available in the environment.
B. they are reflective of modern energy conservation demands.
C. they are mass produced by construction companies.
D. they reflect cultural preferences of migrating populations.
E. they reflect the emerging global culture of designs.

KEY ISSUE 3

Why Is Access to Culture Unequal?

Learning Outcome 4.3.1: Compare the diffusion of TV and the Internet.

TV diffused during the twentieth century from the United States to Europe and then to developing countries. The diffusion of the Internet is following the same pattern as the TV, but at a more rapid pace.

Learning Outcome 4.3.2: Compare the distribution of social media platforms.

The United States has dominated the use of social media but will continue to diffuse to the rest of the world.

Learning Outcome 4.3.3: Evaluate threats to freedom in the use of electronic media.

Access to electronic media is not universal. Only 19 of 65 countries are considered to have free access to the open Internet. Restrictions on the free use of the Internet come from banned technology, censorship, and restrictions on individual usage and access.

Learning Outcome 4.3.4: Describe geographic features of cyberattacks and other misuse of social media.

Social media and electronic devices make it easier for people to interact across the distance of space, thus altering a distance decay concept; however, there are those who take advantage of this connectivity.

Culture is also examined at a global scale and is shaped by a popular culture. Pop culture is shaped by the changing preferences in styles of music, dress, foods, and the interaction of people from all regions of the world. Each element of pop culture changes or evolves as new technologies are developed and as development increases, allowing more populations to engage in the elements of pop culture. The expansion of popular culture is reflective of changing technology as well. Exposure to emerging pop culture between the 1960s and 1980s was predominately through television. Since the 1990s, the expansion of the Internet, increased availability of computer technology, and "smart" devices has allowed virtually all regions of the populated world to have access to a well-diffused global pop culture.

Popular culture diffuses rapidly where high levels of technology allow people to acquire material possessions. The increasingly global world allows for the rapid diffusion and acceptance of the material and nonmaterial elements of popular culture. For example, as a result of the diffusion of popular culture, there are less regional differences in housing, clothing, and food in more developed countries. Television has played a major role in the diffusion of popular culture, especially since World War II. International rates of TV ownership have climbed rapidly in LDCs in the early twenty-first century, but there are still international differences in TV ownership.

In the last decade, other electronic media have become important transmitters of popular culture. According to internetlivestats.com, Internet service has diffused at a rapid pace, from 40 million Internet users worldwide in 1995 to 3.4 billion in 2016. Since their beginnings, Facebook, Twitter, and You Tube have also diffused rapidly, and what once was a phenomenon in the United States continues to diffuse rapidly.

Key Issues Revisited

4.3. Why Is Access to Culture Unequal?

- Popular culture diffuses rapidly across the world, aided by modern communications, especially through electronic media.

- Many countries limit the ability of their citizens to access electronic media in order to prevent anti-government actions.

- Electronic devices have made it easier to communicate but also easier to commit cybercrime and spread misinformation.

Review Questions

4.3.1. What is the most important electronic media format?
A. The Internet
B. The TV
C. The cell phone
D. The radio
E. The computer

4.3.2. Which population dominates the use of social media?
A. Canada
B. China
C. United States
D. India
E. Brazil

4.3.3. According to Freedom House, what content do governments sometimes block on the Internet?
A. Political content
B. Social content
C. Security content
D. Google
E. All of the above

4.3.4 Which country is both the most victimized and the primary source of cyberattacks?
A. Canada
B. United States
C. Russia
D. China
E. Australia

KEY ISSUE 4

Why Do Cultures Face Sustainability Challenges?

Learning Outcome 4.4.1: Summarize challenges for folk culture from diffusion of popular culture.
Popular culture threatens traditional elements of cultural identity in folk culture.

Learning Outcome 4.4.2: Summarize two principal ways that popular culture can adversely affect the landscape.
Popular culture can deplete scarce resources and pollute the landscape.

Learning Outcome 4.4.3: Describe how popular culture can vary by region.
Traditional cultural differences among vernacular regions can be reinforced by contemporary social media and reflect a cultural divergence from popular culture.

The traditional role of women in developing counties is changing as a result of the diffusion of popular culture. It is leading to the advancement of women through education and economic and social opportunities. However, it may also lead to negative impacts such as sex crimes against women, and it challenges centuries-old cultural customs.

The diffusion of popular culture threatens the survival of folk culture. It is one example of **cultural imperialism**, causing people to lose their traditional ways of life in favor of the material elements of popular culture from more developed countries. Folk cultures **assimilate** into more popular cultural practices with each generation if the popular culture is dominant in that place. In the process of losing all of the folk cultural practices, members will create a **syncretic** culture or a blending of both the folk and popular cultural aspects. This process, known as **acculturation**, is a gradual process and differs among generations of the population.

The creation of uniform landscapes through the diffusion of popular culture can negatively impact the environment by depleting natural resources and polluting the landscape. Uniform landscapes create a product recognition increasing consumption. It creates a standard pattern in any developed area around the world to create a sense of comfort away from home, which leads to a landscape of "placelessness," or **cultural homogenization**. Golf courses remake the environment, as do some types of commercial agriculture, creating an increased demand for some products and placing a strain on natural resources. The demand for products from popular cultures such as fast-food restaurants generates more waste and leads to the pollution of the environment.

Key Issues Revisited

4.4. Why Do Cultures Face Sustainability Challenges?

- Popular culture, usually originating in Western MDCs, may cause the elimination of some folk culture traditions (globalization versus local diversity).

- Popular culture may adversely affect the environment through altering an area for product recognition and consumer demand for products.

Review Questions

4.4.1. Why are Amish folk culture regions predominately located in the Midwest?
A. There were no jobs in the eastern United States that accommodated their folk culture practices.
B. They did not support government ideology and sought out lands outside of the territorial states in the early 1800s.
C. They are an agricultural-based society whose practices and traditions center on self-preservation.
D. They were removed from the cities of the east due to their refusal to assimilate into U.S. culture.
E. They could not work in the industrial sector because their belief system prohibited working with machinery.

4.4.2. What causes landscape pollution?
A. Communities desire to promote the sale of a product or play a round of golf.
B. Excess trash is created from global markets and the demand for identification with popular culture.
C. Cultural practices justify eliminating environmental areas that are perceived as unsightly.
D. High-rise buildings and large areas of paved surface alter climatic conditions in a high-density area.
E. All of the above are contributors to landscape pollution.

4.4.3 Traditional cultural differences are reinforced by social media in _____.
A. vernacular regions
B. formal regions
C. functional regions
D. homogenized landscapes
E. syncretic landscapes

Key Terms

Accommodation	**Hearths**
Assimilation*	**Hierarchical diffusion***
Built environment*	**Indigenous architecture**
Cultural hearth*	**Material culture**
Cultural homogenization	**Placelessness**
Cultural imperialism	**Popular culture**
Custom	**Relocation diffusion**
Folk culture	**Social media**
Folk housing	**Sustainability**
Folklore	**Taboo**
Folk music	**Uniform landscape**
Habit	

*Term is in 2019 College Board Curriculum & Exam Description.

Think Like a Geographer Activities

Research McDonald's fast-food restaurant (www.corporate.mcdonalds.com/corpmcd/about-us/around-the-world.html) in four different countries around the world. Explain the effects of popular culture on each, as well as clues that illustrate their local diversity. Identify how McDonald's assimilates and accommodates its menu to the local culture.

Quick Quiz

4.1. A group's material culture is produced by:
A. its geographic location.
B. its habits.
C. its food choices.
D. its food taboos.
E. a collection of social customs.

4.2. In what area are folk culture habits and the environment most linked together?
A. Dress
B. Religious practice
C. Housing designs
D. Food
E. Occupations

4.3. Why is access to culture unequal?
A. Lack of water
B. Lack of income
C. Lack of electricity
D. Lack of access to electronic media
E. Lack of Internet

4.4. In what ways does popular culture threaten environmental sustainability?
A. Through recycling plans
B. Because of increased demand for animal products
C. Through curbside programs
D. Because of increased demand for golfing
E. Because people are becoming vegans

4.5. Briefly describe how social media can affect a country's folk culture. Do you have any contemporary examples of where this has occurred?

Free Response

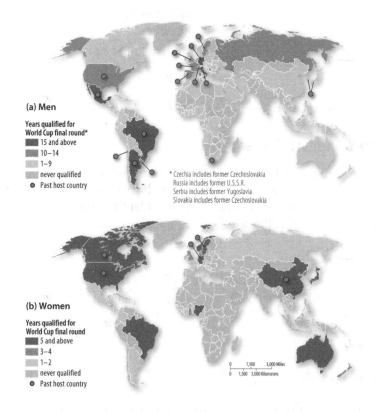

Figure 4-1 Popular Sports: World Cup Soccer

1. From the World Cup Soccer map, describe how a sport, such as soccer, can be transformed from a folk custom to part of the global popular culture.
2. What evidence supports the global popularity of soccer?
3. Explain the pattern of diffusion and popularity between the global popularity of women's and men's soccer.

On the Web

www.geography.about.com/od/culturalgeography/a/culturehearths.htm

www.pcaaca.org/

www.washingtonpost.com/graphics/national/how-diverse-is-america/?hpid=hp_no-name_graphic-story-a%3Ahomepage%2Fstory

www.news.mit.edu/2014/network-maps-global-fame-different-language-speakers-1216

TED Talks

Chimamanda Adichie. The Danger of a Single Story: misunderstanding of one version of cultural explanation
www.ted.com/talks/chimamanda_adichie_the_danger_of_a_single_story

James H Kunstler dissects Suburbia Pop/Folk Culture, Urban. Classic about space and human interaction.
www.ted.com/talks/james_howard_kunstler_dissects_suburbia.html

Wade Davis on the worldwide web of ritual Culture
www.ted.com/talks/wade_davis_on_the_worldwide_web_of_belief_and_ritual.html

Wade Davis on endangered cultures Culture
www.ted.com/talks/wade_davis_on_endangered_cultures.html

Phil Borges on endangered cultures Culture
www.ted.com/talks/phil_borges_on_endangered_cultures.html

Key Figures

Figure 4-6 Diffusion of Popular Culture
Figure 4-8 Cell Phones
Figure 4-10 Most Popular Social Network
Figure 4-14 Popular Music Clusters
Figure 4-17 Popular Sports: World Cup Soccer
Figure 4-18 Regions of Baseball Fans
Figure 4-22 Restrictions on Women's Religious Dress
Figure 4-30 Folk Housing: U.S. Hearths
Figure 4-32 Diffusion of TV
Figure 4-33 Diffusion of the Internet
Figure 4-34 Diffusion of Facebook
Figure 4-40 Internet Freedom
Figure 4-50 Distribution of Amish

AP® *Human Geography Outline of Culture*

Unit 3: Cultural Patterns and Processes

Topic	APHG Topic No. Title	Suggested Skills	Enduring Understandings	Learning Objective	Big Ideas
4.1.1; 4.1.2; 4.2.4; 4.2.5	3.1: Introduction to Culture	4.A: Identify the different types of information presented in visual sources.	PSO-3: Cultural practices vary across geographical locations because of physical geography and available resources.	PSO-3.A: Define the characteristics, attitudes, and traits that influence geographers when they study culture.	BI-1: Patterns and Spatial Organization
4.1.3	3.4: Types of Diffusion	1.D: Describe a relevant geographic concept, process, model, or theory in a specified context.	MP-3: The interaction of people contributes to the spread of cultural practices.	MP-3.A: Define the types of diffusion.	BI-2: Impacts and Interactions
4.2.1; 4.2.2; 4.2.3	3.5: Historical Causes of Diffusion	2.C: Explain a likely outcome in a geographic scenario using geographic concepts, processes, models, or theories.	SPS-3: Cultural ideas, practices, and innovations change or disappear over time.	SPS-3.A: Explain how historical processes impact current cultural patterns.	BI-3: Spatial Processes and Societal Change
4.3.1; 4.3.2; 4.3.3; 4.3.4	3.6: Contemporary Causes of Diffusion	5.B: Explain spatial relationships across various geographic scales using geographic concepts, processes, models, or theories.	SPS-3: Cultural ideas, practices, and innovations change or disappear over time.	SPS-3.A: Explain how historical processes impact current cultural patterns.	BI-3: Spatial Processes and Societal Change

4.4.1	3.8: Effects of Diffusion	2.B: Explain spatial relationships in a specified context or region of the world, using geographic concepts, processes, models, or theories.	SPS-3: Cultural ideas, practices, and innovations change or disappear over time.	SPS-3.B: Explain how the process of diffusion results in changes to the cultural landscape.	BI-3: Spatial Processes and Societal Change
4.4.2; 4.4.3	3.2: Cultural Landscapes	PSO-3: Cultural practices vary across geographical locations because of physical geography and available resources.	PSO-3.B: Describe the characteristics of cultural landscapes.	PSO-3.B.1: Cultural landscapes are combinations of physical features, agricultural and industrial practices, religious and linguistic characteristics, evidence of sequent occupancy, and other expressions of culture including traditional and postmodern architecture and land-use patterns.	BI-1: Patterns and Spatial Organization

Source: College Board AP Human Geography Course Description, effective Fall 2019

FRQ's From College Board

2002 FRQ #3
2002 FRQ #2
2007 FRQ #2
2009 FRQ #1
2015 FRQ #2

Chapter

5 Languages

Where Are Languages Distributed?

Language, together with religion and ethnicity, is one of the three traits that best distinguishes cultural values. The chapter looks at where languages are spoken and why there are distinctive distributions. As well as addressing the diffusion and globalization of English, the chapter also examines attempts to preserve local languages. Reasons for dialectical differences and multilingual states that contribute to unique cultural influences at regional levels of scale are discussed. The global distribution of languages results from a combination of interaction and isolation while allowing the sustainability of some languages and the demise of others.

Learning Outcome 5.1.1: Explain how geographers classify languages.
Languages are classified as institutional, developing, vigorous, threatened, and dying. Languages are organized into families, branches, and groups.

Learning Outcome 5.1.2: Locate on a map the distribution of principal language families.
The two largest language families are Indo-European and Sino-Tibetan.

Learning Outcome 5.1.3: Identify the world's most used languages and language families.
Indo-European is the predominant language family of Europe, Latin America, North America, South Asia, and South Pacific. Sino-Tibetan is the predominant language family of East Asia.

Learning Outcome 5.1.4: Identify the distribution of Indo-European languages.
The four largest branches of Indo-European are Indo-Iranian, Romance, Germanic, and Balto-Slavic. Balto-Slavic predominates in Eastern Europe, Romance in Southern Europe and Latin America, Germanic in Northern Europe and North America, and Indo-Iranian in South Asia and Central Asia.

Learning Outcome 5.1.5: Describe the distribution of language families other than Indo-European.
In addition to Indo-European and Sino-Tibetan, most of the world's remaining major language families are centered in Asia. The third and fourth largest language families are in Africa.

Language is one of the oldest and most geographically diverse cultural traits on Earth. It is a system of communication through speech. The distribution of language around the world is the direct result of migration and the interaction or isolation of language speakers. The diffusion of language is also an example of contagious diffusion and the concepts of adaptation and assimilation of culturally diverse peoples.

Languages are classified as institutional, developing, and endangered. Of the world's 7,099 languages, 576 are designated as **institutional languages** used in government, law, education, and media. An institutional language is an **official language** that also has a literary tradition with a system of grammar rules. Some countries have two official languages because the language of the former colonial is not spoken by much of the population. **Developing languages** also have a literary tradition but may not be widely distributed or the official language. **Threatened languages** typically do not have a literary element, and the numbers of speakers are declining because another language is spoken by a predominately younger population.

Languages are organized into **language families**, a collection of languages related through a common ancestral language existing before recorded history. A **language branch** is a collection of languages within a family related through a common ancestral language within the past several thousand years. The smallest organization and the most recent is the **language group,** a collection of languages within a branch with a common origin in the recent past and containing similar grammar and vocabulary.

All languages belong to a **language family**, which is a collection of many languages that were originally related through a common ancestor. Seven language families contain languages that are spoken by 90 percent of the world's population. More than 1 billion people speak a language that is part of the Indo-European or Sino-Tibetan families. The **Indo-European family** is the world's most spoken language family. Nine percent of the world's population speaks a language that belongs to one of 134 smaller language families.

Languages of the Indo-European family are spoken on all continents but are dominant in Europe and the Americas. There are eight branches of the Indo-European family. Large numbers of people speak a language of one of the following four branches: Indo-Iranian, Romance, Germanic, and Balto-Slavic. German and English are both part of the Germanic branch of Indo-European. The branch of Indo-European with the most speakers is Indo-Iranian, which is divided into an eastern group (Indo-Aryan) and a western group (Iranian). Hindi is the most spoken of the eastern group, and Pakistan's principal language, Urdu, is essentially the same but written in the Arabic alphabet. The major Iranian group languages include Persian, Pashto, and Kurdish. The Balto-Slavic languages are largely those of Eastern Europe, especially Russian.

The Romance languages, including Spanish, Portuguese, French, Italian, and Romanian, all developed from the Latin language of the Romans. Provincial people in the Roman Empire spoke a common form of Latin known as **Vulgar Latin**. Latin diffused with the expansion of the Roman republic and empire, and much later, during the era of Spanish and Portuguese imperialism in the Americas.

There are 11 language families that include 50 million speakers in addition to the Indo-European languages. The largest of the East Asian language families is Sino-Tibetan, which also is the second-largest language family. Mandarin is the most commonly used of the languages. Japanese and Korean are separate languages and have their own language family; however, they are significantly influenced by Chinese linguistic structure. Dravidian and Turkic languages are predominate in south and central Asia. Afro-Asiatic in North Africa is the third-largest language family, with Arabic the largest of the languages in the family. Niger-Congo in sub-Saharan Africa is the fourth-largest language family, with Yoruba and Igbo in Nigeria and Swahili in Kenya, Tanzania, Rwanda, and Uganda. More than 95 percent of the people in sub-Saharan Africa use languages of the Niger-Congo family, making it the largest spoken and institutional language.

Key Issues Revisited

5.1. Where Are Languages Distributed?

- Languages are classified as institutional, developing, vigorous, threatened, and dying.

- Languages are organized into families and branches.

- Ninety percent of the world's population speak a language from one of the seven language families.

Review Questions

5.1.1. How many languages exist in the world today?
A. 4,206
B. 7,099
C. 2,479
D. 1,598
E. 916

5.1.2. Which is the predominant language family of the Western Hemisphere?
A. Germanic
B. Indo-European
C. Quechuan
D. Spanish
E. English

5.1.3. Which language family represents almost 46 percent of the world's population?
A. Sino-Tibetan
B. Niger-Congo
C. English
D. Indo-European
E. Germanic

5.1.4. What is the most widely used language in the eastern branch of the Indo-European language family?
A. Turkic
B. Arabic
C. Hindi
D. Urdu
E. Dravidian

5.1.5. What is the most commonly used Sino-Tibetan language?
A. Han
B. Tibetan
C. Mandarin
D. Thai
E. Laotian

KEY ISSUE 2

Why Do Languages Diffuse?

Learning Outcome 5.2.1: Identify processes of origin and diffusion of a language branch and a family.

Indo-European language originated before recorded history. There are two competing theories on whether origin and diffusion occurred primarily because of conquest (war) or through peace (agriculture). The diffusion of Romance languages 2,000 years ago is well documented through the spread of the Roman Empire.

Learning Outcome 5.2.2: Analyze processes underlying current distribution of English.

English is a Germanic branch language because German-speaking tribes invaded England more than 1,500 years ago. Romance branch words entered English after French-speaking Normans invaded England nearly 1,000 years ago.

Learning Outcome 5.2.3: Explain the concept of lingua franca.

English is a lingua franca. As a global language, English has facilitated the diffusion of popular culture, trade, and scientific understanding.

There are two theories about the origin and diffusion of Indo-European. The **nomadic warrior theory** of Kurgan origin states that the first Indo-European speakers were Kurgans who lived near present-day Russia and Kazakhstan. They migrated westward into Europe, southward to Iran and South Asia, and eastward into Siberia, largely by military conquest. The **theory of Anatolian origin**, or **sedentary farmer theory**, states that the first speakers of Proto-Indo-European lived in eastern Anatolia 2,000 years before the Kurgans and that they migrated west into Europe and east into Asia with their agricultural practices, rather than by military conquest. Regardless of how Indo-European diffused, communication was poor and the result was isolation. Ultimately, distinct languages evolved from distinct groups.

Modern English evolved out of the early language of the Angles from southern Denmark, the Saxons from northwestern Germany, and the Jutes from northern Denmark during the fifth to ninth centuries. After the Norman Conquest, the official language of England for 300 years was French. German was spoken by the working class, while French was the language of the court. In 1489, a new language combining the simpler words with Germanic roots with the more elegant words of French emerged as the modern language of English. Modern English diffused around the world as the British Empire expanded, and then later as the United States extended its realm of influence.

The most important language for international communication is English. English is diffused by popular culture, scientific research, and globalization of trade. A **lingua franca** is a language of international communication typically used to communicate between two different language speakers. A simplified form of English or another lingua franca is a **pidgin language** which is a mix of grammar and words of a lingua franca and a local language. Swahili of East Africa, Hindi in South Asia, Indonesian in Southeast Asia, and Russian are modern lingua franca languages.

Key Issues Revisited

5.2. Why Do Languages Diffuse?

- Indo-European family includes four widely spoken branches.

- English is one of the most important lingua franca and a means of global diffusion of popular culture.

- Indo-European languages developed from a single ancestor through migration, followed by isolation of one group from others.

Review Questions

5.2.1. The origins of the Indo-European language are thought to have developed in:
A. Italy.
B. Kurgan hearth in southern Russia.
C. Angleland.
D. Central Asia.
E. Greece.

5.2.2. Which of the following did not contribute to the formation of "old English" between the fifth and ninth centuries?
A. French
B. Saxons
C. Jutes
D. Angles
E. All of the above contributed

5.2.3. Which language is the global lingua franca of technology and the Internet?
A. Swahili
B. Chinese
C. French
D. Hindi
E. English

KEY ISSUE 3

Why Do Languages Vary Among Places?

Learning Outcome 5.3.1a: Explain the concept of official languages.
English is the official language in 56 countries, representing 2 billion people.

Learning Outcome 5.3.1b: Explain the concept of informal languages.
Mixing languages for simplicity or understanding creates informal languages.

Learning Outcome 5.3.2: Analyze the way that dialects vary.
British and American dialects vary by vocabulary, spelling, and pronunciation.

Learning Outcome 5.3.3: Describe the distribution of principal U.S. dialects.
U.S. English is divided into four main dialects, North, South, Midland, and West. Differences can be traced to patterns of migration to the American colonies from various parts of England.

Learning Outcome 5.3.4: Summarize challenges in distinguishing between some languages and dialects.
Political decisions rather than the actual characteristics of the languages or dialects sometimes distinguish a language from a dialect. Desire for local cultural identity has led to the emergence of distinct languages that were once considered dialects.

Learning Outcome 5.3.5: Give examples of countries that embrace more than one language.
Multilingual states present cultural and political challenges.

English is an official language in 56 countries consisting of 2 billion people. An official language is used for government and public business. In the United States, English is used for all official documents, but the country does not have an official language. There are six official languages of the United Nations: Arabic, Chinese, English, French, Russian, and Spanish. Informal languages develop to simplify or to make difficult words more familiar. A simplified form of English or another lingua franca is a pidgin language, which is a mix of grammar and words of a lingua franca and a local language. Swahili of East Africa, Hindi in South Asia, Indonesian in Southeast Asia, and Russian are modern lingua franca languages.

Different dialects of a language develop through isolation from other speakers of the same language as well as by interaction with other speakers of that language. English has many dialects, but **Received Pronunciation (RP)**, the dialect associated with upper-class Britons, is recognized as

England's **standard language**, which is the most accepted dialect for mass communication. In France, the Parisian dialect became the standard form of French.

There are major dialect differences in English within Britain and the United States. Early colonists in America were responsible for the language patterns that make up the English-speaking parts of the Western Hemisphere. U.S. English differs from British English in vocabulary, spelling, and pronunciation. New objects and experiences were given new names in their location, resulting in different interpretation of the objects and different spellings. Vocabulary that is not used on a national scale has boundaries that limit its word usage. This word-usage boundary is known as an **isogloss**. An isogloss is the boundary area for identifying words and word usage. Sometimes, the boundaries are caused by physical isolation or from cultural enclaves.

English spread across the United States first with the colonists and then with westward expansion after crossing the Appalachians. The four dialect regions, North, South, Midland, and Western, reflect the influence of migration routes and the assimilation of new immigrants into the standard pronunciation. **Creole or creolized language** results from the mixing of a colonizer's language with an indigenous language. A creole language develops when the colonized population adopts the colonists' language and simplifies the grammar and speech patterns. Eventually, creole languages are significantly different from the original language of the colonists and are classified as separate languages. French creole in Haiti and Papiamento (Spanish creole) in the West Indies are examples of creolized languages.

A **monolingual state** will only have one official language that is used in this capacity. **Multilingual states**, such as Kenya (Swahili and English) and Switzerland (German, French, Italian, and Romansh), have more than one official language. Belgium is a multilingual state because French and Flemish (a dialect of the Germanic language of Dutch) are both official languages, but the country has had more difficulty reconciling the interests of the different language speakers. Switzerland has a traditionally decentralized government, which fosters tolerance of multiple languages because decisions are made at local levels, avoiding conflicts with culturally different populations. Canada is a bilingual state recognizing both English and French as national languages. Increased cooperation and development has occurred since the official recognition of both languages and their historic significance to the settlement of Canada.

Conflict also develops from multilingual states. Nigeria has 529 distinct languages, but only three languages are spoken by more than 10 percent of the population and four others are spoken by 1–10 percent of the country's population. Belgium is divided between the southern French speakers and the northern Flemish (a Dutch dialect). Language differences compound political and cultural tensions among the regions.

Key Issues Revisited

5.3. Why Do Languages Vary Among Places?

- The United States has several major dialects representing regional variation.

- Each language has a distinctive distribution, resulting from a combination of migration and isolation.

- Multilingual states can experience political turmoil due to cultural conflict caused from multiple official languages.

Review Questions

5.3.1. Franglais and Spanglish are examples of:
A. official language.
B. creole language.
C. pidgin language.
D. a working language.
E. an isogloss.

5.3.2. A regional variation of a language is known as a _____.
A. bilingual language
B. creole
C. standard language
D. dialect
E. pidgin

5.3.3. Why would geographers use an isogloss?
A. To determine climate zones
B. To determine global warming
C. To determine word choices
D. To identify polar melting rates
E. To identify isolated groups

5.3.4. What is the benefit of standardizing languages?
A. To promote cultural identity
B. To create political stability
C. To increase trade within the state
D. To eliminate uneven development
E. To prevent the development of a pidgin language

5.3.5. Why is Switzerland a successful multilingual state?
A. It has a lack of economic development.
B. A decentralized government allows for a regional decision-making process.
C. All languages are actually dialectical versions of German.
D. Each region is physically isolated from each other, eliminating contact.
E. It is an authoritarian government, prohibiting cultural individuality.

KEY ISSUE 4

Why Do Languages Survive or Perish?

Learning Outcome 5.4.1: Define endangered languages and relate the concept to language policies in Australia and New Zealand.

An **endangered language** is used infrequently and not studied by the youth. Preservation of indigenous languages is important; however, all immigrants are required to learn English.

Learning Outcome 5.4.2: Analyze geographic factors resulting in isolated and extinct languages.

Thousands of languages once in use are now extinct. Isolation has preserved some languages.

Learning Outcome 5.4.3: Describe how some lesser-used languages are being protected.

Celtic languages were widely spoken in the British Isles before the Germanic invasions. These languages are being preserved through the efforts of advocacy groups and government agencies.

Learning Outcome 5.4.4: Summarize processes of growing and reviving languages.

New languages are being invented, others revived, and more preserved in an attempt to maintain local cultures.

Of more than 7,000 living languages, 2,447 are considered to be endangered today. Of these endangered languages, 916 are considered dying languages. Endangered languages, such as those belonging to the Celtic branch of Indo-European, are experiencing resurgence today. The revival of Irish Gaelic, Scottish Gaelic, and Welsh is linked to nationalistic movements in these parts of the British Isles and examples of preservation of languages. Other Celtic languages include Cornish and Breton. **Isolated languages** occur as the speakers of languages that have no common language family are also limited in their interaction with speakers of other languages. Basque is the only isolated language of Europe.

Languages can become **extinct** through the loss of an entire people or through linguistic evolution over time. However, the pressures of economic and social **acculturation**, the **assimilation** of cultural traits such as language by one group under the influence of another, are responsible for most of today's losses. An **extinct language** is one that was once used by people in their daily activities but is no longer in use. The United Nations identifies 228 languages as recently extinct. Many African languages have become extinct because of the linguistic effects of European colonialism. Economic and cultural globalization has led to the demise of many traditional and indigenous languages.

New languages develop and ancient languages are revived. Hebrew is a rare example of an extinct language that has been revived. The revival of Hebrew is associated with the Zionist movement and the creation of the state of Israel in 1948. It is one symbol of Israeli nationalism.

Key Issues Revisited

5.4. Why Do Languages Survive or Perish?

- Many languages have become extinct and others are threatened with extinction.

- Some endangered languages are being preserved and protected.

Review Questions

5.4.1. A concentration of endangered languages can be found in the _____.
A. eastern United States
B. southern United States
C. Appalachia region
D. Great Lakes Region
E. western United States

5.4.2. Which of the following is an example of an isolated language?
A. English
B. Hebrew
C. Gaelic
D. Basque
E. Gothic

5.4.3. Attempts to preserve the Gaelic language can be found in which of the following regions?
A. England and Wales
B. Ireland and Scotland
C. Cornwall and Wales
D. Breton and Cornwall
E. Orkneys and Hebrides

5.4.4. Which of the following is a growing language?
A. Gaelic
B. Hebrew
C. Celtic
D. Flemish
E. Romansch

Key Terms

Acculturation*	Language group
Assimilation*	Lingua franca*
Centrifugal force	Literary tradition
Centripetal force	Monolingual country
Creole or creolized language	Multilingual country
Dialect	Nomadic Warrior theory
Dying language	Official language
Endangered language	Oral tradition
Extinct Language	Pidgin language
Indo-European family*	Received Pronunciation (RP)
Isogloss	Sino-Tibetan family
Isolated language	Standard language
Kurgan hearth	Threatened language
Language*	Theory of Anatolian origin
Language branch	Toponyms*
Language family*	Vulgar Latin

* Term is in 2019 College Board Curriculum & Exam Description.

Think Like a Geographer Activities

www.ethnologue.com
Go to the previous link and explore languages that are extinct or on the verge of going extinct. Can you explain the impact of language extinction in terms of a country's culture, literary traditions, and local diversity? Describe how the diffusion of a lingua franca has changed over time.

Quick Quiz

5.1. Which language family does English belong to?
A. Sino-Tibetan
B. Sino-European
C. Indo-European
D. Indo-Caucasian
E. Niger-Congo

5.2. Which is not an Indo-European branch?
A. Romance
B. Germanic
C. Balto-Slavic
D. Khoisan
E. Indo-Iranian

5.3. An example of a dialect becoming a distinguished language is _____.
A. Catalan
B. Canadian
C. Breton
D. Creole
E. Pidgin

5.4. Which region has the largest number of dying languages?
A. South Pacific
B. Canada
C. Central Europe
D. Eastern Russia
E. Southern China

Free Response

1. Compare the spatial distribution of languages in Switzerland and Belgium.
2. Discuss how Switzerland prevents the diversity of language from dividing the state.
3. Identify how a dual-language country would be economically beneficial.
4. Explain that under certain situations, language can be a centrifugal factor.

On the Web

www.masteringgeography.com
www.infoplease.com/ipa/A0855611.html
www.geography.about.com/od/culturalgeography/a/linguafranca.htm
www.culturalsurvival.org/programs/elc/program
www.unesco.org/languages-atlas/
youtu.be/KdQwalCPNAs
www.thepoke.co.uk/2011/12/23/english-pronunciation/
www.washingtonpost.com/news/worldviews/wp/2015/04/23/the-worlds-languages-in-7-maps-and-charts/
Regional Words: www.youtube.com/watch?v=qXGuCaApR7U
Ohio Valley:
www.youtube.com/watch?v=0mSstSG0O9U&index=31&list=PLTlwKRGStTCjQ9S1bfJBrdgq4isIN2mRk
British vs. American English: www.youtube.com/watch?v=DjOVeESuFJg

TED Talks

Wade Davis: Dreams from endangered cultures

www.ted.com/talks/wade_davis_on_endangered_cultures?language=en

Key Figures

Figure 5-2 Writing Systems of Europe and Southwest Asia

Figure 5-4 Distribution of Language Families

Figure 5-7 Language Families by Share of World Population

Figure 5-9 Language Family Trees

Figure 5-10 Indo-European Branches

Figure 5-11 Languages of India

Figure 5-12 Germanic and Balto-Slavic Branches

Figure 5-13 Romance Branch

Figure 5-14 Language Families of Southwest, East, and Southeast Asia Other Than Indo-European

Figure 5-15 African Languages

Figure 5-16 Origin and Diffusion of Indo-European: Nomadic Warrior Theory

Figure 5-17 Origin and Diffusion of Indo-European: Sedentary Farmer Theory

Figure 5-24 Languages of Websites

Figure 5-25 Languages of Internet Users

Figure 5-27 English-Speaking Countries

Figure 5-31 U.S. Dialects and Subdialects

Figure 5-36 Language Diversity in Switzerland

Figure 5-37 Language Diversity in Belgium

Figure 5-38 Language Diversity in Nigeria

Figure 5-39 Language Diversity in Canada

Figure 5-40 Levels of Endangered Languages

Figure 5-45 Languages in The United States Extinct Since 1950

AP® Human Geography Outline of Culture-Language

Unit 3: Cultural Patterns and Processes

Topic	APHG Topic No. Title	Suggested Skills	Enduring Understandings	Essential Knowledge	Big Ideas
5.1.1; 5.1.3	3.7: Diffusion of Religion and Language	4.E: Explain how maps, images, and landscapes illustrate or relate to geographic principles, processes, and outcomes.	IMP-3: The interaction of people contributes to the spread of cultural practices.	MP-3.B.1: Language families, languages, dialects, world religions, ethnic cultures, and gender roles diffuse from cultural hearths.	BI-2: Impacts and Interactions
5.1.2; 5.1.4; 5.1.5	3.7: Diffusion of Religion and Language	4.E: Explain how maps, images, and landscapes illustrate or relate to geographic principles, processes, and outcomes.	IMP-3: The interaction of people contributes to the spread of cultural practices.	IMP-3.B.2: Diffusion of language families, including Indo-European, and religious patterns and distributions, can be visually represented on maps, in charts and toponyms, and in other representations.	BI-2: Impacts and Interactions
5.2.1; 5.2.2; 5.2.3	3.7: Diffusion of Religion and Language	4.E: Explain how maps, images, and landscapes illustrate or relate to geographic principles, processes, and outcomes.	IMP-3: The interaction of people contributes to the spread of cultural practices.	MP-3.B.1: Language families, languages, dialects, world religions, ethnic cultures, and gender roles diffuse from cultural hearths.	BI-2: Impacts and Interactions
5.3.1; 5.3.2; 5.3.3; 5.3.4; 5.3.5	3.7: Diffusion of Religion and Language	4.E: Explain how maps, images, and landscapes illustrate or relate to geographic principles, processes, and outcomes.	IMP-3: The interaction of people contributes to the spread of cultural practices.	MP-3.B.1: Language families, languages, dialects, world religions, ethnic cultures, and gender roles diffuse from cultural hearths.	BI-2: Impacts and Interactions

5.4.1; 5.4.2; 5.4.3; 5.4.4	3.7: Diffusion of Religion and Language	4.E: Explain how maps, images, and landscapes illustrate or relate to geographic principles, processes, and outcomes.	IMP-3: The interaction of people contributes to the spread of cultural practices.	MP-3.B.1: Language families, languages, dialects, world religions, ethnic cultures, and gender roles diffuse from cultural hearths.	BI-2: Impacts and Interactions

FRQ's From College Board

2002 FRQ #2
2007 FRQ #2
2009 FRQ #1
2016 FRQ #2
2018 FRQ #3

Chapter

6 Religions

Where Are Religions Distributed?

The focus of the chapter is the distribution, diffusion, and influence of major religions. The chapter also examines the impact of religion on the landscape, influences shaping selected cultures, and lastly, the role that religion plays in political and ethnic conflict.

Learning Outcome 6.1.1: Identify the world's major religions and classify them by type.

Four major religions account for 78 percent of the world's population. Geographers classify the world's religions as universalizing or ethnic.

Learning Outcome 6.1.2: Summarize the distribution of major religions.

Christianity predominates in Europe and the Western Hemisphere, Buddhism in East Asia, Hinduism in South Asia, and Islam in other regions of Asia, as well as North Africa.

Learning Outcome 6.1.3: Analyze regional variations in the distribution of Christian branches.

Christianity is divided into three main branches: Roman Catholic, which predominates in southwest Europe and Latin America; Protestant, which predominates in northwest Europe and North America; and Orthodox, which predominates in Eastern Europe.

Learning Outcome 6.1.4: Describe the distribution of the major branches of Islam and Buddhism.

Islam's two major branches are Sunni and Shiite. The largest populations of Muslims are in Southeast and South Asia. The three largest branches of Buddhism are Mahayana, Theravada, and Vajrayana. Adherents of Buddhism predominately stretch from Nepal through Southeast and East Asia.

Learning Outcome 6.1.5: Describe the distribution of Hinduism and other ethnic religions.

Hinduism is clustered primarily in India. Other ethnic religions with the largest numbers of followers are clustered elsewhere in Asia. Traditional folk religions have large numbers of followers in sub-Saharan Africa and Southeast Asia.

Learning Outcome 6.1.6: Identify religions other than the most numerous ones.

The religions with at least 2 million adherents are mostly located in Asia, the largest of these being Sikhism, Juche, Spiritism, and Judaism.

As a cultural trait, **religion** helps define people and how they interpret the world around them. There are essentially two major types of religions, universalizing and ethnic. **Universalizing religions** appeal to people of many cultures, regardless of where they live in the world. Nearly 58 percent of the world's population adheres to a universalizing religion. **Ethnic religions** appeal primarily to one group of people living in one place. About 26 percent of the world's population follows an ethnic religion. Some religions are monotheistic, teaching the primacy of one god, whereas other religions are polytheistic, teaching that there are numerous gods. **Atheists** do not believe in any god. The universalizing religions include three of the five largest, Buddhism, Christianity, and Islam, while Hinduism, **Shintoism**, and Judaism are ethnic religions centered around a core location and contained within a particular ethnic population.

Religion in some cases dominates a region and comprises a large majority of the population in that region. The large majority of people in North America, Latin America, and Europe identify with different branches of Christianity. Central Asia, Southwest Asia, and North Africa are predominately Muslim. In comparison, the regions of East Asia, South Asia, Southeast Asia, and Sub-Saharan Africa represent a larger mix of universalizing and ethnic religions.

Christianity has about billion adherents and is the world's most geographically widespread religion. Christians believe in one God and that his son, Jesus, was the promised Messiah, delivering salvation to all people. Christianity has three major branches: Roman Catholic, Eastern Orthodox, and Protestant. The Roman Catholic Church, with its hearth in Vatican City in Rome, is the most important religion in large parts of Europe and North America and is dominant in Latin America. Catholicism also exists on other continents. The Protestant Church began in the 1500s with Martin Luther's protests against the abuses of the Catholic Church.

Christianity is divided into branches, denominations, and sects. A **branch** is a fundamental division within a religion. A **denomination** is a division of a branch; this term is most commonly used to describe groups such as Baptists or Lutherans, divisions within the Protestant faith. A **congregation** is a local assembly of believers in a particular religion. A **sect** is a group that is smaller than a denomination and has broken away from the denomination. At a country scale, Christian denominations are distributed across the United States in significant regional patterns, with pockets of smaller numbers of other denominations appearing within these regions. In Europe, regional distribution is even more evident: northwestern Europe is predominately Protestant, Southern and Central Europe is Roman Catholic, and Eastern and southeastern Europe adheres to Orthodox Christianity.

Buddhism is the oldest of the world's universalizing religions, with millions of adherents clustered in Eastern and Southeast Asia. Founded by Siddhartha Gautama in the sixth century B.C.E., Buddhism teaches that suffering originates from our attachment to life and other worldly possessions. The key concepts of Buddhism are outlined in the Four Noble Truths. Buddhism split into three main branches, Vajrayana, Theravada, Mahayana, as followers disagreed on interpreting statements by Siddhartha Gautama. Theravada Buddhism is found mainly in Cambodia, Laos, Myanmar, Sri Lanka, and Thailand. Mahayana Buddhism is more prevalent in China, Japan, and Korea. The Vajrayanist are found mainly in Mongolia and Tibet. Unlike Christians and Muslims, most Buddhists also follow an ethnic religion, too.

Islam, with more than 1.5 billion followers, is the dominant religion in North Africa and Southwest Asia and parts of Central Asia, as well as Bangladesh and Indonesia. The Muslim population in North America and Europe has increased dramatically in recent years. Islam is a monotheistic religion, based on the belief that there is one God, Allah, and that Mohammed was Allah's prophet. The word *Islam* in Arabic means *submission to the will of God,* and an adherent is a Muslim, *one who surrenders to God.* Islam is divided into two branches: *Sunni,* which is by far the larger of the two, and *Shiite.* In recent years, there has been a rise in radical **fundamentalism** that has caused more division and conflict in the Muslim world. Most fundamentalists accept the holy book of Islam, the Quran, (Koran), as the unquestioned guide on both religious and secular matters. Islamic fundamentalism avoids any sort of Western influence and can contribute to intense conflict.

Sikhism and **Baháí** are the two universalizing religions other than Buddhism, Christianity, and Islam with the largest number of followers. Most Sikhs are located in the Punjab region of India, whereas Baha'is are dispersed among many countries, especially in Africa and Asia.

Ethnic religions have much more clustered distributions than universalizing religions. **Hinduism**, with nearly 900 million adherents, is the largest ethnic religion and the world's third largest religion. The vast majority of Hindus live on the Indian subcontinent. For thousands of years, Hindus in India have developed a unique society that integrates spiritual practices with daily life. Hindus believe that there is more than one path to reach God; there are thousands of deities in the Hindu belief system. Many Hindu scholars believe that the many deities are manifestations of the god Brahma and thus the religion is monotheistic.

The other major ethnic religion is **Judaism**, which was the first major monotheistic religion. Both Christianity and Islam have roots in Judaism; the ancestry of Jesus traces back to Abraham, considered the father of the Jewish people, and Mohammed likewise traced his ancestry to Abraham. Judaism is based on a sense of ethnic identity to the land of Israel. Jews have returned to this land since the end of the nineteenth century, and in 1948, the United Nations recognized the Jewish state of Israel. Today, most Jews live in Israel and the United States.

Other ethnic religions, particularly some found in China, are **syncretic**, meaning they are a combination of several different religions or traditional practices. **Confucianism** and **Taoism** (sometimes spelled Daoism) are sometimes distinguished as philosophies rather than ethnic religions. There is a lot of mixing of these philosophies and religions. Some Africans still practice **animism**, or traditional ethnic religions, although there has been a rapid decline in African animism because of the increase in the numbers of Christians and Muslims in Africa.

Key Issues Revisited

6.1. Where Are Religions Distributed?

- Religions are classified as either universalizing or ethnic.

- The world has three large universalizing religions—Christianity, Islam, and Buddhism.

- Hinduism is the largest ethnic religion, and most of its adherents are clustered in India.

- Other major religions have clustered distributions.

Review Questions

6.1.1. There are four religions that claim 78 percent of the world's people. Which one is NOT one of those religions?
A. Judaism
B. Christianity
C. Islam
D. Hinduism
E. Buddhism

6.1.2. What two religions are dominant in South Asia?
A. Christianity and Hinduism
B. Islam and Sikhism
C. Buddhism and Christianity
D. Hinduism and Islam
E. Daoism and Buddhism

6.1.3 All of these are part of the Christian church EXCEPT _____.
A. Daoism
B. Roman Catholic
C. Protestant
D. Eastern Orthodox
E. Russian Orthodox

6.1.4. Which country has the largest concentration of Muslims?
A. Indonesia
B. India
C. Saudi Arabia
D. Iran
E. Egypt

6.1.5. The largest ethnic religion by far is _____.
A. Judaism
B. Baha'ism
C. Shintoism
D. Hinduism
E. Islam

6.1.6. The first monotheistic religion was _____.
A. Christianity
B. Islam
C. Judaism
D. Buddhism
E. Jainism

KEY ISSUE 2

Why Do Religions Have Distinctive Distributions?

Learning Outcome 6.2.1: Recount the origins of Christianity and Islam.

Christianity began in Southwest Asia. Christianity developed from the teachings of Jesus, recounted in the works of Matthew, Mark, Luke, and John. Islam traces its origins to Judaism and Christianity and centers its development on the Prophet Muhammad, a descendant of Ishmael, the son of Abraham.

Learning Outcome 6.2.2: Discuss the origin of Buddhism and the reason why the origin of Hinduism is unknown.

Buddhism is based on the life teachings of Siddhartha Gautama and his life in Nepal. Hinduism traces its origins to the Indus Valley civilization; however, it evolved over ancient times due to influences from Aryan invaders.

Learning Outcome 6.2.3: Analyze the process of diffusion of universalizing religions.

Universalizing religions have diffused from their place of origin, their hearths, to other regions of the world.

Learning Outcome 6.2.4: Describe the distinctive migration patterns of Christian groups in modern times.

Christianity diffused with migration. Christian migrants account for one-half of the world's international migrants.

Learning Outcome 6.2.5: Trace the distinctive migration patterns of Muslims and Jews.

The largest numbers of Muslim migrants travel to Saudi Arabia, while 34 percent who migrate internationally are going to Europe. Because it is the world's only state with a Jewish majority, Israel is the primary destination for Jews who migrate internationally. However, the largest number of Jewish adherents is in the United States.

The three universalizing religions diffused from **hearths**, or places of origin that are associated with the lives of their founders. Christianity diffused through relocation diffusion where **missionaries** carried the teachings of Jesus around the Mediterranean world. Expansion diffusion was also important as **pagans**, followers of ancient polytheistic religions, were converted to Christianity. It diffused beyond the European realm during the age of colonialism beginning in the early 1500s.

Islam diffused from its hearth at Makkah through military conquest across North Africa, Southern Europe, and other parts of Southwest Asia. Arab traders brought the religion to sub-Saharan Africa and later Indonesia. The core Islamic beliefs are the Five Pillars of Faith, which address the ritualistic acts of a follower of Islam.

Buddhism diffused from its hearth in northern India to Sri Lanka and eastwards into East and Southeast Asia as a result of missionary activity and trade. The foundation of Buddhism is centered on the concepts of the Four Noble Truths, which guide followers toward Nirvana.

Hinduism, originating in the Indus River valley, dates back to 2500 B.C.E. The expansion of Hinduism was carried by the Aryan invasion into the Ganges River valley as far east as Bangladesh today.

Christianity spread from its hearth through a combination of relocation, expansion hierarchical, and contagious diffusion. Relocation diffusion takes Christianity out of Judea through the Roman Empire. Christianity expands in Eastern Europe through hierarchical diffusion through the conversion of leaders and through contagious diffusion along migration and trade routes. Much like Christianity, Buddhism diffused in a hierarchical manner, expanding to Sri Lanka, Kashmir, and Myanmar, and in the first century C.E. through contagious diffusion along the trade routes extending into China and Korea.

Since Roman times, Jews have been forced to leave the eastern Mediterranean and disperse throughout the world, an action known as the **diaspora** (from the Greek word for *dispersion*). Historically, Jews have been persecuted and forced to live in **ghettos**, city areas set up by law to be inhabited only by Jews in many European countries. Since the Nazi Holocaust, many Jews have returned to Israel, although Judaism, unlike other ethnic religions, is practiced in many countries.

Europe attracts 34 percent of the international migration of Muslims. The source areas of these migrants are Turkey and the former French colonies in Africa. The contagious diffusion of Islam was also the result of trade routes and the expansion of Muslim empires.

Key Issues Revisited

6.2. Why Do Religions Have Distinctive Distributions?

- Universalizing religions have a known origin and clear pattern of diffusion.

- Ethnic religions usually have unknown origins and little diffusion.

- Universalizing religions diffuse from their place of origin, while ethnic religions tend to stay near their place of origin.

- Contemporary migration patterns of some religious groups differ from the concentration of their adherents.

Review Questions

6.2.1. The core of Islamic belief involves the acts of the _____.
A. Eight Fold Path
B. Four Noble Truths
C. Ten Commandments
D. Five Pillars of Faith
E. Forty Years of Wander

6.2.2. Hinduism traces its origins to which region?
A. Tigris River valley
B. Indus River valley
C. Huang He River valley
D. Mississippi River valley
E. Euphrates River valley

6.2.3. Which religions diffused in a hierarchical pattern?
A. Buddhism and Islam
B. Judaism and Sikhism
C. Shintoism and Daoism
D. Hinduism and Christianity
E. Zoroastrianism and Sikhism

6.2.4. The largest number of international migrants is _____.
A. Muslim
B. Buddhist
C. Christian
D. Hindu
E. Jewish

6.2.5. Which population was forced to disperse throughout the world in an action known as the diaspora?
A. Orthodox Christians in 1054 C.E.
B. Jews in 70 C.E.
C. Buddhist in 257 B.C.E.
D. Muslims in 622 C.E.
E. Roman Catholics in 1492 C.E.

KEY ISSUE 3

Why Do Religions Organize Space in Distinctive Patterns?

Learning Outcome 6.3.1: Describe places of worship in various religions.

Religions have places of worship, but these places play differing roles for the various religions.

Learning Outcome 6.3.2: Describe places to which Buddhists and Muslims make pilgrimages.

Eight places in northeastern India and southern Nepal are pilgrimage sites associated with the events of Buddha's life. Holy places are associated with the life of Muhammad and include the cities of Makkah (Mecca) and Madinah (Medina).

Learning Outcome 6.3.3: Give examples of religious settlements and of religious toponyms.

Some communities, such as utopian settlements, are built to reflect the distinctive religious beliefs of a particular group. Places with religious significance are named to recognize the importance of religious principles.

Learning Outcome 6.3.4: Compare the administrative organization of hierarchical and locally autonomous religions.

Religions can be divided into those that are administered through a hierarchy and those that are locally autonomous.

Learning Outcome 6.3.5: Discuss the importance of the physical geography in ethnic religions.

In ethnic religions, holy places derive from the physical geography where the religion's adherents are clustered.

Learning Outcome 6.3.6: Understand the roles of holidays and calendars in various religions.
Universalizing religions commemorate events in the founder's life while ethnic religions connect religious celebrations with the seasons and life in the area.

Places of worship create a landscape reflective of the religious belief system of its adherents.

These sacred structures are designed for congregational worship or for individual meditation. Christian

churches, Muslim mosques, Sikh gurdwaras, Jewish synagogues, and Baha'i houses of worship are all

designed for the followers to join together in common worship. In comparison, the Buddhist pagoda,

Shinto shrine, and Hindu temple are designed for contemplation with the spirits and gods. Christian churches were originally modeled after Roman basilicas. Mosques are the most important religious buildings in the Islamic world, and they also serve as places for the community to gather. Most Hindus worship at home, although Hindu temples serve as shrines to one or more of their gods. The pagoda is the most visible religious architecture of the Buddhist and Shinto landscape and contains the relics of Buddhism.

Religious places of worship are considered sacred if declared as such by the followers. Buddhist holy places or shrines mark the location of important events in Buddha's life and are located in northern India and southern Nepal. Lumbini in southern Nepal is where Buddha was born and is considered the holiest site for Buddhist. The holiest locations in Islam are associated with the life of Mohammed and include, in order of importance, Makkah (Mecca), Madinah (Medina), and Jerusalem. Holy places in ethnic religions are closely tied to physical geography. For example, the River Ganges is the holiest river to Hindus in India, and they believe that bathing in its waters will achieve purification.

Utopian settlements that were built based on the religious way of life are best exemplified by the Latter-day Saints (Mormons) in their settlement of Salt Lake City in 1848. The layout of the city was designed to accommodate the hand carts that were used by the early pioneers in a grid pattern, with church-related structures at strategic points. The layout of some settlements is reflective of their faith by the placement and predominance of the church in the center of the settlement. Many utopian communities have disappeared because of celibacy or poor economic opportunities, but some of their buildings have been repurposed or preserved as museums. Many colonial settlements emphasized the importance of faith by placing the church at the center of the community, often near an open park known as a common.

Religious place names (toponyms) are also reflective of the importance of faith on the landscape. Names of religious leaders or sacred places from the culture hearth are often seen as place names, such as San Antonio, Los Angeles, and Notre Dame, among others.

The Roman Catholic Church is a good example of a **hierarchical religion**, with its well-defined geographical structure and division of territory into local administrative units. Archbishops report to the pope and each heads a province, which includes several dioceses. Bishops report to archbishops and administer a **diocese**, which is the basic unit of the geographic organization of the Roman Catholic Church. The headquarters of a bishop is called a *see* and is usually the largest city in the diocese. A priest reports to a bishop and heads a **parish**. The pope is the bishop of the Diocese of Rome and oversees the *Holy See,* which is in the Vatican City.

Islam and some Protestant denominations are good examples of **autonomous religions** because they are relatively self-sufficient with little interaction among communities within the religion. Islam has the most local autonomy of the three largest universalizing religions.

Universalizing and ethnic religions have a different understanding of the relationship between people and their environment. This is exemplified in their different attitudes toward **cosmogony**, the set of religious beliefs that concern the origin of the universe, and the calendar, which for ethnic religions is very much tied to physical geography. The **solar calendar** corresponds to the position of the sun in relation to the stars. A **lunar calendar** corresponds to the cycles of moon phases. A **lunisolar calendar** has lunar months brought into alignment with the solar year through periodic adjustment. The **solstice** has special significance in some ethnic religions and has its origins in some pagan religions.

The calendar is also an important part of life in both universalizing and ethnic religions. Judaism is considered an ethnic rather than a universalizing religion partly because its major religious holidays are based on its agricultural calendar. Universalizing religions' calendars are based on events dealing with the founder's life.

Burial practices of different religions are also visible on the landscape. Christians, Muslims, and Jews usually bury their dead in cemeteries. In Hinduism, cremation is believed to release the soul from the body for departure to the afterworld. The cremation is an act of purification and ideally should occur near the Ganges River, but not every cremation can be held there or near Varanasi. In contrast, the Chinese government orders cremation due to the loss of agricultural land from burial practices. Age-old practices blend the challenges of the environment with the spiritual understanding of life and death.

Key Issues Revisited

6.3. Why Do Religions Organize Space in Distinctive Patterns?

- Religious structures create a landscape designed around the influence of the religion.

- Religions affect the landscape in other ways too, including the building of religious communities, toponyms marking the landscape, and land reserved for burying the dead.

- Some universalizing religions organize their territory into a rigid administrative structure.

- Universalizing religions celebrate events in the life of the founder of the prophet.

- Ethnic religions are more closely tied to their physical environment than are universalizing religions.

- The calendar revolves around the physical environment in ethnic religions and the founder's life in universalizing religions.

Review Questions

6.3.1. Which is not a place for assembly worship?
A. Church
B. Mosque
C. Synagogue
D. Pagoda
E. Cathedral

6.3.2. Pilgrimages to Buddhist shrines occur in _____.
A. India and Nepal
B. China and Nepal
C. Bangladesh and India
D. Saudi Arabia and Israel
E. Thailand and Japan

6.3.3. Which of the following identifies a utopian settlement?
A. It is built around a religious way of life.
B. It is built around an economic way of life.
C. It is built around a socioeconomic distribution of the people.
D. It is built around the town square.
E. It is built around an artistic style.

6.3.4. Which of the following represents a hierarchical religion?
A. The Church of Jesus Christ of Latter-day Saints
B. The United Church of Christ
C. Hinduism
D. Islam
E. Shinto

6.3.5. What is the holiest river for Hindus?
A. Po
B. Lena
C. Ganges
D. Indus
E. Brahmaputra

Why Do Territorial Conflicts Arise Among Religious Groups?

Learning Outcome 6.4.1: State reasons for geographic conflicts between religious and secular cultural groups.
Religions can come into conflict with government policies, social changes, or other religions.

Learning Outcome 6.4.2: Understand geographic elements of conflicts among religious groups in Southwest Asia.
Combatants in the Middle East have different perspectives on the division of land in the area, stemming from their shared heritage.

Learning Outcome 6.4.3: Explain Israeli and Palestinian perspectives on Israel.
Both Israelis and Palestinians claim the same lands.

Learning Outcome 6.4.4: Explain the importance of Jerusalem to Jews and Muslims.
The most sacred space in Jerusalem for Muslims was built on top of the most sacred space for Jews.

Religious identification can lead to religious conflict. When looking at religious conflict, geographers tend to look at these conflicts as being caused by one of the following: religion versus government policies, religion versus social change, religion versus religion, or religious wars in the Southwest Asia. The Hindu **caste system**, which was the hereditary class into which a Hindu was placed according to religious law, has led to social and ethnic conflict in India. Although caste-based discrimination still exists, these issues are less significant now that the caste system has been legally abolished. The rise of communism has also been a challenge to organized religion, especially in Eastern Europe and Asia.

Religious conflict continues in many parts of the world, especially at the boundaries among different religions, branches, and denominations. These conflicts have complex historical, social, and ethnic roots and must also be understood in the context of political geography. The intense religious conflict in Central Asia is the result of the resurgence of religious fundamentalism, the strict and intense adherence to the basic principles of a religion. Fundamentalists believe that their interpretation is the only correct one and their practice is all that should be allowed. Conflict arises when they claim areas of those that do not believe in or agree with this interpretation.

For example, there has been long-standing conflict in the Southwest Asia. The city of Jerusalem contains sites that are sacred to Judaism, Christianity, and Islam. There have also been religious wars in Ireland between Catholics and Protestants that have their origins in the English conquest of Ireland centuries ago. Tibetan Buddhism has been undermined by Chinese Communism since the latter's takeover of Tibet in 1950. There is concern that many Tibetan Buddhist traditions will be lost forever when the Dalai Lama and current generation of priests die.

Key Issues Revisited

6.4. Why Do Territorial Conflicts Arise Among Religions Groups?

- Expansion of the territory occupied by one religion may reduce the territory of another.

- Religions must compete for control of territory with nonreligious ideas, such as economic modernization.

- Religious groups have opposed government policies, especially those of Communist governments.

- Israel/Palestine is an area of long-standing and intractable conflict, as the area is considered holy by Jews, Christians, and Muslims.

Review Questions

6.4.1. Which religion supports the caste system but is illegal under the law?
A. Buddhism
B. Catholicism
C. Islam
D. Hinduism
E. Baha'ism

6.4.2. Conflict in Southwest Asia involves all of the following EXCEPT _____.
A. Jews
B. Christians
C. Muslims
D. Hindus
E. All of the above are exceptions.

6.4.3. Jerusalem is a sacred place to all of the following EXCEPT _____.
A. Christians
B. Buddhists
C. Muslims
D. Jews
E. None of the above; Jerusalem is sacred to all religions.

6.4.4. The conflict in Jerusalem between the Jews and Muslims is over what holy sites?
A. Garden of Gethsemane and the Mount of Olives
B. Church of the Ascension and the Church of the Holy Sepulchre
C. Yad Vashem and Givat HaTanakh
D. The Western Wall and the Dome of the Rock
E. Mount Zion and Masada

Key Terms

Agnosticism	Hierarchical religion*
Animism	Hinduism*
Atheism	Islam*
Autonomous religions	Judaism*
Bahái	Lunar calendar
Branch	Missionary
Buddhism*	Monotheism
Caste system	Pagan
Christianity*	Pilgrimage
Confucianism	Polytheism
Congregation	Religion*
Cosmogony	Sacred spaces
Denomination	Sect
Diaspora	Shintoism
Diocese	Sikhism*
Ethnic religion*	Solstice
Fundamentalism	Syncretic*
Ghetto	Taoism
Hearth*	Universalizing religion*

* Term is in 2019 College Board Curriculum & Exam Description.

Think Like a Geographer Activities

Research the recent conflict between Buddhists in Tibet and the Communist government of China, as well as the conflict in Northern Ireland between the Catholics and the Protestants. Explain the impact of religion on the cultural landscape.

Quick Quiz

Who Am I?

6.1. Born in Lumbini, Nepal

6.2. Bishop of the Diocese of Rome

6.3. Born in Makkah

6.4. Father of three major world religions

6.5. Father of Sikhism

A. Guru Nanak

B. Buddha

C. Abraham

D. The Pope

E. Muhammad

Free Response

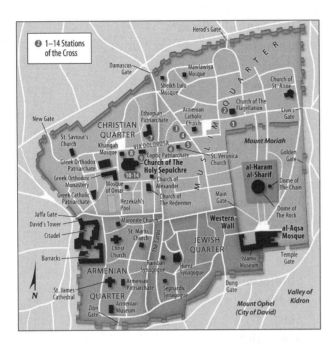

Figure 6-1

Figure 6-2

1. Identify the religious conflict that is illustrated in the photo in Figure 6-2.
2. Using the map in Figure 6-1 and the photo in Figure 6-2, identify and describe three places that are sacred spaces.
3. Explain how religious places impact the socioeconomic landscape.

On the Web

www.masteringgeography.com

www.religioustolerance.org/var_rel.htm

www.religionfacts.com/

www.infoplease.com/ipa/A0855613.html

www.adherents.com/

Around the World in 80 Faiths, America: www.dailymotion.com/video/x3ehb5d_around-the-world-in-80-faith-america_tv

Around the World in 80 Faiths, Middle East: www.dailymotion.com/video/x3bef5n_around-the-world-in-80-faiths-middle-east_tv

www.vox.com/2015/7/13/8950979/religion-map

Animated Map Shows How Religion Spread Around The World: www.m.youtube.com/watch?reload=9&v=AvFI6UBZLv4

The Pyres of Varanasi: Breaking the Cycle of Death and Rebirth: www.nationalgeographic.com/photography/proof/2014/08/07/the-pyres-of-varanasi-breaking-the-cycle-of-death-and-rebirth/

TED Talks

Rick Warren on a life of purpose
www.ted.com/talks/rick_warren_on_a_life_of_purpose.html

Let's Teach Religion—All Religion—in School. Dan Dennett's response to Rick Warren
www.ted.com/talks/dan_dennett_s_response_to_rick_warren.html

AJ Jacob's year on living biblically www.ted.com/talks/a_j_jacobs_year_of_living_biblically.html

Is There a God? theme page, God
www.ted.com/themes/is_there_a_god.html

Key Figures

Figure 6-1 Percentages Adhering to Various Religions

Figure 6-5 Most Numerous Religions by Country

Figure 6-7 Most Numerous Religions by Region

Figure 6-8 Most Numerous Religions and Branches in Europe

Table 6-1 Religions of the United States, 2014

Figure 6-11 Distribution of Branches of Buddhism

Figure 6-12 Distribution of World's Muslims

Figure 6-13 Distribution of Branches of Islam

Figure 6-17 Distribution of Primal-Indigenous Religions in Southeast Asia

Figure 6-19 Distribution of African Traditional Religions

Figure 6-20 Clustered Religions with At Least 2 Million Adherents

Figure 6-22 Distribution of Jews

Figure 6-23 Distribution of Baha'is

Figure 6-25 Origin of Islam

Figure 6-26 Origin of Buddhism

Figure 6-27 Unknown Origin of Hinduism

Figure 6-29 Diffusion of Universalizing Religions

Figure 6-30 Diffusion of Buddhism

Figure 6-31 Diffusion of Islam

Figure 6-32 Diffusion of Christianity

Figure 6-37 Most Numerous Christian Branches in Canada

Figure 6-39 Largest Flows of Islamic Migrants

Figure 6-42 Distribution of Jews, 1910 and 2012

Figure 6-66 Territorial Changes in Israel and Its Neighbors

Figure 6-70 Old City of Jerusalem

Figure 6-71 Western Wall and Dome of The Rock

AP® Human Geography Outline of Culture-Religion

This is part of the section on Cultural Patterns and Processes outlined in Chapter 4.

Unit 3: Cultural Patterns and Processes

Topic	APHG Topic No. Title	Suggested Skills	Enduring Understandings	Essential Knowledge	Big Ideas
6.1.1; 6.1.2; 6.1.3; 6.1.4; 6.1.6	3.7: Diffusion of Religion and Language	4.E: Explain how maps, images, and landscapes illustrate or relate to geographic principles, processes, and outcomes.	IMP-3: The interaction of people contributes to the spread of cultural practices.	IMP-3.B.3: Religions have distinct places of origin from which they diffused to other locations through different processes. Practices and belief systems impacted how widespread the religion diffused.	B1-2: Impacts and Interactions
6.1.5	3.7: Diffusion of Religion and Language	4.E: Explain how maps, images, and landscapes illustrate or relate to geographic principles, processes, and outcomes.	IMP-3: The interaction of people contributes to the spread of cultural practices.	IMP-3.B.5: Ethnic religions, including Hinduism and Judaism, are generally found near the hearth or spread through relocation diffusion.	B1-2: Impacts and Interactions
6.2.1; 6.2.2; 6.2.3; 6.2.4; 6.2.5	3.7: Diffusion of Religion and Language	4.E: Explain how maps, images, and landscapes illustrate or relate to geographic principles, processes, and outcomes.	IMP-3: The interaction of people contributes to the spread of cultural practices.	IMP-3.B.3: Religions have distinct places of origin from which they diffused to other locations through different processes. Practices and belief systems impacted how widespread the religion diffused.	B1-2: Impacts and Interactions
6.3.1; 6.3.2; 6.3.3; 6.3.4; 6.3.5; 6.3.6	3.3: Cultural Patterns	4.C: Explain patterns and trends in visual sources to draw conclusions.	PSO-3: Cultural practices vary across geographical locations because of physical geography and available resources.	PSO-3.D.1: Regional patterns of language, religion, and ethnicity contribute to a sense of place, enhance placemaking, and shape the global cultural landscape.	B1-2: Impacts and Interactions

6.4.1; *6.4.2;* *6.4.3;* *6.4.4*	3.3: Cultural Patterns	4.C: Explain patterns and trends in visual sources to draw conclusions.	PSO-3: Cultural practices vary across geographical locations because of physical geography and available resources.	PSO-3.D.2: Language, ethnicity and religion are factors in creating centripetal and centrifugal forces.	B1-2: Impacts and Interactions

Source: College Board AP Human Geography Course Description, effective Fall 2019

FRQ's From the College Board

2009 FRQ#1
2002 FRQ#2

Chapter

7 Ethnicities

Where Are Ethnicities Distributed?

The geographic distribution of ethnicities is initially considered in this chapter. Ethnic groups are tied to particular places because members of the group, or their ancestors, were born or raised there. Another important consideration is ethnic conflict in specific areas and certain places of the world. The attempt to retain distinct ethnic identity is one example of the preservation of local diversity, while some regions experience ethnic conflict leading to forced migration or genocide. The AP Human Geography course is asking students to examine patterns and landscapes influenced by ethnic patterns. The ethnically influenced landscape looks at attitudes toward different ethnic groups, reasons for concentration of ethnic groups in places outside of their homeland, influences on global and popular culture, and how ethnic conflict leads to centripetal and centrifugal forces.

Learning Outcome 7.1.1: Distinguish between ethnicity and race.

Ethnicity is the cultural group or nation one identifies with. Race is distinguished by physiological traits.

Learning Outcome 7.1.2: Summarize changes in the classification of race and ethnicity in the United States.

The U.S. Bureau of the Census classifies people in the United States by race as white, black or African American, American Indian or Alaska Native, Asian, and Pacific Islander.

Learning Outcome 7.1.3: Compare the distribution of U.S. ethnicities.

Hispanics are clustered in the Southwest, African Americans in the Southeast, and Asian Americans in the West. African Americans and Hispanics are highly clustered in urban areas, especially in inner-city neighborhoods.

Learning Outcome 7.1.4: Compare race and ethnicity in Brazil.

Brazil has a distinctive regional difference in the distribution of races because of its colonial and slave history.

Learning Outcome 7.1.5: Describe the distribution of ethnicities within urban areas.

Immigrants tend to migrate to the same areas in a city as previous members of the same ethnic community. This pattern creates an ethnic enclave and influences the cultural landscape of a city.

Ethnicity comes from the Greek root *ethnos,* which means *national.* Ethnicity is identity with a group of people who share a common identity with a specific homeland or hearth. It is distinct from **race**, which is identity with a group of people who share a biological ancestor. Biological classification by race is the basis for **racism**, which is the belief that racial differences produce an inherent superiority of a particular race. A **racist** is someone who follows the beliefs of racism. The characteristics of ethnicity derive from the distinctive features of specific geographic locations, whereas those of race are not rooted in particular places. **Nationality** is the group of people who share legal attachment to a particular country. Race and ethnicity are not synonymous with each other. Ethnicity and nationality are spatially defined, whereas the concept of race is biologically defined. The U.S. Census regards *Hispanic American* as an ethnicity, while it classifies *Asian American* and *African American* as races.

With the exception of non-Hispanic European-Americans, the largest ethnicities in the United States are Hispanics (or Latinos) at 17 percent of total population, African Americans at 12 percent, and Asian

Americans at 5 percent. An additional 2 percent are American Indian, Native Hawaiian, or Alaskan Native. The remaining 62 percent of the population are descendants of non-Hispanic Europeans.

On a regional scale, African Americans are clustered in the Southeast, Hispanics in the Southwest, Asian Americans in the West and major American cities, and American Indians in the Southwest and Plains states. At the urban level, African Americans and Hispanics are highly clustered in ethnic neighborhoods, also known as an ethnic enclave, in cities. At the same time, these cities are also **multicultural**. This cluster pattern is seen in many large cities outside the United States that have experienced large-scale migration from foreign countries.

Previously in the United States, ethnic enclaves were created by European immigrants who developed the areas with their own cultural footprint on the landscape of businesses, restaurants, and stores that appealed to the needs of the particular ethnic population. The concept of Little Italy, Chinatown, and the Jewish section of Brooklyn in New York City are examples of ethnic enclaves. The second and third generation of descendants of these European immigrants were fully assimilated into American life and moved out to suburban communities. The suburbs developed a cluster pattern of settlement identified through local religious, food, and services for the various ethnic populations. These clustered patterns are known as **ethnoburbs**. Examples of ethnoburbs are found in Chicago, New York City, Houston, and Detroit, among many others.

Other countries that are composed of large numbers of migrants historically or currently have a similar pattern of regional and urban ethnic differences like those of the United States. The cities of London, Paris, Brussels, and Cape Town are just a few, and the countries of Brazil, South Africa, Singapore, Canada, and regions such as South Asia, Central Asia, and West Asia all experience ethnic diversity that appears on the cultural landscape in clustered ethnic settlements.

Section 7.1.4 of the textbook addresses the challenges of classifying race identification at the national level in Brazil. The complexity of Brazilian ethnic and racial classification stems from Brazil's colonial origin and periods of immigration from other parts of the world.

Key Issues Revisited

7.1. Where Are Ethnicities Distributed?

- Ethnicity, race, and nationality are not the same concepts.

- Large numbers of non-European ethnicities in the United States are Hispanic, African American, and Asian American.

- These ethnic groups are clustered in regions of the country and within urban areas.

Review Questions

7.1.1. The most important feature of ethnicity that geographers look at is:
A. migration routes.
B. the spatial distribution of common cultural traditions.
C. the legal identity of a population.
D. physiological traits of a population.
E. facial features.

7.1.2. The most important feature of race that geographers look at is:
A. skin color.
B. hair type.
C. blood type.
D. religious identity.
E. facial features.

7.1.3. At what scale would the distribution of African Americans and Hispanics be most notable because they are so clustered together?
A. Local scale
B. Regional scale
C. County scale
D. State scale
E. National scale

7.1.4. Which of the following countries reflects a multiethnic and multiracial society?
A. Iceland
B. Poland
C. Brazil
D. Mongolia
E. Japan

7.1.5. Where is an ethnoburb located?
A. In the heart of the inner city
B. In the suburban real of the city
C. In the hinterlands away from the city
D. Predominately in an urban region composed of one ethnicity
E. Along the original settlement areas of a region

KEY ISSUE 2

Why Do Ethnicities Have Distinctive Distributions?

The AP Human Geography course is asking students to examine patterns and landscapes influenced by ethnic patterns. The ethnically influenced landscape looks at attitudes toward different ethnic groups and reasons for concentration of ethnic groups in places outside of their homeland.

Learning Outcome 7.2.1: Describe forced migration from Africa.
Many African Americans trace their ancestry to forced migration from Africa for slavery. By contrast, many Hispanics and Asian Americans trace their heritage to people who migrated in the late twentieth century for economic prospects and political freedom.

Learning Outcome 7.2.2: Describe the patterns of migration of African Americans within the United States.
African Americans migrated in large numbers from the South to the North and West in the early twentieth century. African Americans clustered in inner-city ghettos that have expanded in recent decades.

Learning Outcome 7.2.3a: Explain the laws once used to segregate races in the United States.
The U.S. Supreme Court upheld "separate but equal" laws in *Plessy v. Ferguson* in 1896. The high court rejected this principle in 1954.

Learning Outcome 7.2.3b: Explain the laws once used to segregate races in South Africa.
Apartheid created legal separation of the races in South Africa. Apartheid ended in 1991.

Learning Outcome 7.2.4: Describe how ethnicities can be divided among more than one nationality.
Political boundaries can divide ethnicities into more than one nationality, which can cause centrifugal factors.

The distribution of African Americans in the United States illustrates a pattern of both international and intraregional migrations.

Three major migration patterns have shaped the current distribution of African Americans within the United States. The first was the forced migration from Africa that was part of the **triangular**

slave trade. After slavery, most African Americans remained in the rural South working as **sharecroppers**, which is farming land rented from a landowner and paying rent in the form of crops. Blacks were still separated from whites in the South through laws that followed the Supreme Court's "separate but equal" treatment of the races. The second major migration pattern was the migration to northern cities at the beginning of the twentieth century. In these cities, African American immigrants lived in **ghettos,** named for the term for neighborhoods where Jews were forced to live in medieval Europe. Segregation laws were eliminated during the 1950s and 1960s. The third migration pattern was their movement from ghettos into neighborhoods immediately adjacent during this time. This was made possible by "white flight" to the suburbs, which, in turn, was encouraged by **blockbusting**, where real estate agents convinced white homeowners living near a black area to sell their houses to the agents at low prices.

Discrimination by race was the cornerstone of the South African legal system of apartheid. **Apartheid** was the physical separation of different races into separate geographic areas. It was instituted by the white Afrikaners government in 1948 and was particularly designed to subjugate the black majority by forcing them to live in impoverished homelands. The apartheid laws were repealed in 1991, but although South Africa now has black majority rule, it will take many years to redress their geographic impact.

Ethnic division among independent countries can lead to independence movements by ethnic minority population and cause an escalation of tensions in the neighboring countries from the same supporters. Examples of this centrifugal force include the Kurds separated into Turkey, Iran, Iraq, and Syria and the Hindu and Muslim populations separated from their ethnic majority in India and Pakistan. All of these areas continue to have political and cultural conflict today.

Key Issues Revisited

7.2. Why Do Ethnicities Have Distinctive Distributions?

- Ancestors of some African Americans immigrated to the United States as slaves.

- African Americans migrated from the South to the North and West during the early-twentieth century seeking jobs.

- Laws allowed for the segregation of races for much of the twentieth century in South Africa and the United States.

Review Questions

7.2.1. What amendment to the U.S. Constitution outlawed slavery?
A. Amendment 19
B. Amendment 14
C. Amendment 5
D. Amendment 13
E. Amendment 1

7.2.2. What prompted the migration of African Americans from the South to the North and West in the 1920s and 1950s?
A. Available housing
B. Factory jobs
C. Open farm land
D. Expanding settlement areas in cities
E. Civil rights and freedoms

7.2.3. The policy of legally separating races and moving them into designated homeland areas in South Africa was known as _____.
A. racism
B. apartheid
C. separate but equal
D. Homeland Act
E. Civil Rights Act

7.2.4. Which area in India is contested due to ethnic conflict from the imposition of a political boundary with Pakistan?
A. Tamil Nadu
B. Rajasthan
C. Uttar Pradesh
D. Jammu and Kashmir
E. Punjab

KEY ISSUE 3

Why Might Ethnicities Face Conflicts?

Learning Outcome 7.3.1: Explain differences between ethnicities and nationalities.
Nationality is the identification with a group of people who share legal attachment and personal allegiance to a particular country. **Nationalism** is loyalty and devotion to a nationality.

Learning Outcome 7.3.2: Identify the principal ethnic conflicts in Western Asia.
The lack of correspondence between the territory occupied by ethnicities and nationalities is especially severe in western Asia.

Learning Outcome 7.3.3: Identify the principal ethnic conflicts in West-Central Asia.
Dozens of ethnicities are divided between eight nations and 4 million square kilometers.

The AP Human Geography course is asking students to examine patterns and landscapes influenced by ethnic patterns. The ethnically influenced landscape looks at attitudes toward different ethnic groups and how ethnic conflict leads to centripetal and centrifugal forces.

Nationality, which comes from the Latin word *nasci,* meaning *to have been born,* is the identity with a group of people who share legal attachment and personal allegiance to a country. The desire for self-rule or **self-determination** has transformed ethnic groups into nationalities. A **nation-state** is a state whose territory corresponds to that occupied by a particular ethnicity. There are numerous nation-states in Europe, including France, Slovenia, and Denmark. For example, there are some German speakers in Denmark and some Danish speakers in Germany.

Nationalism refers to the degree of loyalty that one has for a nationality. This could be instilled by promoting symbols of nationalism such as flags and songs. Nationalism is an example of a **centripetal force**, which is one that tends to unify people behind the state. **Centrifugal forces** do exactly the opposite and may lead to the breakup of a state.

Multiethnic states contain more than one dominant ethnicity. For example, Belgium is divided among the Dutch-speaking Flemish and the French-speaking Walloons. They are also called **multinational states**, and each ethnic group will generally recognize each other as distinct nationalities. This is true of the United Kingdom today with its four major nationalities—English, Welsh, Scottish, and (northern) Irish. The former Soviet Union was the largest multinational state with 15 republics that represented many different ethnic groups. The breakup of the Soviet Union created independent states in the Baltic, Eastern Europe, Central Asia, and the Caucasus. There are geopolitical problems in the Caucasus because the boundaries of Armenia, Azerbaijan, and Georgia do not completely match the territories occupied by these ethnicities. For example, there are minorities of Armenians in Azerbaijan, and vice versa. Russia is still the largest multinational state with 39 nationalities, many of which, like Chechnya, want to be independent.

Conflicts also arise when one ethnicity is split among more than one country. A **stateless** nation is a group of people with common cultural ties that are contained in one or more states of other cultural groups that they do not identify with. The Kurds are an example of a stateless nation occupying lands in Iraq, Iran, Turkey, and Syria. The desire to create an independent state uniting the Kurdish people has lead to nationalist uprisings in the region. There have also been major ethnic disputes between India and Pakistan since these countries became independent from Britain in 1947. Even though there was massive forced migration at the time of independence, there are still minorities of Hindus in Pakistan and minorities of Muslims in India. In addition, the two countries never agreed on the location of their boundary in the northern region of Kashmir.

Movements for self-determination are fueled by **ethnonationalism**, a strong feeling of belonging to a nation that is a minority within a state or prevalent in the western Asian countries from Turkey to Afghanistan. In Lebanon, Syria, Iraq, and Iran, the foundation for nationalist uprisings is based on conflicts of religious identity; in Turkey, Afghanistan, and Pakistan the nationalist conflict centers around large numbers of ethnicities who have suffered under harsh and discriminatory laws. Lebanon has experienced civil war because of ethnic and religious divisions. The country is comprised of numerous Christian sects, as well as Muslims belonging to both the Shiite and Sunni sects. The island country of Sri Lanka has been torn by fighting between the Sinhalese Buddhists, who speak an Indo-European language, and the Tamil Hindus, who speak a Dravidian language. The long war between the ethnicities ended in 2009 with the defeat of the Tamil.

Many of these uprisings are based on irredentist motivations. **Irredentist** movements or **irredentism** is the attempt to claim territory on the basis of (real or imagined) historic or ethnic affiliations. Irredentist movements are active in the Caucasus region.

Key Issues Revisited

7.3. Why Might Ethnicities Face Conflicts?

- Conflicts can develop when a country contains several ethnicities that vie for political control based on irredentist or nationalist motivations.

- Conflicts can also develop when an ethnicity is divided among more than one country.

Review Questions

7.3.1. Nationalities share all BUT which of the following?
A. Passports
B. Voting
C. Civic duty
D. Religion
E. Loyalty

7.3.2. The Kurds are an example of a _____.
A. multinational state
B. nation-state
C. stateless nation
D. centripetal force for Iraq
E. centrifugal force for India

7.3.3. What has contributed to most of the conflicts between ethnicities in West and Central Asia?
A. Religious differences
B. State boundaries
C. Economic barriers to trade
D. Civil war
E. Dialects of language that prevents effective communication

KEY ISSUE 4

Why Do Ethnic Cleansing and Genocide Occur?

Learning Outcome 7.4.1: Analyze current and past examples of ethnic cleansing and genocide.

Ethnic cleansing is the deliberate policy of one ethnic or religious group to remove by violent and terror-inspiring means another ethnic or religious group from certain geographic areas.

Learning Outcome 7.4.2: Describe the breakup of Yugoslavia and its consequences for Balkan ethnic groups.

Balkanization is a process by which a state breaks down through conflicts among its ethnicities. This led to further ethnic cleansing in Kosovo and Croatia.

Learning Outcome 7.4.3: Explain the concept of ethnic cleansing in Bosnia & Herzegovina.

Ethnic cleansing is the forced removal of the population outside of the territory and destruction of the remaining settlement.

Learning Outcome 7.4.4: Identify the principal recent episodes of genocide in Africa.

Genocide is the mass killing of a group of people in an attempt to eliminate the entire group from existence.

Learning Outcome 7.4.5: Identify the principal recent episodes of genocide in Central Africa.

Genocide has been practiced in several places in Central Africa, including Rwanda, Burundi, and the Democratic Republic of Congo. Ethnic conflicts have resulted in genocides.

Throughout history, conflict between ethnic groups has led to forced migration. Ethnic cleansing is the process by which a more powerful ethnic group forcibly removes a less powerful one in order to create their own nation or nation-state. Geographers look at ethnic cleansing because it alters the cultural landscape and the spatial distribution of the ethnic population that was attacked.

The most recent ethnic cleansing, as declared by the United Nations, has occurred in Myanmar toward the Rohingya population that migrated from Bangladesh during the British colonial period. The Myanmar government sought to eliminate the Rohingya by forcing them to flee the region.

In the 1990s, the ethnic cleansing in Bosnia and Herzegovina is a classic example of the devolution into ethnically homogeneous areas. Bosnia was the most multiethnic republic of former Yugoslavia. At the time of the breakup of Yugoslavia in the early 1990s, the population of Bosnia consisted of 44 percent Bosnian Muslim, 31 percent Serb, and 17 percent Croat. Serbs and Croats fought to unite their ethnicity in Bosnia with their respective republics; this is called irredentism. The Serbs in Bosnia were **irredenta** of Serbia. To reunite the Serb and Croat ethnicities, they both engaged in ethnic cleansing of Bosnian Muslims.

After the breakup of Yugoslavia, Serbia remained a multiethnic state. The southern **province** of Kosovo is 90 percent ethnic Albanian. Serbia launched a campaign of ethnic cleansing of the Albanian majority. Eventually, Serbia withdrew its troops from Kosovo as a result of a North Atlantic Treaty Organization (NATO) air attack. Kosovo declared its independence from Serbia in 2008. In 1991, Serbians tried to break apart the eastern section of Croatia. With only 12 percent of the population, the Serbs forcibly removed the Croats and entered a four-year war that resulted in Serbian leaders being prosecuted for war crimes connected to the ethnic cleansing of Croats.

The Balkans has always been a region of ethnic conflict. The political geography term **Balkanized** is used to describe a geographic area that cannot be organized into one or more stable states inhabited by multiple ethnicities. The term Balkanization is the process by which a state breaks down through ethnic conflict. A shatterbelt refers to an area or region that is constantly in a state of conflict.

Genocide is the mass killing of a group of people in an attempt to eliminate the entire population. As a result of colonialism and the division of the African nations among the European colonists, ethnic populations of portions of Africa were divided and separated. After independence from colonial powers, several of these countries fell into ethnic conflict because of the division of the ethnic populations and inclusion of others in foreign territories. Sudan is one of the areas that has been at war since the 1980s, resulting in genocide and ethnic cleansing particularly in the region of Darfur and South Sudan. Darfur lost 300,000 people to genocide and 3 million to ethnic cleansing most of which are now living in refugee camps. A 22-year war in south Sudan resulted in 1.9 million killed and another 700,000 displaced. The north-south war resulted from a religious conflict where the north was trying to impose a strict Islamic legal system on the non-Muslim southerners.

Ethnic cleansing led to genocide in Rwanda in the 1990s because of longstanding conflict between the Hutus and the Tutsis. The Hutus were farmers and the Tutsis were cattle herders. Historically, the Tutsi took control and made the Hutus their serfs. Previously, the region was colonized by the Belgians and Germans. In 1962, shortly before independence, the Hutus launched an ethnic cleansing against the Tutsis. Then in 1994, Tutsi descendants returned to the country, setting off a civil war. The assassination of the presidents of Rwanda and Burundi sparked the genocide of more than 800,000 Tutsis in Rwanda and 300,000 in Burundi. Another wave of ethnic cleansing and genocide occurred when Tutsis defeated the Hutu army and killed half a million Hutus. This conflict has spilled into neighboring countries, especially the Democratic Republic of the Congo, and the region is still very unstable because of ethnic conflict.

Key Issues Revisited

7.4. Why Do Ethnic Cleansing and Genocide Occur?

- Ethnic cleansing is an attempt by one ethnic group to remove all members of another ethnic group in order to create an ethnically homogeneous region.

- Genocide is the mass killing of a group of people in an attempt to eliminate the entire group from existence.

- Ethnic cleansing was practiced in the conflict in Yugoslavia during the 1990s, in Sudan in the 1980s, and in Central Africa since 1994.

Review Questions

7.4.1. The policy to deliberately remove one ethnic or religious group by violence or terror is _____.
A. genocide
B. civil war
C. ethnic cleansing
D. Balkanization
E. nation building

7.4.2. Geographers study ethnic cleansing because:
A. it results in the alteration of a place and its use by a different population.
B. maps have to be redrawn.
C. it changes the names of leadership.
D. it can negatively change the economic structure of the country.
E. it creates a syncretic society.

7.4.3. What is the process of a state breaking down through conflicts among its ethnicities?
A. Shatterbelt
B. Genocide
C. Centripetal
D. Centrifugal
E. Balkanization

7.4.4. What was the cause of the ethnic cleansing in Sudan?
A. Civil war
B. Ethnic diversity between Arab and non-Arab ethnicities
C. Loss of government control by the ethnic minority population
D. Expansion into non-Arab lands by the Arab majority
E. Control of water access by the Christian Dinka population

7.4.5. Which area of sub-Saharan Africa has suffered from the world's deadliest wars in the past 70 years?
A. Sudan
B. Rwanda
C. The Congo
D. Ethiopia
E. Burundi

Key Terms

Apartheid	**Multicultural**
Balkanization	**Multiethnic state**
Balkanized	**Multinational state* (unit 4)**
Blockbusting*	**Nationalism* (unit 4)**
Centripetal forces*	**Nationality**
Centrifugal forces*	**Nation-state* (unit 4)**
Contagious diffusion*	**Province**
Ethnic cleansing*	**Race**
Ethnic neighborhoods*	**Racism**
Ethnicity*	**Racist**
Ethnonationalism* (unit 4)	**Relocation diffusion***
Genocide	**Self-determination* (unit 4)**
Ghettos	**Sharecropper**
Hierarchical diffusion*	**Shatterbelt* (unit 4)**
Irredenta	**Stimulus diffusion***
Irredentism*	**Triangular slave trade**

* Term is in 2019 College Board Curriculum & Exam Description.

Think Like a Geographer Activities

Go to www.washingtonpost.com/wp-srv/national/longterm/meltingpot/melt0222.htm

If you go to the above link, read the article and attempt to answer the question, "Is America a melting pot even though there is the appearance of ethnic segregation?"

Quick Quiz

7.1. Which U.S. region has the highest population concentration of Hispanics?
A. Northeast
B. Midwest
C. Ohio Valley
D. Pacific Northwest
E. Southwest

7.2. Race is:
A. characterized by Caucasian, African American, and Hispanic/Latino.
B. self-identification with a group sharing a biological ancestor.
C. determinable from physical characteristics, like DNA.
D. evenly distributed around the world.
E. determined by the country you come from.

7.3. In the United States, which is shared by all Americans?
A. Nationality
B. Language
C. Ethnicity
D. Race
E. DNA

7.4. Which of the following is an example of irredentism?
A. Balkanization
B. Shatterbelt
C. Genocide
D. Nationalism
E. Segregation

Free Response

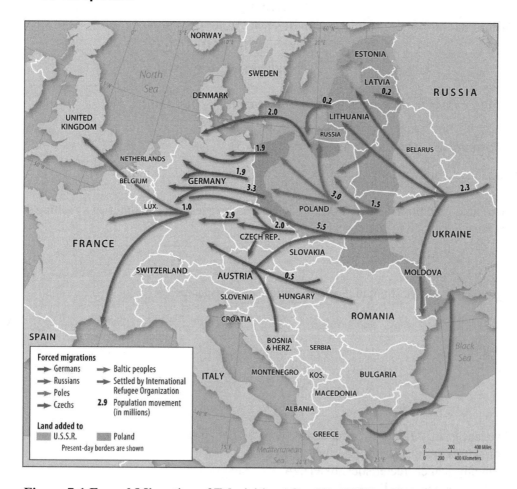

Figure 7-1 Forced Migration of Ethnicities After World War II

1. Using the map above (Figure 7-49 in your textbook) describe the socioeconomic and political impact of forced migration in Europe.

2. Explain how migration impacts the nationalistic identity of a state. Provide one example.

3. Identify two centripetal and two centrifugal factors affecting the sociopolitical development of a multiethnic society.

On the Web

www.masteringgeography.com

www.diffen.com/difference/Ethnicity_vs_Race

www.infoplease.com/ipa/A0855617.html

www.washingtonpost.com/graphics/national/how-diverse-is-america/?hpid=hp_no-name_graphic-story-a%3Ahomepage%2Fstory

www.nytimes.com/2016/01/03/world/asia/xinjiang-seethes-under-chinese-crackdown.html?smid=fb-nytimes&smtyp=cur&_r=0

www.nytimes.com/2016/01/03/world/asia/xinjiang-seethes-under-chinese-crackdown.html

TED Talks

The "Ethnic Cleansing" of Myanmar's Rohingya Muslims, published by VOX
www.youtube.com/watch?v=04axDDRVy_o

The Middle East's Cold War, Explained
www.youtube.com/watch?v=veMFCFyOwFI

Stefan Wolff: The Path to Ending Ethnic Conflicts
www.youtube.com/watch?v=UfM7t_oqNDw&feature=youtu.be

Ngozi Okonjo-Iweala: Aid versus Trade
www.ted.com/talks/ngozi_okonjo_iweala_on_aid_versus_trade.html

Ngozi Okonjo-Iweala: Want to Help Africa? Do Business Here
www.ted.com/talks/ngozi_okonjo_iweala_on_doing_business_in_africa.html

Bono: My Wish: Three Actions for Africa
www.ted.com/talks/bono_s_call_to_action_for_africa.html

Bill Gates: Mosquitos, Malaria and Education
www.ted.com/talks/bill_gates_unplugged.html

Key Figures

Figure 7-5 Hispanics by Place of Origin
Figure 7-6 Distribution of Hispanics in the United States
Figure 7-7 Asian Americans by Country of Origin
Figure 7-8 Distribution of Asian Americans in the United States
Figure 7-9 Distribution of African Americans in the United States
Figure 7-10 Distribution of American Indians, Alaska Natives, and Native Hawaiians in the United States
Figure 7-22 Ethnic Enclaves, London
Figure 7-24 Origins and Destinations of Slaves
Figure 7-25 Triangular Slave Trade
Figure 7-26 Interregional Migration of African Americans
Figure 7-32 South Africa's Apartheid Homelands
Figure 7-35 Ethnic Division of South Asia
Figure 7-37 Kurdistan
Figure 7-43 Ethnicities in Western Asia
Figure 7-46 Ethnicities in West-Central Asia
Figure 7-51 Destinations of Ethnically Cleansed Rohingya as of 2018
Figure 7-53 Breakup of Yugoslavia
Figure 7-58 Africa's Many Ethnicities and Nationalities
Figure 7-62 Rwanda and Burundi
Figure 7-64 Ethnicities in the Democratic Republic of Congo

AP® Human Geography Outline of Culture-Ethnicity

This is part of the section on Cultural Patterns and Processes outlined in Chapter 4.

Unit 3: Cultural Patterns and Processes

Unit 4 Political Organization of Space: *(topics related to the political topic of ethnicity)*

Topic	APHG Topic No. Title	Suggested Skills	Enduring Understandings	Essential Knowledge	Big Ideas
7.1.1; *7.1.2;* *7.1.3;* *7.1.4;* *7.1.5;* *7.2.1;* *7.2.2;* *7.2.3;* *7.2.4;* *7.3.1;* *7.3.2;* *7.3.3*	3.3: Cultural Patterns	4.C: Explain patterns and trends in visual sources to draw conclusions.	PSO-3: Cultural practices vary across geographical locations because of physical geography and available resources.	PSO-3.C.1: Attitudes toward ethnicity and gender, including the role of women in the workforce; ethnic neighborhoods; and indigenous communities and lands, help shape the use of space in a given society. PSO-3.D.2: Language, ethnicity, and religion are factors in creating centripetal and centrifugal forces.	BI-1: Patterns and Spatial Organization

7.4.1; 7.4.2; 7.4.3; 7.4.4; 7.4.5	4.8: Defining Devolutionary Factors	3.E: Explain what maps or data imply or illustrate about geographic principles, processes, and outcomes.	SPS-4: Political, economic, cultural, or technological changes can challenge state sovereignty.	SPS-4.A.1: Factors that can lead to the devolution of states includ the division of groups by physical geography, ethnic separatism, ethnic cleansing, terrorism, economic and social problems, and irredentism.	BI-3: Spatial Processes and Societal Change

Source: College Board AP Human Geography Course Description, effective Fall 2015

FRQ's From College Board

2002 FRQ #2
2002 FRQ #3
2005 FRQ #1
2006 FRQ #3
2007 FRQ #2
2009 FRQ #1
2010 FRQ #2
2014 FRQ #2

Chapter

8 Political Geography

Where Are States Distributed?

This chapter examines the spatial distribution of the Earth's land area and how it is divided into state divisions. Cultural interpretation of the role of the state leads to political turmoil and challenges to control within the state. The location of boundaries gives some indication as to potential instability and boundary disputes between countries. Boundaries also create connections between neighboring states. The chapter concludes with the discussion of the changing nature of political conflict, shifting from global war to the rise of terrorist attacks, and the relationship between terrorism and political geography.

Learning Outcome 8.1.1: Explain the difference between a state of the world and a state within the United States.

A **state** is an organized political unit with an established and sovereign government.

Learning Outcome 8.1.2: Explain why it is difficult to determine whether some of Earth's land areas are sovereign states.

Sovereignty is the control of a state's internal affairs by the national government and independent of other state interference. When a land area is claimed by more than one state, its sovereignty is tested.

Political geography can be studied at a number of different scales, including local, national, and international politics. The division of the Earth into occupied and defined space is the most fundamental cultural characteristic. A state is a defined territory with a permanent population and an established government. The largest state is Russia, occupying 11 percent of the Earth's surface. The Vatican is the smallest of the microstates at 0.6 square miles. A state is ruled by an established government that has sovereignty over its internal and external affairs from outside influence. A state is also an example of a formal region.

This definition of a state is tested in some places, notably Korea, China, and Taiwan, Western Sahara (Sahrawi Republic), and the Polar Regions. North and South Korea were admitted to the United

Nations as separate countries, but both are committed to reunification into one sovereign state. China has claimed Taiwan since the establishment of that country when Nationalists fled there from China in the late 1940s. Taiwan is considered a rogue province of China by the Chinese government. The government of the Republic of China is the officially recognized government by the United Nations. Morocco still claims Western Sahara, although most African countries recognize it as a sovereign state. Tensions over the sovereignty claims of the Senkaku/Diaoyu islands in the East China Sea are currently increasing between Japan and the People's Republic of China. Neglect by China prior to 1895 prompted Japan to claim the islands and, with the exception of 1945–1972, when the United States administered them following Japan's defeat in World War II, they remain a claim of Japan.

Key Issues Revisited

8.1. Where Are States Distributed?

- A state is a political unit, with definite territory, an organized government, and sovereignty.

- Most of Earth's surface is allocated to states, and only a few colonies and areas of unorganized territory remain.

Review Questions

8.1.1. A state is a good example of what type of region?
A. Vernacular
B. Functional
C. Traditional
D. Formal
E. Perceived

8.1.2. Which of the following does NOT define a state?
A. It consists of defined territory with a recognized boundary.
B. It contains an established population.
C. An established government administers it.
D. It contains administrative subdivisions.
E. It possesses sovereignty over internal affairs.

KEY ISSUE 2

Why Are States Challenging to Create?

Learning Outcome 8.2.1: Summarize how states developed historically.

The first states developed in Mesopotamia as city-states. Periodically, a city or tribe would exert military dominance over adjacent territory, creating an empire.

Learning Outcome 8.2.2: Describe the modern development of nation-states.

Creating political divisions along distinctive cultural characteristics or ethnicities is a relatively recent concept. A multinational state contains multiple ethnicities rather than a single ethnicity.

Learning Outcome 8.2.3: Describe challenges in creating nation-states in the former Soviet Union.

Russia is the world's largest multinational state, with numerous ethnic groups, especially in areas that border other states. The Caucasus region contains a complex array of ethnicities divided among several small states.

Learning Outcome 8.2.4: Explain Russia's status as a multinational state.

The country's largest ethnicities were organized into 15 republics that are now independent states.

Learning Outcome 8.2.5: Explain the concept of colonies and describe their current distribution.

A **colony** is territory legally tied to a state. Into the twentieth century, much of the world consisted of colonies, but few remain.

The concept of dividing the world into a collection of independent states is relatively recent, dating from eighteenth-century Europe, but the concept of **territoriality** can be traced to the ancient Middle East. The first city-states that developed in Mesopotamia in the ancient Fertile Crescent had clearly defined walled-boundaries and control of agricultural lands. A **city-state** is a sovereign state that consists of a town or city and the surrounding countryside.

Later, the Roman Empire provided the best example of the power of political unity. After the collapse of the Roman Empire in the fifth century C.E., Europe was divided into a large number of feudal estates. Ultimately, powerful kings gained control and consolidated neighboring estates under unified control in Western Europe. Their kingdoms formed the basis for the development of the modern states that included England, France, and Spain.

A **nation** consists of a group of people with a common ethnic and cultural identity. A **nation-state** is where political boundaries coincide with the territory occupied by a particular ethnicity that has been transformed into a nationality. A nation can be a state, but a state cannot be a nation. Today, a nation-state will consist of a very large majority of the population identifying with the nationality of that country.

At the international geopolitical level, three theories have been important in the development of the nation-state concept in the last-two hundred years. In the late - nineteenth century, Friedrich Ratzel proposed his **organic theory** of the evolution of nations. According to Ratzel, states that did not expand their land area would disintegrate "like an organism that fails to find food." Sir Halford Mackinder developed the **Heartland Theory** at the beginning of the twentieth century. He believed that the Eurasian landmass was the world's heartland for the food supply and thus the key to world domination. Nicholas Spykman disagreed and argued that the **rimland** area surrounding the **heartland** and including the world's oceans was the key to world political power; this was his **Rimland Theory**.

In post–WWI, Europe was divided into nation-states using language as the identifying feature of the ethnic group. Ethnic groups have the desire for **self-determination**, that is, to govern themselves as a nation-state. There is no nation-state that corresponds precisely to the areas of a particular ethnicity. In Europe, the principle example of a failed nation-state is Yugoslavia. A **multiethnic state** is a state that contains more than one ethnicity; this describes almost every state in the world. A **multinational state** is a state that contains more than one ethnicity with goals of self-determination and self-government. Ethnic identity has become important to Europe and is reflective in the division of Yugoslavia, the Soviet Union, and Czechoslovakia. Czechoslovakia divided in 1993 in the peaceful Velvet Revolution into the nation-states of Czechia (formerly the Czech Republic) and Slovakia. The breakup of the Soviet Union resulted in the formation of 15 new independent states. Russia is the largest multiethnic state, recognizing 39 ethnic groups that make up 19 percent of the Russian state. The most recent ethnic conflict in the region resulted in the Russian annexation of Crimea after it seized the area from Ukraine in 2014. Russia argued that the residents are ethnic Russians and from 1783 to 1954 had been part of Russian territory. Other regions of the former Soviet Union continue to see challenges by ethnic populations to create their own nation-states. The Caucasus region continues to experience border disputes based on ethnic and historical claims. However, Armenia is the most ethnically homogeneous country in the region.

European states controlled much of the world through **colonialism** beginning in the early 1500s. They established colonies by imposing their political, economic, and cultural control on territories in Latin America, Asia, and Africa that became legally tied to a sovereign state. The United Kingdom had colonies on every continent proclaiming that the "Sun never sets" on the British Empire. Some states that remained independent became **buffer states**, separating areas of colonial control. For example, until 1947, Thailand was a buffer state between British India and French Indochina. Latin American countries became independent in the first half of the nineteenth century, and **decolonization** proceeded rapidly across Africa and Asia after World War II. Today there are only a few remaining colonies, and these are generally only very small territories around the globe. Today there are only 17 places considered as "non-self-governing territories" or colonies in the world.

Key Issues Revisited

8.2. Why Are States Challenging to Create?

- Nation-states evolved from the division of feudal estates and kingdoms in Europe.

- Russia is the largest multinational state.

- Boundary disputes still exist between ethnicities in the regions of the former Soviet Union and Eastern Europe.

Review Questions

8.2.1. What is the first type of political organization?
A. Nation-state
B. Kingdom
C. City-state
D. Colony
E. Multinational state

8.2.2. Which of the following is an example of self-determination?
A. Creation of Czechia and Slovakia
B. Formation of Yugoslavia
C. Seizure of Crimea
D. The nation-state of Japan
E. The division of Germany in 1946

8.2.3. What is the largest multinational state?
A. Germany
B. Ukraine
C. China
D. Russia
E. Brazil

8.2.4. Which state is the most ethnically homogeneous country in the former Soviet Union?
A. Russia
B. Ukraine
C. Kazakhstan
D. Armenia
E. Moldova

8.2.5. Who had a worldwide empire in 1900?
A. France
B. Germany
C. United States
D. Holland
E. United Kingdom

KEY ISSUE 3

Why Do States Face Threats?

Learning Outcome 8.3.1: Describe the functions of the United Nations.
All but a handful of states are members of the United Nations. UN membership grew rapidly in 1955 when many European states joined, in 1960 when many African states joined, and in the 1990s when states formerly part of the Soviet Union and Yugoslavia joined.

Learning Outcome 8.3.2: Explain differences among three regime types.
Regimes can be democratic, anocratic, or autocratic; the trend has been toward more democratic regimes. Local governments can be organized according to unitary or federal state principles; the trend has been toward more federal states.

Learning Outcome 8.3.3: Describe the distribution of nuclear weapons.
Countries with the most nuclear warheads include Russia, the United States, United Kingdom, France, China, India, Pakistan, North Korea, and Israel.

Learning Outcome 8.3.4: Describe the principal alliances in Europe.
NATO is the European military alliance, and the European Union is the economic alliance of 28 European nations.

Learning Outcome 8.3.5: Explain the concept of terrorism and cite U.S. examples.
Terrorism is the systematic use of violence to intimidate a population or coerce a government. Terrorism against the United States culminated in the 9/11 attacks.

Learning Outcome 8.3.6: Identify the major terrorist organizations.
Most terrorist activities have been carried out by members of terrorist organizations. In recent years, al-Qaeda, the Taliban, the Islamic State, and Boko Haram have claimed multiple terrorist attacks.

One of the most important trends in international politics is the development of international and regional alliances. **International organizations** are alliances of two or more countries seeking cooperation. The **United Nations (UN)** and the **North American Free Trade Agreement (NAFTA)** are both examples of international alliances. The United Nations is a global organization that focuses on peace and security, whereas NAFTA is a regional economic alliance. The **European Union (EU)** is also a regional economic union, but it includes elements of political unity as well. All of these organizations are **supranational organizations** that include the membership of two or more states that relinquish some degree of sovereignty for the benefits of an alliance with other states.

When a large number of states were of roughly equal strength, no single state could dominate. This was the geopolitical situation in Europe before the First World War, where European states formed opposing alliances and a **balance of power** was maintained. This changed after the Second World War, when the **Warsaw Pact** and the **North Atlantic Treaty Organization (NATO)** became the opposing military alliances of the Cold War. Balance of power became bipolar. Most Eastern European countries were controlled by the Soviet Union during the Cold War and were known as **satellite states**.

Confederations are similar to international organizations in that they bring several states together for a common purpose. The **Commonwealth of Independent States (CIS)**, a confederacy of independent states of the former Soviet Union for common economic and administrative needs, is an example of such an alliance. There are numerous other regional organizations in the world that combine political, military, and economic goals. Other prominent regional organizations include the **Organization on Security and Cooperation in Europe (OSCE)**, the **Organization of American States (OAS)**, the **African Union (AU)**, and the **Commonwealth**.

National governments can be classified as **democratic** where citizens elect leaders and can run for office, **autocratic** in which a country is run according to the interests of the ruler, or **anocratic**, which is a mix of democratic and autocratic. The government structure within a country is arranged in a unitary state or in a **federal state**. A **unitary state** places the power of the state in the hands of a central government. Essentially, a unitary government has a strong central government and weak local governments that have very limited ability to make laws. Unitary states work best in relatively small nation-states. The best examples of unitary states are those of Western Europe such as France. **Centripetal forces**, such as the reliance on a strong central government, strong national institutions, and a sense of common history, bind countries together.

In contrast, a federal state power is delegated to local governments and works well in multinational states where there is potential ethnic conflict. In the United States, the power is distributed to the state and municipal governments. In recent years, there has been a global trend toward federal government. In addition to the United States, most of the world's largest states are federal governments, including Brazil, Russia, Canada, and India.

Centripetal forces, such as the reliance on a strong central government, strong national institutions, and a sense of common history, bind countries together. Thus, in spite of greater global political cooperation, local diversity has increased in political affairs, and individual ethnic groups are demanding more control over territory. The pressures for independence within a multinational state from various ethnic groups are also known as **devolution** or **devolutionary pressures**. These pressures are also referred to as **centrifugal forces** because they pull countries apart. Devolution is the process of areas within a state demanding and gaining political power extending to autonomy limiting the control of the central government. Devolution is frequently compared with balkanization. The term balkanization symbolizes the division of the former Yugoslavia on the Balkan Peninsula along ethnic lines creating new states based on the majority ethnic populations. The distinction between devolution, balkanization and a shatterbelt need to be understood in terms of their spatial impact and eventual outcomes.

A region experiencing continued pressures from internal and external forces resulting in conflict, separatist movements, and division is known as a **shatterbelt**. A shatterbelt is defined as a region "whose internal, geographical, cultural, religious, and political fragmentation is compounded by pressures from external major powers attracted by the region's strategic location and economic resources" (Cohen, 1982). The centrifugal forces outlined in this unit are the contributing factors leading to geopolitical shatterbelt regions. Southwest Asia, southeastern Europe, Caucasus region, Southeast Asia, and Central Asia are shatterbelt regions. The Caucasus region is splintered by territorial conflict of competing cultural groups, a global demand for available resources in the case of Southwest Asia, ethnic conflicts from superimposed boundaries in southeastern Europe and Central Asia, and territorial demands of minority populations in areas of Southeast Asia. In summary a region can be a shatterbelt leading to devolution within a country of the region and ultimately the creation of another state or balkanization.

Terrorism is the systematic use of violence by a group in order to intimidate a population or coerce a government into granting its demands. It is sometimes hard to distinguish terrorism from other acts of political violence. This is the case with some of the actions of the Palestinians against Israel and Chechen rebels against Russia.

There have been a number of terrorist attacks against the United States in recent years, but the most devastating was on September 11, 2001. The terrorist group al-Qaeda has been implicated in many of these attacks, including the September 11, 2001, attack. Founded by Osama bin Laden, al-Qaeda consists of numerous cells, unites jihad fighters, and has used fundamentalist Islam to justify attacks, especially against the United States. Members of the Yemen affiliate of al-Qaeda were responsible for the January 7, 2015, attack on the offices of *Charlie Hebdo* in Paris.

The Islamic State (ISIS/ISIL) became affiliated with al-Qaeda in 2004 but split apart in 2014. More recently, ISIS claimed responsibility for the November 13, 2015, attack on the Bataclan and soccer stadium in Paris and the March 22, 2016, attack at the Brussels, Belgium, airport and train station. ISIS seeks to impose strict religious laws throughout Southwest Asia, but they also claim to have authority to rule Muslims around the world.

Boko Haram is responsible for terrorist activities in Northern Nigeria and Western Africa in an attempt to unite the region under strict fundamentalist Islamic law. Since 2014, Boko Haram has allied itself with ISIS. Several states in the Middle East have also provided support for terrorism at three levels. Some have provided sanctuary for terrorists wanted by other countries. They have supplied weapons, money, and intelligence to terrorists, and some countries have planned attacks using terrorists. These countries have included Libya, Afghanistan, Yemen, Iraq, and Iran at various times in recent years.

Terrorist attacks led by ultra-nationalist sympathizers are responsible for terrorist attacks in the United States, the United Kingdom, Germany, and most recently in New Zealand. These attacks were targeted toward ethnic minorities, usually recent immigrants, based on the fear that the white majority and society as it was previously known is subject to change as a result of the newer immigrants. **Ethnonationalism** has resulted in actions that are leading to terror attacks against ethnic minority populations, many of which are recent immigrants, for cultures that are not part of the familiar region and culture. These migrant populations are targeted because of their cultural, religious, linguistic, and places of origin.

In the United States, domestic terrorists have targeted government institutions or individuals responsible for various government actions. The 1993 attack on the Murrah Federal Building in Oklahoma City by Timothy McVeigh was an example of this type of domestic terrorism.

Key Issues Revisited

8.3. Why Do States Face Threats?

- Boundaries are physical and cultural.

- Geometric and ethnic borders are cultural boundaries.

- Boundaries affect the shape of countries and affect the ability of a country to live peacefully with its neighbors.

- The government of a state is classified as democratic, autocratic, or anocratic.

- Boundaries within states can be manipulated to favor one political party over another.

- Terrorism has been a global challenge targeted at governmental and societal change.

Review Questions

8.3.1. What is the most important global forum for cooperation among states?
A. NATO
B. NAFTA
C. UN
D. EU
E. UNCLOS

8.3.2 What is the most stable state of North America?
A. The United States of America
B. The United Mexican States
C. The Republic of Costa Rica
D. Canada
E. The Republic of Cuba

8.3.3. All of the following identify weapons of mass destruction EXCEPT
A. The term was originally applied to chemical weapons.
B. They can cause great damage to people, structures, and the biosphere.
C. The abbreviation WMD is usually used to describe these weapons.
D. There is a clear definition that includes only nuclear, biological, and chemical weapons.
E. The Nuclear Non-Proliferation Treaty has prevented development of weapons of mass destruction.

8.3.4. The main purpose of the European Union is to:
A. promote human rights.
B. punish war criminals.
C. provide military aid.
D. stop rebellions in former colonies.
E. promote economic and political cooperation.

8.3.5. A terrorist attack must _____.
A. be intentional on the part of the perpetrator
B. occur in Southwest Asia
C. originate over religious conflict
D. disrupt local government and economic activities
E. lead to the death of over 100 people

8.3.6. What is the goal of Boko Haram?
A. Unite world Muslims under one system of laws, government, and culture.
B. Transform Nigeria into an Islamic State.
C. Unite the Islamic world under Sharia law.
D. Impose strict Sharia law throughout Southwest Asia.
E. Eliminate all democratic governments from the Middle East.

KEY ISSUE 4

Why Do States Have Distinctive Geographic Structure?

Learning Outcome 8.4.1: Describe the types of cultural boundaries between states.
Geometry and ethnicities can be used to delineate cultural boundaries between states.

Learning Outcome 8.4.2: Describe types of physical boundaries between states.
Physical features used to delineate boundaries include deserts, mountains, and bodies of water.

Learning Outcome 8.4.3: Describe types of geometric boundaries between states.
Boundaries define the outer limits of a state's territorial control. Geometric boundaries are based on treaties and are sometimes disputed

Learning Outcome 8.4.4: Describe the five shapes of states.
States take five forms: compact, elongated, prorupted, fragmented, and perforated. Landlocked states have no access to the sea.

Learning Outcome 8.4.5: Explain the practice of gerrymandering and ways in which it is done.
Gerrymandering is the redrawing of electoral districts to benefit the party in power. Three forms of gerrymandering are wasted vote, excess vote, and stacked vote.

Learning Outcome 8.4.6: Describe approaches to reducing gerrymandering.
North Carolina has the most gerrymandered districts. Independent commissions typically try to reduce gerrymandering by creating compact districts without regard to voting preferences.

Borders, called boundaries, separate states from each other. A **boundary** is an invisible line that completely surrounds a state, marks the outer limits of its territorial control, and gives it a distinctive shape. Prior to the establishment of formal boundaries, frontiers separated states. A **frontier** is a zone or area between states where no state exercises complete control. Frontiers still exist between states on the Arabian Peninsula, where the borders are virtually uninhabited desert regions.

Political boundaries are delimited, defined, and demarcated. When political boundaries are established, they are **delimited**, or drawn on a map. Normally, a formal agreement will establish a treaty setting up and **defining** the border. The border can also be **demarcated** by using some visible means to indicate the boundary on the ground.

There are a number of different types of **cultural boundaries** between states. When British India became independent in 1948, the boundary that was created between the newly independent states of India and Pakistan was essentially a **religious boundary**. It separated a predominantly Muslim

Pakistan from a predominantly Hindu India. Religious reasons also form the boundary between the Republic of Ireland and Northern Ireland. **Language boundaries** have always been important cultural boundaries between ethnic groups. Linguistic differences became the basis of the borders of France, Portugal, Spain, Germany, and Italy. Borders based on ethnicity is the rationale between the Greek Cypriots and the Turks with the establishment of the U.N. buffer zone along the "Green line" in Cyprus. In Central Africa, the division between Burundi and Rwanda is along ethnic divisions, as is that between Slovenia and Croatia in Southern Europe. Ethnic boundaries define the territory of a population that has a shared heritage, including a common ethnicity, language, religion, and culture. In some areas where the majority ethnicity feels threatened by a minority ethnic group, ethnonationalism may arise.

Geometric boundaries follow straight lines and have little to do with the physical or cultural landscape. The boundaries between many African states today are geometric. They are also called **superimposed boundaries** because they were drawn by European colonial powers that did not pay any attention to the social, cultural, or ethnic compositions of African people.

Physical boundaries follow important physical features on the landscape, such as water, mountains, and deserts. For example, the boundary between France and Spain is the crest of the Pyrenees Mountains, and the boundary separating Uganda, Kenya, and Tanzania runs through Lake Victoria. Part of the boundary between the United States and Mexico is the Rio Grande River. The boundary between Canada and the United States is both a geometric and a physical boundary. Physical boundaries are often **antecedent boundaries** because they were natural boundaries long before those areas became populated.

The **United Nations Convention on the Law of the Sea (UNCLOS)** established maritime boundaries agreed upon by 168 countries. The United States did not sign UNCLOS. Each state with an ocean boundary can set regulations in the **territorial waters** up to 12 nautical miles from its shore and certain other laws in the 12- to 24-mile contiguous zone. Up to 200 nautical miles, a state has an **exclusive economic zone (EEZ)** over which it has certain economic rights. Where the water distance between two countries is less than 24 miles, sometimes called **choke points**, **median lines** delimit the boundary between the two countries equidistant from each shore. Beyond this 200-nautical-mile limit lie the **high seas** that are beyond national jurisdiction and are free and open for all countries to use. Maritime boundary disputes are addressed in the International Court of Justice.

State (or territorial) **morphology**, or the shape of a state, can be a **centripetal** (uniting) or **centrifugal** (separating) factor for a country. As a centripetal factor, the shape can add to the identity and global recognition, as in the case of the United States, Italy, or Canada. The shape can influence the ease of internal administration or allow for the development of social disunity and potential political challenges.

Countries like Poland, which are relatively rounded, are **compact states**. This shape enhances communications between all regions, especially when the capital is centrally located.

Prorupted states are compact states with a large projecting extension. Proruptions can disrupt, like the Afghanistan proruption (the Wakhan Corridor), which denies Russia a shared boundary with Pakistan. They can also provide access, such as Namibia's proruption (the Caprivi Strip) which was originally designed to give this former German colony access to the Zambezi River in Southwest Africa.

Elongated states, such as Chile, Vietnam, and The Gambia, are long and thin. Such states often suffer from poor internal communications.

A state that is divided into several discontinuous pieces of territory is called a **fragmented state**. The United States is fragmented because Alaska and Hawaii are separated from the contiguous lower 48 states. Kaliningrad is separated from the rest of Russia by the independent states of Lithuania and Belarus. Island states like Indonesia are fragmented because of water. In addition, some states have fragmented territory that lies completely within the boundary of another state. This was the case with West Berlin during the Cold War and is called an **exclave**. The boundary between East and West Berlin, as well as the boundary between East and West Germany, is now a **relic boundary** because it no longer exists. An **enclave** is a piece of territory that is surrounded by another political unit of which it is not a part. Lesotho is an enclave because it is completely surrounded by South Africa.

States like Italy and South Africa that completely surround other states are known as **perforated states**. The states that are completely surrounded, such as Lesotho by South Africa, are also **landlocked states** that lack access to the ocean or a sea.

The various shapes of states provide both centrifugal and centripetal factors. Some states occupy strategically important locations on the Earth's surface. This is true of Singapore on the tip of Malaysia in Southeast Asia and Panama on the isthmus between North and South America. The various shapes of states provide both advantages and disadvantages.

National governments can be classified as **democratic**, **autocratic**, or **anocratic**. Since the 1980s, the world has become increasingly more democratic. In democracies, politics must follow legally prescribed rules. However, parties to the political process often find ways to bend those rules to their advantage. The boundaries separating legislative districts in the United States and other countries have to be redrawn from time to time in order to account for changing population. For example, the 435 districts of the U.S. House of Representatives are redrawn after the census every 10 years. This is called **reapportionment**; this is followed by **redistricting**, when states that either gained or lost population must redraw their districts. In most U.S. states, this is done by the state legislature, and historically, the political party in control has tried to do this. The redrawing of legislative boundaries to benefit a specific political party in power is called gerrymandering. The term was named for Elbridge Gerry, a nineteenth-century politician from Massachusetts, who tried to do this in his state and created an oddly shaped district that looked so much like a salamander that his opponents called it a "gerrymander."

There are three types of gerrymandering. "Wasted votes" spreads opposition supporters across many districts; "excess votes" concentrates opposition in few districts, and "stacked votes" link distant areas of similar voters through oddly shaped boundaries. Although the Supreme Court has ruled gerrymandering illegal, stacked vote gerrymandering is still a reality. According to a study by the *Washington Post*, the state with the most gerrymandering is North Carolina.

Key Issues Revisited

8.4. Why Do States Have Distinctive Geographic Structure?

- After the Second World War, the United States and the Soviet Union, the world's two superpowers, formed military alliances with other countries.
- Economic alliances have become more important in Europe since the end of the Cold War.
- Terrorism initiated by individuals, organizations, and states has increased, especially against the United States.

Review Questions

8.4.1. Before defined boundaries, what separated states?
A. Demarcated borders
B. Frontiers
C. Greenbelts
D. Water
E. No man's land

8.4.2. According to the Law of the Sea, the territorial limits for most countries is:
A. 3.5 nautical miles.
B. 12 nautical miles.
C. 3.5 land miles.
D. 5.5 kilometers.
E. 158 miles.

8.4.3. Which of the following land masses has only geometric boundaries?
A. North America
B. South America
C. Europe
D. Russia
E. Antarctica

8.4.4. Most landlocked states would be found in _____.
A. Asia
B. Europe
C. South America
D. Africa
E. The Middle East

8.4.5 What is the manipulation of legislative boundaries to benefit one party over another called?
A. Democracy

B. Gerrymandering
C. Independent commissions
D. Congressional plan
E. Political cooperation

Key Terms

African Union (AU)

Antecedent boundaries*

Balance of power*

Balkanization*

Berlin Conference*

Boundary

Buffer state

Centrifugal forces*

Centripetal forces*

Choke point*

City-state

Colonialism*

Colonies

Commonwealth

Commonwealth of Independent States (CIS)

Compact state

Confederation

Consequent Boundaries*

Cultural boundaries

Decolonization

Defined boundary*

Delimitation*

Demarcation*

Devolution*

Elongated state

Enclave

European Union (EU)

Ethnonationalism*

Exclave

Exclusive economic zone (EEZ)

Federal states*

Fragmented state

Frontier

Geometric boundaries*

Geopolitics

International organizations

Irredentism*

Landlocked state

Maritime boundaries*

Median lines

Microstates

Multinational state*

Nation*

Nation-state*

Neocolonialism*

North American Free Trade Association (NAFTA)

North Atlantic Treaty Organization (NATO)*

Operational boundary

Organic theory

Organization of American States (OAS)

Perforated state

Physical boundaries

Prorupted state

Reapportionment

Redistricting*

Relic boundary*

Religious boundaries

Rimland theory

Satellite states

Self-determination

Shatterbelts*

Sovereignty*

State*

Stateless*

State morphology

Subsequent boundaries*

Superimposed boundaries*

Supranational organizations*

Territorial sea*

Territoriality*

Terrorism*

Gerrymandering*

Heartland theory

High seas

Imperialism*

Unitary state*

United Nations (UN)*

United Nations Convention on the Law of the Sea (UNCLOS)*

Voting districts*

* Term is in 2019 College Board Curriculum & Exam Description.

Think Like a Geographer Activities

DATA ACQUISITION CHART FOR ANALYZING NATO AND THE EUROPEAN UNION

	NATO	EU
Purposes and Principles		
Political Functions		
Economic Functions		
Admissions Issues		
Major Successes		
Failures, Problems, and Critical Issues		

1. What are the major similarities and differences between NATO and the EU?

2. Write a **Critique of NATO and the European Union** for the Council of Europe, comparing the purpose and role played by each of these organizations in postwar Europe. Your critique should include an analysis of the spatial development of these organizations and address the political and economic functions of both NATO and European Union as they relate to cooperation and conflict in Europe.

Quick Quiz

8.1. Why are Senkaku/Diaoyu islands important to China, Japan, and Taiwan?
A. They are a good location to expand a growing population.
B. They have valuable minerals and oil that are needed.
C. They are in a tropical location that allows for tropical aquaculture.
D. The islands extend the territorial maritime boundaries further into the East China Sea.
E. Population migration can be exclusively controlled to the islands.

8.2. What would be the effect of a further split of European states into multiple states?
A. NATO could ensure better military defense.
B. It would create nation-states.
C. The European Union would expand the number of member states in the European Union.
D. Larger countries would have less economic control.
E. It would create more problems securing international borders.

8.3. Where did the Taliban develop, and why?
A. In Afghanistan, in response to the Soviet Union invasion
B. In Iraq, in response to the attack by the United States
C. In Iran, in response to the attack by Iraq
D. In Saudi Arabia, home of Osama bin Laden
E. In Iran as a result of the Islamic Revolution

8.4. Which of the following is separated by a mountain boundary?
A. United States and Canada
B. Chile and Argentina
C. Brazil and Uruguay
D. France and Germany
E. Iceland and Norway

Free Response

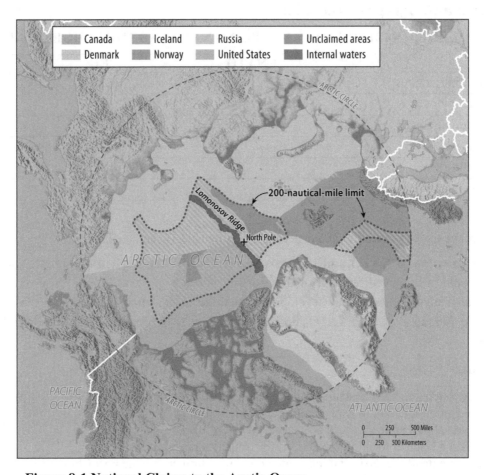

Figure 8-1 National Claims to the Arctic Ocean

1. Using Figure 8-1, identify four countries with claims to the Arctic Ocean.

2. Discuss the significance of the 200-nautical-mile limit of the United Nations Convention on the Law of the Seas.

3. Discuss the economic and political impact of the melting of Arctic ice.

On the Web

Here are some useful websites for this chapter:

www.pearsonmylabandmastering.com/northamerica/masteringgeography/

www.sheppardsoftware.com/Geography.htm

www.geography.about.com/od/politicalgeography/Political_Geography.htm

www.un.org/en/

www.education.nationalgeographic.org/topics/ap-human-geography-political-patterns/

www.visionofhumanity.org/app/uploads/2018/12/Global-Terrorism-Index-2018-1.pdf

www.storymaps.esri.com/stories/terrorist-attacks/

www.ourworldindata.org/terrorism

www.ourworldindata.org/democracy

www.ourworldindata.org/peacekeeping

www.visionofhumanity.org/app/uploads/2018/12/Global-Terrorism-Index-2018-1.pdf

TED Talks

ParagKhanna,_Mapping_the_Future_of_Countries:
www.ted.com/talks/parag_khanna_maps_the_future_of_countries.html

The Middle East's Cold War, Explained: www.youtube.com

China Is Erasing Its Border with Hong Kong: www.youtu.be

How 156 years of British rule shaped Hong Kong: www.youtu.be

The Most Complex International Borders in the World: www.youtu.be

Gerrymandering Explained: www.youtu.be

Key Figures

Figure 8-1 States of the World

Figure 8-8 Fertile Crescent

Figure 8-14 Europe, 1924

Figure 8-15 Europe, 1980

Figure 8-19 Ethnic Diversity

Figure 8-23 Ethnicities in Russia

Figure 8-27 Remaining Colonies

Figure 8-29 Colonial Possessions, 1914

Figure 8-34 Regime Types

Figure 8-36 Fragile States Index

Figure 8-42 European Union

Figure 8-43 NATO Members in Europe

Figure 8-47 Terrorist Attacks in the United States

Figure 8-48 Terrorist Attacks with at Least 100 Fatalities, 2000–2017

AP® Human Geography Outline of Political Organization of Space

Unit 4 Political Organization of Space: *(topics related to the political topic of ethnicity)*

Topic	APHG Topic No. Title	Suggested Skills	Enduring Understandings	Essential Knowledge	Big Ideas
8.1.1	4.1: Introduction to Political Geography	4.A: Identify the different types of information presented in visual sources.	PSO-4: The political organization of space results from historical and current processes, events, and ideas.	PSO-4.A.1: Independent states are the primary building blocks of the world political map.	BI-1: Patterns and Spatial Organization
8.1.2	4.2: Political Processes	3.E: Explain what maps or data imply or illustrate about geographic principles, processes, and outcomes.	PSO-4: The political organization of space results from historical and current processes, events, and ideas.	PSO-4.B.1: The concepts of sovereignty, nation-states, and self-determination shape the contemporary world.	BI-1 Patterns and Spatial Organization
8.2.1; 8.2.2; 8.2.3	4.1: Introduction to Political Geography	4.A: Identify the different types of information presented in visual sources.	PSO-4: The political organization of space results from historical and current processes, events, and ideas.	PSO-4.A.2: Types of political entities include nations, nation-states, stateless nations, multinational states, multistate nations, and autonomous and semiautonomous regions, such as American Indian reservations.	BI-1 Patterns and Spatial Organization
8.2.4; 8.2.5	4.2: Political Processes	3.E: Explain what maps or data imply or illustrate about geographic principles, processes, and outcomes.	PSO-4: The political organization of space results from historical and current processes, events, and ideas.	PSO-4.B.2: Colonialism, imperialism, independence movements, and devolution along national lines have influenced contemporary political boundaries.	BI-1 Patterns and Spatial Organization

8.3.1	4.9: Challenges to Sovereignty	5.C: Compare geographic characteristics and processes at various scales.	SPS-4: Political, economic, cultural, or technological changes can challenge state sovereignty.	SPS-4.B.3: Global efforts to address transnational and environmental challenges and to create economies of scale, trade agreements, and military alliances help further supranationalism.	BI-3: Spatial Processes and Societal Change
8.3.2	4.7: Forms of Governance	2.A: Describe spatial patterns, networks, and relationships.	IMP-4: Political boundaries and divisions of governance, between states and within them, reflect balances of power that have been negotiated or imposed.	IMP-4.D.1: Unitary states tend to have a more top-down, centralized form of governance, while federal states have more local-based, dispersed power centers.	BI-2: Impacts and Interactions
8.3.3; 8.3.5; 8.3.6	4.8: Defining Devolutionary Factors	3.E: Explain what maps or data imply or illustrate about geographic principles, processes, and outcomes.	SPS-4: Political, economic, cultural, or technological changes can challenge state sovereignty.	SPS-4.A.1: Factors that can lead to the devolution of states include the division of groups by physical geography, ethnic separatism, ethnic cleansing, terrorism, economic and social problems, and irredentism.	BI-3: Spatial Processes and Societal Change
8.3.4	4.8: Defining Devolutionary Factors	5.C: Compare geographic characteristics and processes at various scales.	SPS-4: Political, economic, cultural, or technological changes can challenge state sovereignty.	SPS-4.B.4: Supranational organizations—including the United Nations (UN), North Atlantic Treaty Organization (NATO), European Union (EU), Association of Southeast Asian Nations (ASEAN), Arctic Council, and African Union can challenge state sovereignty by limiting the economic or political actions of member states.	BI-3: Spatial Processes and Societal Change

8.4.1; 8.4.2; 8.4.3	4.4: Defining Political Boundaries	5.D: Explain the degree to which a geographic concept, process, model, or theory effectively explains geographic effects across various geographic scales.	IMP-4: Political boundaries and divisions of governance, between states and within them reflect balances of power that have been negotiated or imposed.	IMP-4.B.1: Boundaries are defined, delimited, demarcated, and administered to establish limits of sovereignty, but they are often contested. IMP-4.B.2: Political boundaries often coincide with cultural, national, or economic divisions. However, some boundaries are created by demilitarized zones or policy, such as the Berlin Conference. MP-4.B.3: Land and maritime boundaries and international agreements can influence national or regional identity and encourage or discourage international or internal interactions and disputes over resources. IMP-4.B.4: The United Nations Convention on the Law of the Sea defines the rights and responsibilities of nations in the use of international waters, established territorial seas, and exclusive economic zones.	BI-2: Impacts and Interactions
8.4.4	4.9: Challenges to Sovereignty 4.10: Consequences of Centrifugal and Centripetal Forces	5.C: Compare geographic characteristics and processes at various scales.	SPS-4: Political, economic, cultural, or technological changes can challenge state sovereignty.	SPS-4.B.1: Devolution occurs when states fragment into autonomous regions; subnational political-territorial units, such as those within Spain, Belgium, Canada, and Nigeria; or when states disintegrate, as happened in Sudan and the former Soviet Union.	BI-3: Spatial Processes and Societal Change

8.4.5; 8.4.6	4.6: Internal Boundaries	5.A: Identify the scales of analysis presented by maps, in quantitative and geospatial data, images, and landscapes.	IMP-4: Political boundaries and divisions of governance, between states and within them, reflect balances of power that have been negotiated or imposed.	SPS-4.C.1: Centrifugal forces may lead to failed states, uneven development, stateless nations, and ethnic nationalist movements. SPS-4.C.2: Centripetal forces can lead to ethnonationalism, more equitable infrastructure development, and increased cultural cohesion.	
				IMP-4.B.5: Voting districts, redistricting, and gerrymandering affect election results at various scales.	BI-2: Impacts and Interactions

Source: College Board AP Human Geography Course Description, effective Fall 2019

FRQ's From College Board

2002 FRQ #1
2005 FRQ #1
2006 FRQ #3
2010 FRQ #2
2012 FRQ #1
2014 FRQ #2s
2016 FRQ #2
2017 FRQ #3
2019 FRQ #3 set 1
2019 FRQ #3 set 2

Chapter

9 Food & Agriculture

This chapter deals with the major primary sector economic activity—agriculture. The origins of agriculture are examined for the characteristics of each agricultural hearth and the diffusion across space of food consumption. Farming varies around the world because of a variety of cultural and environmental factors creating unique agricultural regions. Agriculture is very different in less developed and developed regions. In less developed regions, dominated by subsistence agriculture, farm products are usually consumed near to where they are produced. Commercial farming is the norm in more developed countries, and farmers sell what they produce. Farmers face numerous problems in each type of region. Trade in agricultural products creates global connections and challenges farmers with concerns of sustainable practices and production levels.

KEY ISSUE 1

Why Do People Consume Different Foods?

Learning Outcome 9.1.1: Explain differences between developed and developing countries in food consumption.
Most humans derive most of their dietary energy through cereal grains, especially wheat, rice, and maize. The primary source of protein is meat products in more developed countries and grain in developing countries.

Learning Outcome 9.1.2: Describe the distribution of undernourishment.
The United Nations estimates that 795 million people are undernourished, with one-half in South and East Asia.

Learning Outcome 9.1.3: Explain differences between more developed and developing countries in source of nutrients.
Meat products account for one-third of protein in more developed countries compared to one-tenth in developing countries. Cereal grains make up the largest amount of proteins in developing countries.

People need food to survive; however, the types of foods people eat around the world vary greatly. The diet of people is dependent on the level of development of a country, the physical environment, and also cultural preferences. Wheat, rice, and maize (corn) account for 90 percent of all grain production and 40 percent of all dietary energy consumed worldwide. The United Nations estimates that approximately 10 percent of the people on Earth do not have **food security**. Results at the end of the U.N. Millennium Development initiative in 2015 revealed that the proportion of undernourished people in the developing regions had fallen by almost half since 1990; however, about 850 million people are estimated to be undernourished according to the United Nations.

Food security is defined as the physical, social, and economic access to safe and nutritious food sufficient to meet dietary needs and food preferences for an active and healthy life. Ninety-eight percent of the world's undernourished people are in developing countries. China and India have the largest numbers of undernourished people, but it is more prevalent in sub-Saharan Africa, with one-fourth of the population undernourished. The current U.N. **Sustainable Development Goals** aim to end all forms of hunger and malnutrition by 2030 using sustainable agricultural practices and promoting international cooperation through investment in infrastructure and technology to improve agricultural productivity, (www.sdgfund.org/goal-2-zero-hunger).

Challenges facing food production and distribution today are concerned with food prices, insufficient nutrient value in the available food supply, incorporating sustainable practices in food production, and the growing demand for organic and specialty crops. Food prices dipped in 2015 after 10 years of steady increase and have continued to rise since 2017. Increased population creates an increased demand as incomes rise in developing countries, especially in China and India. Additionally, the use of grain crops raised for biofuel has caused an increase in food prices for both animal feed and human consumption.

In more developed countries, food demands are shifting from availability to concern for how plants and animals are raised and potential health risks, in addition to the ethical issues of animal welfare in the food production system. Developed populations acquire protein through the consumption of meat products (beef, pork, and chicken), whereas in developing nations, they get most protein from cereal products. Africa experiences the greatest extent of undernourishment due to the fact that population growth has put a strain on food production. The challenge to world food security, particularly in the developing countries, is the price of food and not the actual food supply.

Key Issues Revisited

9.1. Why Do People Consume Different Foods?

- Most food is consumed in the form of cereal grains, especially wheat, rice, and maize.

- More calories and more animal products are consumed in more developed countries.

- Undernourishment is common in Asia and sub-Saharan Africa.

Review Questions

9.1.1. Where is the threat of famine the greatest?
A. Central Asia
B. South Asia
C. South Africa
D. East Africa and the horn of Africa
E. North Africa

9.1.2. The access to safe and nutritious food sufficient to lead an active and healthy life is known as _____.
A. food security
B. protein insecurity
C. protein sufficiency
D. overnourishment
E. obesity

9.1.3. The main source of protein in more developed countries comes from _____.
A. tofu
B. soybeans
C. wheat
D. maize
E. meat

KEY ISSUE 2

Where Did Agriculture Originate?

Learning Outcome 9.2.1: Summarize the Origin of Agriculture.
Deliberate cultivation of plants and raising animals for sustenance and economic gain occurred approximately 10,000 years ago in five hearths.

Learning Outcome 9.2.2: Describe the principal differences between subsistence and commercial agriculture.
Subsistence agriculture, practiced in developing countries, is characterized by a high percentage of farmers in the labor force, limited use of machinery, and small average farm size. A small percentage of farmers in the labor force, heavy use of machinery, and large average farm size characterize commercial agriculture, practiced in more developed countries.

Prior to the invention of agriculture, humans lived as nomadic **hunters and gatherers,** traveling in small groups and collecting food daily. Over thousands of years, plant cultivation evolved through a combination of accident and deliberate experiment. The **Neolithic (or First) Agricultural Revolution** began approximately 10,000 years ago, with the deliberate modification of Earth's surface through the cultivation of plants and **domestication** of animals, for sedentary food production. The word *cultivate* means "to care for," and a **crop** is any plant cultivated by people.

According to the geographer Carl Sauer, there were two initial types of cultivation. The first was **vegetative planting**, which is the reproduction of plants by direct cloning from existing plants. **Seed agriculture** came later; this is the reproduction of plants of seeds. Most farmers practice seed agriculture today.

Cultivation of plants originated in several **agricultural hearths**. Sauer believed that vegetative planting originated in Southeast Asia and diffused from there to other parts of Asia, the Middle East, Africa, and Southern Europe. The earliest crops (barley, wheat, lentils, and olives) were domesticated in Southwest Asia (**Fertile Crescent**). Animals important to agriculture were also domesticated in Southwest Asia. These animals were raised for work, meat, and dairy production.

Sauer identified numerous hearths for seed agriculture. The East Asian hearth domesticated rice and millet. South Asia was the source of chickens while Central Asia domesticated the horse. Sub-Saharan Africa domesticated sorghum around 8,000 years ago, and yams perhaps even earlier. Millet and rice might have emerged in this region as well. Cotton and beans originated in Mexico, potatoes in Peru in the Latin American hearth, and maize might have been domesticated in both regions around the same time. The variety of plants is the result of cultural preferences, as well as climatic and soil conditions within each hearth.

In **subsistence agriculture**, farmers produce goods to provide for themselves and others in the local community in less developed countries. **Commercial agriculture**, found in more developed countries, is the production of food for commercial, free market sale. These crops are known as **cash crops** since they are raised for sale. This type of agriculture emerged as a result of increased farming technology that was developed during the **Second Agricultural Revolution** in the eighteenth century in Europe.

Commercial and subsistence agriculture differ in terms of purpose, labor, use of machinery, and size. The purpose of farming is different in developing and more developed countries. Developing areas depend on subsistence agriculture for personal consumption, while more developed countries focus on commercial agriculture for economic gain. Subsistence agriculture is **labor intensive** rather than **capital intensive**, as in commercial agriculture. Thus, there will always be a higher percentage of the labor force involved in agriculture in the developing world. Agriculture in more developed countries involves more machinery and technology, while the developing world uses animal and human labor.

Farm size is larger in commercial agriculture, especially in the United States and Canada. The large farm size and use of machinery is considered an aspect of **extensive agriculture**. Commercial farms in the United States are large due to the use and cost of machinery where the farmer can produce a higher yield more efficiently on a larger amount of land. This is known as economy of scale. As a result of the costs of land and inputs needed for growing crops, commercial farms have become very large operations with over 1,400 acres under cultivation. Technology has also contributed to the commercial production of food with the use of GPS devices, soil and moisture monitors, and automated equipment, creating greater efficiency and productivity. The loss of very productive farmland is an increasing problem in the United States because of urban sprawl. In commercial agriculture, there is a close relationship between agriculture and other businesses, which is not the case in subsistence agriculture. In more developed countries, the system of commercial farming is known as **agribusiness** because farming is integrated into a large food-production industry.

Key Issues Revisited

9.2. Where Did Agriculture Originate?

- Before the development of agriculture, people survived by hunting and gathering.

- Agriculture evolved from multiple hearths approximately 10,000 years ago.

- Current agricultural practices vary between subsistence practices in developing countries and commercial agriculture in developed countries.

Review Questions

9.2.1. What caused the world's population to grow about 8,000 years ago?
A. Medical advances
B. Cultivation of crops
C. Industrialization
D. Urbanization
E. Migration

9.2.2. Farming with highly mechanized equipment and large amounts of cultivated acreage of one or two cash crops is known as _____.
A. subsistence agriculture
B. extensive agriculture
C. commercial agriculture
D. truck agriculture
E. traditional agriculture

KEY ISSUE 3

Where Is Agriculture Distributed?

Learning Outcome 9.3.1: Describe agricultural regions and their relationships to climate regions.

Agricultural regions are divided into 11 major regions, including 5 in developing countries and 6 in more developed countries. Types of agriculture closely match agricultural regions.

Learning Outcome 9.3.2: Explain the principal forms of agriculture in higher-density developing regions.

The principal crop in the intensive subsistence region is wet rice. Growing rice is an intensive operation that depends primarily on abundant labor. Other crops include wheat, barley, and other grains in high-density areas.

Learning Outcome 9.3.3: Explain the principal forms of subsistence agriculture in lower-density tropical regions.

Shifting cultivation and plantation farming are found in areas of low population in tropical regions.

Learning Outcome 9.3.4: Explain the principal forms of subsistence agriculture in lower-density dry regions.

Pastoral nomadism is the principal form of agriculture adapted to the dry lands of developing countries.

Learning Outcome 9.3.5: Describe the contribution of fishing to the world supply.

Fishing and aquaculture have tripled in 50 years, accounting for 1 percent of calories consumed by humans.

Learning Outcome 9.3.6: Describe the basic principles of several forms of crop-based commercial agriculture.

Commercial agriculture is divided into six main types: grain, Mediterranean, commercial gardening and fruit farming, mixed crop and livestock, dairy, and livestock ranching.

Learning Outcome 9.3.7: Describe dairy and ranching commercial agriculture.

Dairy farming is especially important near major population concentrations in developed countries. Livestock is raised on land that is too dry for growing crops.

Learning Outcome 9.3.8: Describe the basic principles of several forms of mixed crop and livestock agriculture.

Mixed crop and livestock farming is the most common form of agriculture in the center of the United States. Crops like maize and soybeans are grown primarily to feed animals.

The relationship between agricultural regions and climate regions is very similar. Dry land areas are predominately pastoral nomadism in developing countries or are devoted to ranching in more developed countries. Additionally, Mediterranean agriculture occurs in the climatic regions named for the specific climate and agricultural characteristics. There are five agricultural regions that are predominately found in developing countries: intensive subsistence, wet-rice dominant, and intensive subsistence in high-density population areas. Nomadism found in dry land areas is pastoral nomadism. Shifting cultivation and plantation agriculture predominate in tropical regions. There are six agricultural regions in more developed countries: mixed crop and livestock, grains in low density population areas, dairy near population centers, ranching in dry lands, commercial gardening, and Mediterranean agriculture in specific climate regions.

Some subsistence agriculture is **intensive**, where farmers work land more intensively to subsist. **Intertillage** or field clearance is usually very labor intensive because of a lack of modern machinery. **Intensive subsistence agriculture** is practiced in much of Asia on small plots and mostly by hand. **Wet rice** is the dominant crop in Southeast Asia, including China. Wet rice is planted in dry soil in a nursery and then moved to seedlings in a flooded field. The flooded field is called a **sawah** (**paddy** is the Malay word for wet rice). When the rice is harvested, the husks, known as **chaff**, are separated from the seeds when their heads are **threshed** by being beaten on the ground. When the threshed rice is placed on a tray, the lighter chaff is **winnowed**, or blown away by the wind. If the rice is to be consumed by the farmer, the **hull**, or outer covering, is removed by mortar and pestle. In parts of Asia, farmers can get two harvests per year from one field. This is known as **double cropping**. Where wet rice is not dominant in Asia, more than one harvest can be obtained each year through **crop rotation**, which is the practice of using different fields from crop to crop each year to avoid soil exhaustion.

Shifting cultivation is practiced in much of the world's tropical regions. Farmers clear land for planting by slashing vegetation and burning the debris; this is called **slash-and-burn agriculture**. The cleared land is called **swidden**, and crops grown will include rice (Asia), maize and manioc (South America), and millet and sorghum (Africa). Farmers will only grow crops on a cleared field for a few years until the soil nutrients are depleted and then they will leave it **fallow** (nothing planted) so that it can recover. Shifting cultivation occupies about one-fourth of the world's land area but supports less than 5 percent of the world's population. As rain forests are being cut, shifting cultivation is declining, especially in the Amazon basin. Swidden lands are being replaced by logging, cattle ranching, and cash crops. Tropical regions are also areas of **plantation agriculture**. **Plantations** are the only significant large-scale commercial agriculture in the developing world. Plantations will specialize in crops such as sugarcane, tea, rubber, pineapples, bananas, coffee, and spices that will usually be exported to other countries. Most plantations are owned by foreign companies and are very labor intensive.

Pastoral nomadism is a type of **extensive subsistence agriculture** that involves nomadic animal husbandry. It is practiced in the dry climates of the developing world. The livestock provides food, clothing, and shelter. The animals will vary, depending on cultural preferences and physical geography, but may include goats, camels, horses, sheep, or cattle. Pastoral nomads have a strong sense of territoriality, which determines the land that they occupy. Some pastoral nomads practice **transhumance**, which is the seasonal movement of livestock between mountains and lowland pasture areas. A **pasture** is grass or other plants grown for feeding livestock, as well as land used for grazing. This type of agricultural system is on the decline as modern technology is changing and results in the conversion of land from nomadic to sedentary agriculture.

Food from the Earth's waters is obtained through fishing or aquaculture. **Aquaculture** is the deliberate cultivation of seafood under controlled conditions. Fishing is the capture of wild seafood or fish living in waters. Fishing and aquaculture are both subsistence and commercial agricultural practices. Seafood is harvested from the 16 major fishing regions in the oceans, lakes, and rivers. In 50 years, the global fish production has increased from 36 to 202 million metric tons, with only two-thirds used for human consumption. The remaining fish harvest is used in fish meal and fed to livestock. Fish and seafood provide 1 percent of the caloric consumption by humans.

Agribusiness is the integration of commercial farming and food production. **Commercial grain farming**, which includes wheat and corn, takes place in western North America and southern Russia. In North America, there is a **winter wheat** belt in Kansas, Colorado, and Oklahoma where the crop is planted in the autumn. In the **spring wheat** belt, which includes the Dakotas, Montana, and southern Saskatchewan, the crop is planted in the spring. A third important grain-growing region is in the state of Washington. Commercial grain farming is mechanized using a **combine** to reap, thresh, and clean the grain in one operation. Commercial grain farming is a large-scale or **extensive** operation. Wheat is the dominant grain raised in the United States and Canada for international trade.

Mediterranean agriculture, practiced in the Mediterranean, coastal California, south Texas, parts of Chile, Australia, and South Africa, consists of diverse specialty crops such as grapes, olives, nuts, fruits, and vegetables mostly for human consumption. **Horticulture** is the deliberate growing of fruits, vegetables, and flowers. **Commercial gardening and fruit farming** is the dominant form of agriculture in the southeastern United States. It is practiced close to urban areas and is also called **truck farming** because "truck" was the Middle English word for barter or the exchange of commodities. Truck farms grow fruits and vegetables.

Livestock ranching is the extensive commercial grazing of livestock land in semi-arid or arid lands. It is practiced in much of the western United States and the pampas region of Argentina, southern Brazil, and Uruguay. Historically, ranching involved the herding of cattle over open ranges in a semi-nomadic style and later became sedentary farming by dividing open land into ranches. Today, it has become part of the meat-processing industry rather than an economic activity practiced on isolated farms. **Feed lots** are often used for more cost-efficient livestock fattening.

Dairy farming is an important type of commercial agriculture near urban areas in North America and Europe. The ring surrounding a city from which milk can be supplied without spoiling is called the **milkshed**. Increasingly in the more developed world, thanks to modern transportation systems, dairy production can take place further from the market. Dairy farmers are facing economic difficulties because of declining revenues and increasing costs. Other problems inherent to dairy farming include the fact that it is very labor intensive (cows must be milked twice a day) and the cows require expensive **winter feed**.

Mixed crop and livestock farming is practiced in much of the United States and Northern Europe. Most of the crops are fed to animals. Corn (maize) is generally the crop of choice because of its high yields per area. The predominate region, for mixed crop and livestock farming, known as the Corn Belt, extends from Ohio to the Dakotas and is centered in Iowa. Soybeans are the second most important crop in the United States and are raised predominately for animal feed and oil.

The **von Thünen model** helps explain the importance of proximity to market and the choice of crops in commercial agriculture. Johann von Thünen published his model in *The Isolated State* in 1826. According to von Thünen, rent, or land value, will decrease the further one moves away from a market. Thus, the agricultural products that use the land most intensively, have the highest transportation costs, are more perishable, and are in the greatest demand, such as dairying and fruits and vegetables, will be located close to the market. Agriculture that uses the land more extensively, such as livestock ranching, will be further away from the market.

von Thünen placed horticulture and dairying closest to the city, followed by forestry (for fuel and building). The next rings were used for various crops and pasture, becoming more extensive further from the market. The model had various assumptions that may not have been true in reality, such as a uniform landscape, equal ease of transportation in all directions, and a single market. Although *The Isolated State* is a dated and oversimplified model of reality, the principles of agricultural location still apply today, especially at a national or global scale, and it still describes the actual patterns of land use surrounding many cities.

Key Issues Revisited

9.3. Where Is Agriculture Distributed?

- There are five subsistence and six commercial regions of agricultural production.

- The most common type of farm found in more developed countries is mixed crop and livestock.

- Where mixed crop and livestock is not suitable, commercial farmers practice a variety of other types of agriculture, including dairying, commercial grain, and ranching.

- In subsistence regions, pastoral nomadism is prevalent in dry lands, shifting cultivation in tropical forests, and intensive subsistence in regions with high population concentrations.

Review Questions

9.3.1. Which climate and agricultural regions are found between 20N and 20S latitude?
A. Pastoral nomadism and continental climate
B. Plantations and tropical climates
C. Grain farming and continental climates
D. Mixed crop and humid continental
E. Mediterranean and marine West Coast

9.3.2. Intensive subsistence agriculture would be found in:
A. East Asia and Southwest Asia.
B. East Asia and South Asia.
C. Latin America and Southeast Asia.
D. Southeast Asia and sub-Saharan Africa.
E. South Asia and Latin America.

9.3.3. Rubber, tea, coffee, cocoa, and palm oil is raised in:
A. intensive plantation agriculture.
B. extensive mechanized plantations.
C. areas of shifting cultivation.
D. Mediterranean agricultural areas.
E. market gardens.

9.3.4. In which country would you find pastoral nomads?
A. Kazakhstan
B. China
C. Israel
D. Saudi Arabia
E. All of these countries have nomads.

9.3.5. Aquaculture:
A. has caused the decline of native fish species from overfishing.
B. has increased the amount of fish-based protein available in the food supply by two-thirds.
C. has created an increase in the human consumption of fish by 20 percent.
D. has reduced the demand on wild species of fish by allowing populations to reestablish numbers.
E. is restricted to inland waterways.

9.3.6. The vertical integration of food production from the field to the table is known as _____.
A. farming
B. agriculture
C. agribusiness
D. commercial farming
E. niche farming

9.3.7. Who is the largest milk producer and the largest meat producer, respectively?
A. United States and China
B. India and Canada
C. Germany and Russia
D. France and Brazil
E. Argentina and Russia

9.3.8. What country leads the world in corn production?
A. Mexico
B. Brazil
C. China
D. Argentina
E. United States

KEY ISSUE 4

Why Do Farmers Face Sustainability Challenges?

Learning Outcome 9.4.1: Explain the contribution of expanding exports to world food supply.
Global exports move primarily from the Western Hemisphere to the Eastern Hemisphere with the United States, Canada, Brazil, and Argentina the leading exporters.

Learning Outcome 9.4.2: Explain reasons for loss of farmland.
Farmland is lost to expanding urban areas, increased desertification from lack of water, and in some cases, increased water saturation.

Learning Outcome 9.4.3: Describe how farmers and scientists have achieved productivity increases.
The green revolution increased crop yields from the same amount of land, expanding the food supply at a time when the population was increasing rapidly.

Learning Outcome 9.4.4: Discuss the debate over the planting of GMO seeds.
Genetic modification of plants and animals allows for selective reproduction to produce larger yields with more efficiency and desirable qualities.

Learning Outcome 9.4.5: Identify principles of organic farming and sustainable land management.
Organic farming does not use herbicides and pesticides or GMO seeds. Organically raised animals are not confined in pens and have limited use of antibiotics. Sustainable land management prevents wind and water erosion of valuable top soil during fallow periods.

Learning Outcome 9.4.6: Analyze the importance of water in agriculture.
Water is essential for raising plants and animals. Too little water stresses agricultural production and too much causes soil erosion.

According to the World Trade Organization, the global trade in agricultural exports exceeds $769 billion in 2016. Leading exporters of agricultural products from the Western Hemisphere are the United States, Canada, Argentina, and Brazil. However, on a global scale, South east Asia, and the South Pacific are major exporting regions. The increase of agricultural exports from developing countries is the result of the use of modern production methods, high-yield seeds, and the increased use of fertilizers, pesticides, and machinery. Developing countries are faced with a dilemma: the more land that is used for growing export crops, the less land is available for domestic consumption crops. Export crops generate revenue that can be used to develop the economy and move the population from subsistence farming to commercial agriculture. This dilemma is also faced within the labor force. The demand on the world market for agricultural crops uses men who work for wages while women continue the traditional subsistence agricultural practices without pay in order to provide for the family and the community.

The threat to agricultural lands is both the result of expanding population settlements and alteration of the natural environment. As urban areas grow and demand more space, some of the most productive farmland on the periphery is sold and converted into suburban areas of urban sprawl. Some of the most threatened agricultural land in the United States is in Maryland between Baltimore and Washington, D.C. The loss of prime agricultural land to population and urban growth reduces the availability of food supplies in the market area where the population of the United States is most densely distributed. **Desertification** of semi-arid agricultural lands also threatens the production of food supply. Excessive crop production of high-water-demanding plants, animal grazing, and deforestation alter the soil nutrients and the ability of the soils to retain moisture. The demand for cotton production in the former Soviet Union (today in Uzbekistan) has resulted in an 85 percent decline in the size of the Aral Sea, the fourth-largest inland lake in the world, and destruction of a once-thriving ecosystem. Destruction of agricultural areas also occurs when irrigated land has inadequate drainage, leading to oversaturation of soils, damaging plant roots, and potentially increased salinity.

In order to head off a potential famine in Mexico and India in the 1960s, **Norman Borlaug** introduced the use of new technology to change agricultural practices. The **green revolution** began with high-yielding **hybridized** cereal grains, expanding irrigation practices, using synthetic fertilizers and pesticides, and modernizing farming techniques with equipment. Additionally, the International Rice Research Institute in the Philippines in 1966 developed hybrid rice that has a higher yield and is a hardier plant. The new hybridized rice, known as "miracle rice," required the use of fertilizers and pesticides. The Philippines became a supplier of rice in the global market within 20 years by doubling their rice production. By 1971, India experienced a surplus of several million tons in its wheat production and by 2006 was a major exporter of rice in the global market. In order to maintain the levels of production, more fertilizers and machinery are required. The **fertilizers** are composed of nitrogen, potash, and phosphorus. These elements enrich the soil nutrients in order to extract higher yields. However, the production of nitrogen-, potash-, and phosphorus-based fertilizers are dependent on petroleum as a component and a fuel for distribution. Petroleum-based fertilizers and insecticides have environmental impacts, including drying out soils, increasing the demand of water for irrigation, and contributing to air pollution from carbon combustion engines. Commercial productivity has increased yields on decreasing amounts of land as a result of the green revolution and the changes in agricultural production.

According to the Cartagena Protocol on Biosafety, a **genetically modified organism (GMO)** is defined as "any living organism that possesses a novel combination of genetic material obtained through the use of modern biotechnology." GMOs are organisms whose genetic makeup has been altered *without* the addition of genetic material from an unrelated organism but whose DNA is changed to introduce a new trait or suppress a genetic tendency. A "transgenic organism" is one that has the genetic makeup altered by the addition of genetic material from an unrelated organism, usually developed through recombinant DNA technology. Because a transgenic organism carries a gene from an unrelated species, it has undergone a genetic change to its DNA and is also genetically modified. A transgenic organism is a GMO, but not all GMOs are transgenic. **Genetically modified crops** are altered to create a resistance to certain pests, diseases, or environmental conditions to reduce spoilage or resistance to chemical treatments (e.g., resistance to a herbicide), or to improve the nutrient makeup of a crop.

According to the World Health Institute, currently available genetically modified foods stem mostly from plants, but in the future, foods derived from genetically modified microorganisms or genetically modified animals are likely to be introduced in the market. Most existing genetically modified crops have been developed to improve yield, through the introduction of resistance to plant diseases or of increased tolerance of herbicides. In the future, genetic modification could be aimed at altering the nutrient content of food, reducing its allergenic potential, or improving the efficiency of food production systems (www.who.int/topics/food_genetically_modified/en/).

With any science and technological process, there are disadvantages and advantages that create ongoing debates and such is the case with genetically modified organisms. The debate is centered on the potential environmental, health, and cultural impact. Some of the dominant areas of concern are described here:

Environmental disadvantages:

- Causing a lower level of biodiversity with fewer strains of seeds
- Potential danger to other insects that are important to the ecosystem and are eliminated through insect-resistant varieties
- Creating herbicide-resistant weeds
- Cross-pollination between GMO and non-GMOs
- Not proven to be 100 percent environmentally safe

Cultural/Health disadvantages:

- Increased funding for more research
- Concerns on changing the field of agriculture
- Trade concerns with countries that will not allow GMO products
- Allergic reactions to new proteins and unknown genetic material
- Potential decreased antibiotic efficacy

Environmental advantages:

- Can increase yields grown on the same or less acreage
- Can reduce crop damage from weeds, diseases, and insects, which means herbicide applications are more precise or used more efficiently
- Can reduce crop damage from adverse weather conditions
- Can reduce fossil-fuel use

Cultural/Health advantages:

- Allows for more profit from increased yield

- Economically efficient by producing more without expanding acreage (Because GMOs are designed to resist pests, there will be no need for pesticides to be used, which means more savings.)
- Advanced crops and lower costs, leading to cheaper food
- Can potentially improve nutritional value
- Recent advancements in soybeans creating new oil with health benefits for consumers, including less saturated fat

Today, the organic food market accounts for almost 5 percent of the total U.S. food sales. **Organic farming** eliminates the use of petrochemical-based fertilizers, pesticides, herbicides, antibiotics, and growth hormones, as well as concentrated animal feeding operations (C.A.F.O.). The difference between more developed and developing countries in terms of food production is shaped by government policy and financial conditions. In developed countries, farmers are encouraged to grow less food to prevent creating an excess supply while the government pays farmers when certain prices are low and will buy surplus production to sell or donate to foreign governments. By contrast, in developing countries, farmers are encouraged to produce more food to keep up with the rate of population growth.

Sustainable land management in agriculture is concerned with reducing the loss of high-quality topsoil from wind and water erosion and preserving the moisture content of soil. Conservation tillage includes deliberate actions to conserve soil and moisture without adding unnatural products to the land. **No tillage (no-till agriculture)** farming practices leave the chaff on the fields through the winter snows to keep the wind from blowing the soil into water systems. The chaff also preserves moisture and provides nutrients in the soils during nongrowing periods. Contour landscaping and integrated pest management practices are designed to conserve moisture levels in the soils and reduce the amount of petrochemical products used on fields. The U.S. government encourages conservation practices through subsidies for preserving wetland areas in farm acreage, planting clover and alfalfa for animal fodder, and shifting lands back into natural contours and removing tiles that channelize water away from crops.

Key Issues Revisited

9.4. Why Do Farmers Face Sustainability Challenges?

- Agricultural land is lost to competing uses, such as expanding urban areas.

- The green revolution improved the productivity of farming in some countries.

- Some agricultural regions face environmental challenges.

- GMO crops are increasing the yield and nutrient values of some plants yet are controversial.

- Population growth, government policies, and niche farming challenge sustainable agriculture.

Review Questions

9.4.1. Which of the following explains the flow of agricultural products in the global market?
A. Major grain production flows from Russia to Europe and India.
B. China provides grain products to much of Europe.
C. European Union is a major supplier of grain to Latin America.
D. Japan is a major supplier of grain products to the rest of Asia.
E. United States, Canada, and Argentina are major grain suppliers to Europe and Asia.

9.4.2. What is the relationship of global food production to population growth?
A. Food production is well below population growth.
B. Food production exceeds population growth.
C. Food production is about even with population growth.
D. Food production cannot keep up with population growth.
E. None of the above.

9.4.3. Subsistence intensive farming occurs predominately in:
A. rural areas of Canada.
B. the hillsides of South east Asia.
C. the Atlantic Northeast and inland Europe.
D. rural areas of the southern United States.
E. Central and Eastern Europe.

9.4.4. A GMO is:
A. an organism that has had the DNA altered for improved productivity.
B. a dangerous organism that kills off healthy species.
C. an organism that is naturally created.
D. a plant species that is only raised in the United States.
E. a space designed for gender-specific practices.

9.4.5. Which country has the largest share of the world's organic farms?
A. Argentina
B. Australia
C. Austria
D. Azerbaijan
E. Armenia

9.4.6. Which of the following is an example of sustainable land management?
A. Use groundwater instead of rivers for irrigation.
B. Reduce fertilizers and pesticides to conserve fossil fuels.
C. Use conservation tillage to reduce soil erosion.
D. Convert to organic and truck farming.
E. Use GMOs to reduce water usage.

Key Terms

Agribusiness

Agricultural hearths*

Agricultural Revolution*

Agriculture*

Aquaculture*

Biotechnology*

Bio-climatic zones*

Capital-intensive

Cereal grain

Chaff

Columbian Exchange*

Combine

Commercial agriculture*

Commercial gardening and fruit farming*

Commercial grain farming*

Crop*

Crop rotation

Dairy farming

Desertification*

Domestication*

Double cropping

Deforestation*

Dry rice

Extensive agriculture*

Fair trade*

Fallow

Genetic modification (GM)*

Genetically Modified Organism (GMO)*

Grain

Green revolution*

Horticulture

Hull

Hunters and gatherers

Intensive subsistence agriculture*

Intertillage

Irrigation*

Labor-intensive

Livestock ranching*

Large-scale agriculture

Mediterranean agriculture*

Milkshed

Mixed crop and livestock farming*

Neolithic

Nomadic herding*

Organic farming*

Overgrazing

Paddy

Pastoral nomadism*

Pasture

Plantation*

Ranching*

Ridge tillage

Sawah

Second Agricultural Revolution*

Seed agriculture*

Shifting agriculture*

Slash-and-burn agriculture*

Threshing

Soil degradation*	Transhumance*
Specialty crops*	Truck farming
Spring wheat	Vegetative planting
Subsistence agriculture*	von Thünen Model*
Suitcase farming	Wet rice
Sustainable agriculture*	Winter wheat
Swidden	Women in agriculture*
Third Agricultural Revolution	

* Term is in 2019 College Board Curriculum & Exam Description.

Source: College Board AP Human Geography Course Description, effective Fall 2019

Think Like a Geographer

- Using a map of climatic regions, indicate areas that each of the crops or agricultural activities occurs. Explain the patterns that you observe, focusing on the correlation of crops to latitudinal regions.
- Complete a chart indicating which type of agricultural activity each crop is produced for: plantation, truck farms, large-scale commercial, extensive, or intensive.
- Evaluate the map in part one and a map of global population areas. Determine if there is a correlation between population areas and agricultural activities.

apples	corn	olives	rubber
bananas	cotton	oranges	sheep
barley	cranberries	palm	tea
beef cattle	dairy cattle	pineapple	wet rice
cinnamon	dry rice	potatoes	wheat
cocoa	grapefruit	poultry	
coffee	grapes		

Quick Quiz

9.1. What are the three dominant grains in the world?
A. Barley, sorghum, and millet
B. Wheat, rice, and maize
C. Oats, barley, and maize
D. Barley, oats, and soybeans
E. Rice, soybeans, and rye

9.2. Which crops are thought to have originated in Latin America?
A. Maize, beans, cotton, and potatoes
B. Barley, cattle, wheat, and oats
C. Sorghum, yams, rice, and coffee
D. Coconut, mango, taro, and peas
E. Rice, millet, soybeans, corn, and walnut

9.3. Which of the following are plantation crops raised in the tropics at higher elevations?
A. Cotton and hemp
B. Pineapples and bananas
C. Coffee and tea
D. Wheat and barley
E. Cinnamon and cocoa

9.4. Which crop has the highest percentage of genetically modified plants?
A. Cotton
B. Maize
C. Soybeans
D. Rice
E. Wheat

9.5. Which of the following is a sustainable agricultural practice?
A. Desertification
B. Irrigation of marginal lands
C. Using GMOs
D. Increased animal production for protein
E. No-till agriculture

9.6. The most productive agricultural land is known as _____.
A. farmland
B. von Thünen land
C. prime agricultural land
D. productive agricultural land
E. cultivation

9.7. What is another name for commercial agriculture in the more developed world?
A. Truck farming
B. Horticulture
C. Globalized agriculture
D. Agribusiness
E. Market agriculture

9.8. Which country is among the largest exporter of agricultural products?
A. Russia
B. China
C. Chile
D. Brazil
E. Egypt

9.9. Which region has the largest percentage of population that is undernourished?
A. Latin America
B. East Asia
C. Northern Europe
D. Oceania
E. Sub-Saharan Africa

9.10 What type of commercial agriculture is found in developing countries?
A. Plantation farming
B. Mixed crop and livestock
C. Dairy farming
D. Grain farming
E. Commercial gardening

Free Response

1. Evaluate the advantages and disadvantages of genetically modified crops in a more developed country.
2. Analyze the impact of the green revolution in a named developing country.
3. Compare the impact on the landscape between truck farming and extensive grain farming.
4. Compare the impact on the landscape between organic farming and plantation farms.
5. Discuss the advantages of community gardens.

On the Web

www.pearsonmylabandmastering.com/northamerica/masteringgeography/
www.mapsofworld.com/thematic-maps/world-food-consumption-map.htm
www.time.com/8515/hungry-planet-what-the-world-eats/
www.differencebetween.com/difference-between-subsistence-farming-and-vs-commercial-farming/
www.wfp.org/hunger/malnutrition
www.cbd.int/agro/whatstheproblem.shtml
www.sdgfund.org/goal-2-zero-hunger
www.storymaps.esri.com/stories/2017/fast-food-nation/
Resources for Teaching the AP Human Geography Agriculture and Rural Land Use Topic:
www.education.nationalgeographic.org/topics/ap-human-geography-agriculture/
Eat: The Story of Food, National Geographic Channel:
www.youtube.com/watch?v=Q09vB3KVmkU&list=EL9Z6kL5chShmZs-5shbiNyA
Farming First, A global coalition for sustainable agricultural development:
www.farmingfirst.org/portal/gender/
Feeding the World:
www.nationalgeographic.com/foodfeatures/feeding-9-billion/
Food by the Numbers: Feeding Our Hungry Planet:
www.video.nationalgeographic.com/video/food-by-the-numbers/141014-world-food-day-ngfood
How Far Does Your Food Travel?
www.buzzfeed.com/generalelectric/how-far-does-your-food-travel-6ieg
Living in the Shadow of Industrial Farming:
www.geographyeducation.org/2015/08/17/living-in-the-shadow-of-industrial-farming/
Recent Developments: Globalization, Agriculture, and Human Geography:
www.apcentral.collegeboard.com/apc/members/courses/teachers_corner/32449.html

Teaching the Geography of Food:
www.blog.education.nationalgeographic.com/2015/02/25/teaching-the-geography-of-food/
What the World Eats: Compare Diet and Consumption Patterns Over Time:
www.education.nationalgeographic.org/media/dietary-consumption-around-world/
What You Need to Know About Genetically Engineered Food:
www.theatlantic.com/health/archive/2013/02/what-you-need-to-know-about-genetically-engineered-food/272931/
Global Hunger Index
www.globalhungerindex.org/results/
Living in a Food Desert
www.youtube.com/watch?v=jicYbi-8ZNU&t=1135s&list=PLTlwKRGStTCjQ9S1bfJBrdgq4isIN2mRk&index=40

TED Talks

Cary Fowler: One Seed at a Time, Protecting the Future of Food
www.ted.com/talks/cary_fowler_one_seed_at_a_time_protecting_the_future_of_food?language=en

Mark Bittman: What's Wrong with What We Eat
www.ted.com/talks/mark_bittman_on_what_s_wrong_with_what_we_eat

Carolyn Steel: How Food Shapes Our Cities
www.ted.com/talks/carolyn_steel_how_food_shapes_our_cities?language=en

Borut Bohanec: GMO Controversies—Science vs. Public Fear
www.youtube.com/watch?v=mz4_TwdaYeI

Gary Hirshberg: Why Genetically Engineered Foods Should be Labeled—Bottom Up and Top Down
www.youtube.com/watch?v=pGyOwnqpCKk

Tom Wilson: Population Growth and Food Supply
www.youtu.be/f9uJ_cBXEKQ

Key Figures

Figure 9-1 Dietary Energy Consumption, 2013
Figure 9-4 Percentage of Population Who Are Undernourished, 2017
Figure 9-7 Income Spent on Food
Figure 9-10 Dietary Energy by Source
Figure 9-14 Protein by Source
Figure 9-15 Protein from Meat
Figure 9-19 Agriculture Hearths and Dispersal Routes
Figure 9-20 Agricultural Workers, 2017
Figure 9-23 Agricultural Regions
Figure 9-26 Rice Production
Figure 9-35 Plantation
Figure 9-36 Climate and Agriculture Regions

AP® Human Geography

Unit 5: Agriculture and Rural Land-Use Patterns and Processes

Topic	APHG Topic No. Title	Suggested Skills	Enduring Understandings	Learning Objective	Big Ideas
9.1.1; 9.1.2	5.6: Agricultural Production Regions	2.E: Explain the degree to which a geographic concept, process, model, or theory effectively explains geographic effects in different contexts and regions of the world.	PSO-5: Availability of resources and cultural practices influence agricultural practices and land-use patterns.	PSO-5.C: Explain how economic forces influence agricultural practices.	BI-1: Patterns and Spatial Organization
9.1.3	5.1: Introduction to Agriculture	2.D: Explain the significance of geographic similarities and differences among different locations and/or at different times.	PSO-5: Availability of resources and cultural practices influence agricultural practices and land-use patterns.	PSO-5.A: Explain the connection between physical geography and agricultural practices.	BI-1: Patterns and Spatial Organization
9.2.1	5.3: Agricultural Origins and Diffusions	2.B: Explain spatial relationships in a specified context or region of the world, using geographic concepts, processes, models, or theories.	SPS-5: Agriculture has changed over time because of cultural diffusion and advances in technology.	SPS-5.A: Identify major centers of domestication of plants and animals.	BI-3: Spatial Processes and Societal Change
9.2.2; 9.3.1; 9.3.2; 9.3.3	5.6: Agricultural Production Regions	2.D: Explain the significance of geographic similarities and differences among different locations and/or at different	PSO-5: Availability of resources and cultural practices influence agricultural practices and	PSO-5.A: Explain the connection between physical geography and agricultural practices.	BI-1: Patterns and Spatial Organization

		times.	land-use patterns.		
9.3.4	5.10: Consequences of Agricultural Practices	2.E: Explain the degree to which a geographic concept, process, model, or theory effectively explains geographic effects in different contexts and regions of the world.	IMP-5: Agricultural production and consumption patterns vary in different locations, presenting different environmental, social, economic, and cultural opportunities and challenges.	IMP-5.A: Explain how agricultural practices have environmental and societal consequence.	BI-2: Impacts and Interactions
9.3.5	5.11: Challenges of Contemporary Agriculture	2.E: Explain the degree to which a geographic concept, process, model, or theory effectively explains geographic effects in different contexts and regions of the world.	IMP-5: Agricultural production and consumption patterns vary in different locations, presenting different environmental, social, economic, and cultural opportunities and challenges.	IMP-5.B: Explain challenges and debates related to the changing nature of contemporary agriculture and food-production practices.	BI-2: Impacts and Interactions
9.3.6	5.7: Spatial Organization of Agriculture	2.E: Explain the degree to which a geographic concept, process, model, or theory effectively explains geographic effects in different contexts and regions of the world.	PSO-5: Availability of resources and cultural practices influence agricultural practices and land-use patterns.	PSO-5.C: Explain how economic forces influence agricultural practices.	BI-1: Patterns and Spatial Organization
9.3.7	5.1: Introduction to Agriculture	2.D: Explain the significance of geographic similarities and differences among different locations and/or at different times.	PSO-5: Availability of resources and cultural practices influence agricultural practices and land-use patterns.	PSO-5.A: Explain the connection between physical geography and agricultural practices.	BI-1: Patterns and Spatial Organization

9.3.8	5.1: Introduction to Agriculture	2.D: Explain the significance of geographic similarities and differences among different locations and/or at different times.	PSO-5: Availability of resources and cultural practices influence agricultural practices and land-use patterns.	PSO-5.C: Explain how economic forces influence agricultural practices.	BI-1: Patterns and Spatial Organization
9.3.8	5.8: von Thünen Model	5.B: Explain spatial relationships across various geographic scales using geographic concepts, processes, models, or theories.	PSO-5: Availability of resources and cultural practices influence agricultural practices and land-use patterns.	PSO-5.D: Describe how the von Thünen model is used to explain patterns of agricultural production at various scales.	BI-1: Patterns and Spatial Organization
9.4.1	5.10: Consequences of Agricultural Practices	2.E: Explain the degree to which a geographic concept, process, model, or theory effectively explains geographic effects in different contexts and regions of the world.	IMP-5: Agricultural production and consumption patterns vary in different locations, presenting different environmental, social, economic, and cultural opportunities and challenges.	IMP-5.B: Explain challenges and debates related to the changing nature of contemporary agriculture and food-production practices.	BI-2: Impacts and Interactions
9.4.2	5.10: Consequences of Agricultural Practices	2.E: Explain the degree to which a geographic concept, process, model, or theory effectively explains geographic effects in different contexts and regions of the world.	IMP-5: Agricultural production and consumption patterns vary in different locations, presenting different environmental, social, economic, and cultural opportunities and challenges.	IMP-5.A: Explain how agricultural practices have environmental and societal consequences.	BI-2: Impacts and Interactions

9.4.3	5.11: Challenges of Contemporary Agriculture	2.D: Explain the significance of geographic similarities and differences among different locations and/or at different times.	IMP-5: Agricultural production and consumption patterns vary in different locations, presenting different environmental, social, economic, and cultural opportunities and challenges.	IMP-5.B: Explain challenges and debates related to the changing nature of contemporary agriculture and food-production practices.	BI-2: Impacts and Interactions
9.4.3	5.5: The Green Revolution	2.D: Explain the significance of geographic similarities and differences among different locations and/or at different times.	SPS-5: Agriculture has changed over time because of cultural diffusion and advances in technology.	SPS-5.D: Explain the consequences of the green revolution on food supply and the environment in the developing world.	BI-3: Spatial Processes and Societal Change
9.4.4; 9.4.5	5.11: Challenges of Contemporary Agriculture	2.D: Explain the significance of geographic similarities and differences among different locations and/or at different times.	IMP-5: Agricultural production and consumption patterns vary in different locations, presenting different environmental, social, economic, and cultural opportunities and challenges.	IMP-5.B: Explain challenges and debates related to the changing nature of contemporary agriculture and food-production practices.	BI-2: Impacts and Interactions
9.4.6	5.6: Agricultural Production Regions	2.E: Explain the degree to which a geographic concept, process, model, or theory effectively explains geographic effects in different contexts and regions of the world.	PSO-5: Availability of resources and cultural practices influence agricultural practices and land-use patterns.	PSO-5.E: Explain the interdependence among regions of agricultural production and consumption.	BI-1: Patterns and Spatial Organization

Source: College Board AP Human Geography Course Description, effective Fall 2019

FRQ's From College Board

2001 FRQ #1
2004 FRQ #2
2007 FRQ #1
2008 FRQ #1
2012 FRQ #2
2014 FRQ #3
2016 FRQ #3

Chapter

10 Development

Why Does Development Vary Among Countries?

Development is a process of improving a person's prospects of leading a long and healthy life, acquiring knowledge, and obtaining adequate resources. This chapter addresses the locational factors influencing more developed and less developed countries and explains why some regions are more developed than others. More and less developed regions are distinguished by economic, social, and demographic indicators. Development is dependent on government policies and establishing connections between places to make development fair and equitable for all.

Learning Outcome 10.1.1: Explain the concepts of development, developed and developing countries, and the Human Development Index.

The United Nations defines development as a process of enlarging people's ability to lead a long and healthy life, to acquire knowledge, and to have resources needed for a decent standard of living. A developed country has progressed further in development compared to a developing country. The HDI measures the standard of living, life expectancy, and level of education.

Learning Outcome 10.1.2: Explain the HDI standard of living factor.

Standard of living is measured by the GNI per capita at PPP.

Learning Outcome 10.1.3: Explain the HDI education factors.

The years of schooling is considered to be the most critical measure of the ability of an individual to gain access to knowledge needed for development.

Learning Outcome 10.1.4: Identify HDI health factors.

Access to medical care is essential for long and healthy lives. Life expectancy at birth is an indicator used to measure the development level of a country.

Development is the process of improving the conditions of people through diffusion of knowledge and technology. Development is a continuous process, and each country lies somewhere along that continuum. A **more developed country (MDC)**, also known as a **developed country**, will be further along that continuum than a **less developed country (LDC)**, also known as a **developing country**.

The United Nations HDI, (or GDP), identifies **gross national income (GNI)** as its economic indicator of development. The GNI is adjusted by the PPP, the difference in the cost of goods among similar countries of similar GNI. Other economic indicators that help distinguish between levels of development include economic structure, purchasing power, worker productivity, access to raw materials, and availability of consumer goods. GNI is the value of all goods and services produced in a country, including money that leaves and enters the country. The annual per capita GNI in 2015 exceeded $40,000 in more developed countries and was about $10,000 in developing countries, and this gap has been widening.

The percentage of workers in the different sectors of the economy will help show the level of development of a country. Workers in the **primary sector** of the economy extract materials from Earth, usually through agriculture. The share of GDP accounted for by the primary sector has decreased in developing countries, but it remains higher than in more developed countries. The low number of primary sector workers means that only a few produce enough food for the rest of society and presumably with mechanical assistance. The **secondary sector** is the industrial sector of the economy, and the **tertiary sector** is the service sector of the economy. Employment in the secondary sector of more developed countries has decreased below that of developing countries. The highly developed countries have the share of their GDP from the tertiary, quaternary, and quinary sectors. **Quaternary** sector jobs include business services and wholesaling, and **quinary** sector jobs are in health, education, research, government, retailing, and tourism. However, the current practice is to consider all these jobs as groups within the tertiary sector.

Productivity is the value of a particular product compared to the amount of labor needed to make it. It can be measured by the **value added** per worker, which in manufacturing is the gross value of the product minus the costs of raw materials and energy. Productivity is much higher in more developed countries because of higher technology and capital intensive industries. Production in developing countries is still very labor intensive.

Development requires access to raw materials, although some developed countries such as Japan, Singapore, and Switzerland lack significant resources, and some developing countries such as those in sub-Saharan Africa have significant raw materials. Development also requires energy to fuel industry and transform raw materials into finished products.

The **Human Development Index (HDI)** is one measure of development. HDI was created by the United Nations and has been used since 1980. It measures development in terms of human welfare rather than money or productivity. It evaluates human welfare in three areas: economic, social, and demographic. The economic factor is **gross domestic product (GDP)** per capita or gross national income (GNI) per capita at **purchasing power parity (PPP)**. GNI per capita at PPP is the standard used by the United Nations but that some nations have also used GDP to measure the economic progress of a country. The social factors are the literacy rate and amount of education, and the demographic factor is life expectancy. The highest HDI possible is 1.0 or 100%. The closer the measurement is to 1.0, the higher the development status of a country. The countries of the world are categorized by the United Nations into nine regions and three other distinctive regions according to their level of development. Countries fall into four wide human development categories, Very High Human Development includes 58 countries, 53 countries are included in High Human Development, 39 countries are ranked as Medium Human Development, and 38 countries are in the Low Human Development. Six countries are not ranked in the HDI. The five more developed regions include North America, Europe, Russia, Japan, and Oceania. North America has the highest HDI (0.908) and is well endowed with natural resources and agricultural land. It has developed high-tech industries, is a leading consumer, and the world's largest market. Its high percentage of tertiary sector employment has offset the loss of manufacturing.

Education and health are key social indicators of development. High levels of development are associated with high levels of education. The quality of education is typically measured by student/teacher ratio and literacy rates. The **literacy rate** is the percentage of a country's population who can read and write. Literacy rates in more developed countries usually exceed 99 percent, whereas many developing countries have rates that are below 70 percent. There are also huge differences between literacy rates for men and women in developing countries. More developed countries dominate scientific and nonfiction publishing worldwide; however, in developing countries, this knowledge comes from books written in nonnative languages.

The United Nations' HDI includes life expectancy as a measure of development. Other demographic indicators include infant mortality, natural increase, and crude birth rates. Life expectancy is a measure of health and welfare; some more developed countries have life expectancies that are twice as high as developing countries. Infant mortality rates speak to levels of health care in a country. Rates of natural increase are much higher in developing countries and force them to allocate increasing percentages of their GDP to care for a rapidly expanding population. Developing countries have higher rates of natural increase because they have higher crude birth rates. One has to be careful when looking at crude death rates to help measure levels of development for two reasons. First, the diffusion of medical technology from developed to developing countries has reduced death rates in less developed countries. Second, the high crude death rates of some more developed countries are a reflection of their higher percentages of elderly and lower percentages of children.

Countries that produce more quality nonessential consumer goods are able to promote expansion of industry and the generation of additional wealth. Consumer goods such as automobiles, telephones, and televisions are very accessible to many people in more developed countries but only to the wealthy in developing countries.

Key Issues Revisited

10.1. Why Does Development Vary Among Countries?

- Development is the process by which the material conditions of a country's people are improved.

- The Human Development Index (HDI) measures the level of development of each country.

- A more developed country has a higher level of per capita GDP as a result of the structural transformation of the economy from an agricultural to a service-providing society.

- Developed countries use their wealth to provide better health, education, and welfare services, whereas developing countries must use their additional wealth largely to meet the most basic needs of a rapidly growing population.

- The five regions of more developed countries include Europe, North America, Japan, Oceania, and Russia.

- The seven regions of developing countries are Latin America, East Asia, Central Asia, Southwest Asia, Southeast Asia, South Asia, and sub-Saharan Africa.

Review Questions

10.1.1. Which of the following is not a factor for the measurement of the Human Development Index?
A. Standard of living
B. Long and healthy life
C. Access to knowledge
D. Primary sector employment
E. All are factors for HDI.

10.1.2. Countries with the lowest HDI would be found in what region?
A. Southeast Asia
B. Central Asia
C. Europe
D. Sub-Saharan Africa
E. Latin America

10.1.3. The literacy rate of countries in Latin America is at least _____ percent.
A. 99–100
B. 90–98
C. 70–89
D. below 70
E. below 40

10.1.4. Which developed country has a life expectancy like those of developing countries?
A. Russia
B. United States
C. Spain
D. Japan
E. Denmark

KEY ISSUE 2

Where Are Inequalities in Development Distributed?

Learning Outcome 10.2.1: Describe the United Nation's measures of inequality.
The United Nations uses the Inequality-adjusted Human Development Index (IHDI). The IHDI modifies the HDI to account for inequality within a country.

Learning Outcome 10.2.2: Describe patterns of regional inequality within developing and more developed countries.
Inequality within countries can be seen in the difference between the HDI and IHDI and also through differences in per capita GDP among states or provinces.

Learning Outcome 10.2.3: Describe the United Nation's measures of gender inequality.
The **Gender Inequality Index (GII)** measures the extent of gender inequality. The GII combines measures of empowerment, labor force participation, and reproductive rights.

Learning Outcome 10.2.4: Describe empowerment-related components of gender inequality.
Empowerment refers to the ability of women to achieve economic and political power.

Learning Outcome 10.2.5: Describe reproductive health elements of the GII.
The reproductive health component of GII is based on the maternal mortality rate and the adolescent fertility rate.

Development measures access to a decent standard of living, to an education, and to health care. The level of development is not uniform across a country, resulting in levels of inequality within and among countries. Unequal development usually appears in terms of income, gender, and aspects of location. On a global scale, we see uneven development and unequal development occurring at a greater rate in countries that are on the periphery of an economic core. The Inequality-adjusted Human Development Index is a modification of the HDI taking into account acquisition and distribution of wealth, access to education, and health care. More developed countries have values of HDI and IHDI closer together, indicating a modest level of inequality by global standards. Highest inequality is in sub-Saharan Africa and South Asia. Turkey and Brazil provide examples of differing inequality within developing countries. Both have similar HDI scores, but Brazil has a lower IHDI, indicating greater inequality in Turkey. Inequality in development is prevalent in both countries as you move away from the economic core and the dominant cities. Inequality in more developed countries is less extreme and is regionally expressed.

The Gender Inequality Index (GII) combines multiple measures, including empowerment, labor, and reproductive health. A country with complete gender equality would have a GII of 0. A country with a high GII means that there is a great amount of disparity between men and women. The lowest GIIs are found in countries that have a high HDI. The empowerment measure of GII looks at the degree of education and political power held by women. The economic indicator is the percentage of women who have completed high school. This indicator is much higher in more developed countries than in developing countries. One indicator of the political power of women is the percentage of the country's administrative and managerial jobs they hold. This is higher in more developed countries, especially European countries, than in developing countries. The other political indicator of empowerment is the percentage of women elected to public office. Key indicators look better for developing countries now than a generation ago, but the gap in key development indicators between developing countries and more developed countries remains wide.

Analyzing HDI and GII shows that the more developed country will have less gender inequality than a developing country. Additionally, women will have more access to health care, more access to education, and the opportunity to work outside of the home. These opportunities contribute to the ability to increase the overall health, education, and income of the family, which then increases the development levels at the lowest level of the scale.

Immanuel Wallerstein analyzed development at a regional and global scale and described a relationship between more developed and developing countries as a "core" and "periphery" relationship.

The countries of the **core** are those that control the world's economic activity and wealth. The countries of the **semi-periphery** and **periphery** are typically members of the developing world. The semi-peripheral countries border the core countries/regions and directly benefit from this spatial relationship in terms of economic development, trade, and quality of life. Countries on the far periphery benefit the least from the core relationship.

Since the 1990s, gender inequality has declined in all but 4 of 138 measured countries. The greatest improvements are in Southwest Asia and North Africa. The United States is ranked 41st on the GII and 13th on the HDI. The lower ranking on the GII is due to a higher teenage birth rate and a higher maternal mortality rate during childbirth, in addition to a lower empowerment measurement compared to other highly developed countries.

Gender empowerment measures the ability of women to achieve economic and political power. The GII empowerment uses two indicators: the percentage of seats held by women in national legislatures and the percentage of women who have completed some secondary school. Rwanda is the only country with a national parliament that is majority female. In the United States, only 19 percent of senators and 24 percent of representatives in Congress are female. In Canada, 26 percent of the House of Commons are women. Education opportunities are clearly divided along more developed or developing country lines. In developing countries, only 62 percent of eligible girls go on to secondary school, with South Asia and Central Africa having the greatest gender differences. The last measurement of gender empowerment is employment outside of the home. Women in more developed countries tend to hold full-time jobs outside of the home, while women in South and Southwest Asia tend to not be employed outside of the home in primary or secondary sector jobs.

The final measurement of GII is reproductive health, which is determined by the maternal mortality rate and the adolescent fertility rate. The numbers of women who die in childbirth in more developed countries average 16 per 100,000 live births, while in developing countries this rate increases to an average of 171, with the highest rates in sub-Saharan Africa. Access to prenatal health care and medical assistance during the birth process is a significant factor in the mortality rates of mothers and infants. The adolescent fertility rate measures the number of births per 1,000 women 15–19 years of age. Access to contraception, education, family planning, and cultural influences are key to reducing this rate in developing countries, where there is an average of 53 births per 1,000 women 15–19 years old. In more developed countries, this rate is 19 births per 1,000.

Key Issues Revisited

10.2. Where Are Inequalities in Development Found?

- The United Nations has found evidence of gender inequality in every country of the world, measured by the Inequality-adjusted HDI.

- The Gender Development Index measures the gender gap in achievement of income, education, and life expectancy.

- The GII measures the extent of inequality between men and women based on reproductive health, empowerment, and employment.

Review Questions

10.2.1. Inequality in developing countries is most likely found:
A. in the primate city.
B. in the cities located in extreme environments.
C. in areas further away from the large urban core.
D. in the agricultural areas of the country.
E. in the inner city sections of the large cities.

10.2.2. The greatest improvement in the GII since the 1990s has been in _____.
A. Southwest Asia and North Africa
B. Western Europe
C. Sub-Saharan Africa
D. East and Southeast Asia
E. South America

10.2.3. Where would the lowest rate of female participation in the workforce be found?
A. Eastern Europe
B. Central Asia
C. Southwest Asia
D. Latin America
E. North America

10.2.4. According to the United Nations, gender inequality adversely affects which of these?
A. The environment
B. Politics
C. Childbirth
D. Life expectancy
E. Death rates

10.2.5. Which country has a high HDI and a low GII?
A. Russia
B. Canada
C. India
D. China
E. Brazil

KEY ISSUE 3

Why Do Countries Face Development Challenges?

Learning Outcome 10.3.1: Summarize the two paths to development.
To promote development, developing countries choose either the self-sufficiency path or the international trade path.

Learning Outcome 10.3.2: Analyze reasons for the triumph of the international trade approach to development.
International trade has several advantages over self-sufficiency, including improved efficiency, increased competitiveness, and greater government and business transparency.

Learning Outcome 10.3.3: Identify the main sources of financing development.
Finance comes from direct investment by transnational corporations and loans from banks and international organizations.

Learning Outcome 10.3.4: Explain alternate strategies for coping with the costs of development.
Developing countries often have to choose between stimulus and austerity to cope with high debt obligations that can result in financial crisis.

Today, developing countries have to develop much more rapidly than the time it took the currently developed countries to do. Additionally, developing countries have to adopt policies that successfully promote development and find funding to pay for the development. In order to promote development, countries must follow a plan of "development in one country," also known as the path of self-sufficiency or the path to development through international trade. Development by the self-sufficiency plan requires limiting imports, imposing high tariffs and restrictions on foreign suppliers, and supporting new businesses with tax breaks and subsidies. Government investment is spread across all economic sectors, narrowing the gap between the wealthy and the poor. The goal is to replace foreign imports with domestically produced items, and the only way to make it possible is to sell domestic goods for very low prices while imposing high tariffs on foreign products. India initially focused its development plan on this path of self-sufficiency; however, it shifted to the international trade model in the 1990s and entered the global trade market.

W.W. Rostow presented a five-stage model of development in the 1950s. The **Rostow model** of development by international trade argues that a country begins first as a **traditional society** engaged in agriculture and "nonproductive" activities; in its second stage, it develops the **preconditions for takeoff** by creating the initial economic infrastructure with the guidance of well-educated leaders and support from international funding; during the third **takeoff** stage, the country experiences rapid growth in limited economic activities, which utilize modern technology to become productive; the fourth stage is the **drive to maturity** when modern technology is utilized across all of the industries, resulting in a more skilled and specialized workforce; and in the final fifth stage, or the **age of mass consumption**, the economy shifts from heavy industry to the production of consumer products. The international trade model of development allows a country to identify its unique economic assets and then determine what products it can manufacture and distribute on the world market at a lower cost than other countries. The sale of these products in the world market brings in outside monies that are used to invest in additional areas of development.

The international trade model was adopted by South Korea, Singapore, Taiwan, and Hong Kong, or the Four Asian Dragons (also called the Four Asian Tigers). They focused on producing textiles and electronics while offering a low-cost labor market to make the products less expensive on the world market. Saudi Arabia, Kuwait, Bahrain, Oman, and the United Arab Emirates also adopted the international trade model. Their focus was on the extraction of petroleum and using it to finance domestic development, transforming the desert into a modern high-technology-driven society. Trade increased more rapidly than wealth after the 1990s when the international trade model was adopted by several long-time advocates of self-sufficiency, namely, India, Russia, and China.

In 1995, countries that represented 97 percent of the world trade formed the **World Trade Organization (WTO)**. The WTO's purpose was to continue to promote world trade, reduce tariffs and trade barriers, and enforce agreements among member nations.

Since developing countries lack money to fund development, they must obtain financial support from more developed countries through direct investment by transnational corporations and loans from banks and international organizations. **Foreign direct investment** is investment from one country into the economy of another foreign country. The major sources of foreign direct investment are from transnational corporations that operate in all countries except where their corporate headquarters is located. However, only 45.2 percent of FDI funds go to countries in the developing world while 30.5 percent is directed to European countries. Two sources of loans to developing countries are from the World Bank and the **International Monetary Fund (IMF)**. The **World Bank** provides loans for infrastructure and public services. The IMF provides additional loans to countries that have trouble meeting their debt obligations and balance of payments that are preventing further economic expansion. Over $10 billion in assistance has been provided to India, China, Pakistan, Indonesia, Turkey, Brazil, and Mexico. Ideally, monies are loaned to build and improve infrastructure that will then attract new or expanded businesses providing additional tax income for the developing country. The developing country is intended to repay the loan with the additional tax revenue but that does not happen with many of the countries. Some countries are not able to repay the interest on their loans or the principal repayments. When countries cannot repay their debts, future loans and continued construction are halted, thus limiting further development.

In an attempt to fight economic downturns, political leaders have supported either stimulating the economy by increasing government spending and creating government funded work programs or supporting austerity strategies of reducing taxes so that people can spend their tax savings to restimulate the economy. Austerity measure follows a structural adjustment program to implement economic reforms targeting investment on the individual and not at the government level in developing countries. Monies are directed toward improving the quality of life of the poor, promoting private-sector development, direct investment on health and education programs, and reforming government spending. However, critics argue that structural reforms can also cause a greater impact on the poor due to government cutbacks to encourage private development. Counterarguments from international organizations say that the poor suffer more without reforms because it is economic growth over time that benefits the poor. Ultimately, the IMF and World Bank support innovative programs to encourage development of poor populations and developing countries.

Microfinancing is another means of economic development. **Microloans** are small loans made to individuals and small businesses in relatively low amounts. The Grameen Bank of Bangladesh specialized in making small loans to women producing fair trade handcrafted products. With small loan amounts and low interest rates, the microfinancing program has been extremely successful in improving the lives of individual families and stimulating the economic development of the local community.

Key Issues Revisited

10.3. Why Do Countries Face Development Challenges?

- The path to development is through self-sufficiency or international trade.

- Trade increased more rapidly than wealth at the end of the twentieth century under the international trade development model.

- Development is financed through foreign direct investment and loans from international organizations.

- Austerity and stimulus are strategies for fighting economic downturns.

Review Questions

10.3.1. Which was NOT one of the Four Asian Dragons that based its development on international trade?
A. Singapore
B. Taiwan
C. South Korea
D. Vietnam
E. Hong Kong

10.3.2. A country that concentrates on international trade:
A. benefits from exposure to the demands and preferences of the consumers in other countries.
B. is limited by the actions of the trading bloc of the WTO.
C. is exempt from foreign trade tariffs.
D. experiences slow but steady growth.
E. is restricted by foreign trade agreements.

10.3.3. Microsoft loaning money to set up software packaging operations in Ireland would be an example of _____.
A. the International Monetary Fund
B. the World Bank
C. foreign direct investment
D. a multinational corporation relocation program
E. an international development assistance program

10.3.4. Microfinancing is intended:
A. for new corporations moving into developing countries.
B. for women to obtain small loans for cottage industries.
C. for established businesses to secure loans for expansion.
D. to provide substantial loans to multinational corporations to move into less developed countries.
E. to provide loans of less than $100.

KEY ISSUE 4

Why Are Countries Able to Make Progress in Development?

Learning Outcome 10.4.1a: Describe ways in which differences in development have narrowed.
The gap in HDI between more developed countries and developing countries has narrowed since 1980.

Learning Outcome 10.4.1b: Describe ways in which differences in development have increased.
Income inequality among countries, carbon emissions connected to climate change, and threats to biodiversity continue to increase disparity among countries.

Learning Outcome 10.4.2: Explain the principles of fair trade.
Fair trade attempts to protect workers and small businesses in developing countries. Fair trade involves a combination of producer and worker standards.

Fair trade has been proposed as an alternative to the international trade model of development. **Fair trade** means that products are made and traded according to standards that protect workers and small businesses in developing countries. Standards for fair trade are set internationally by the Fairtrade Labelling Organizations International (FLO). Ten Thousand Villages, which specializes in handicrafts, is the largest fair trade organization in North America. Three sets of standards distinguish fair trade; one set applies to workers on farms and in factories, one to producers, and the other to consumers.

To reduce disparity between more developed and developing countries, the United Nations adopted the Sustainable Development Goals, which replaced the Millennium Development Goals. The development goals set targets to reach by 2030. The 17 SDGs can be grouped into four areas: global health (#17), the natural environment (#13, 14, and 15), infrastructures, (#2, 6, 7, 8, 9, 10, 11, and 12), and well-being, (#1, 3, 4, 5, 10, and 16). All 17 of the sustainable development goals are targeted at improving the quality of life, fostering continued development while ensuring resources, and progress for future generations. Current progress in human development has resulted in a narrowing of the gap of the HDI between developed and developing countries. GNI, education, and life expectancy have all increased in both developed and developing countries. More developed countries continue to set new standards for development, creating greater challenges for developing and emerging economic societies.

Key Issues Revisited

10.4. Why Are Countries Able to Make Progress in Development?

- Progress in development indicators has increased in most regions, but gaps between more developed and developing countries still exist.

- Fair trade is an alternative to the international trade model.

Review Questions

10.4.1. Which region has seen the lowest gain in HDI indicators?
A. North America
B. South America
C. Central Asia
D. South Asia
E. Sub-Saharan Africa

10.4.2. What is the main advantage of fair trade?
A. It allows for fair competition between the same producers in a country on the global market.
B. It improves working conditions and global trade opportunities in developing countries.
C. It provides equal trade practices and restrictions among countries.
D. It allows for competition of workers in agricultural industries by controlling wage rates.
E. There is no such thing as fair trade.

Key Terms

Commodity dependence*
Comparative advantage*
Core-periphery model*
Dependency theory*
Developed country
Developing country
Development*
Fair trade*
Foreign direct investment
Gender Empowerment Measure (GEM)*
Gender Inequality Index (GII)*
Gross domestic product (GDP)*
Gross national income (GNI)*
Human Development Index (HDI)*
International Monetary Fund (IMF)
Least cost theory*
Less developed country (LDC)

Literacy rate*
Microloans*
More developed country (MDC)
Periphery*
Primary sector*
Productivity
Purchasing power parity (PPP)
Rostow development model*
Secondary sector*
Semi-periphery*
Sustainable development*
Tertiary sector*
Transnational Corporation*
Value added
Wallerstein's world-systems theory*
World Bank
World Trade Organization (WTO)*

Term is in 2019 College Board Curriculum & Exam Description.

Source: College Board AP Human Geography Course Description, effective Fall 2019

Think Like a Geographer Activities

1. Compare Saudi Arabia's levels of development in terms of gross domestic product, gender inequality, and education. What might account for the discrepancies among these indices?

2. Point–counterpoint: Conduct a class debate on development. Which program works with point–counterpoint positions on self-sufficiency vs. international trade, stimulus vs austerity, and IMF/World Bank loans vs. private sector development. Discuss these options for countries with valuable natural resources and without, countries in strategic locations and those with no locational benefit, and the role of periphery and semi-periphery of a developing country.

3. Investigation: Track all the products purchased in a week and record which are produced as part of fair trade agreements.

Quick Quiz

10.1. Development is:
A. the process that aids people's intellectual ability.
B. the process used to increase a factory's output.
C. the process of improving the material conditions of people through technology and knowledge.
D. the process of manufacturing efficiently.
E. the process of giving children in Africa a free laptop.

10.2. Highly developed countries will have:
A. a shrinking primary sector and emerging quaternary sector.
B. a shrinking secondary sector and established tertiary, quaternary, and quinary sectors.
C. an expanding primary sector.
D. a declining tertiary sector and expanding secondary sector.
E. a GDP dominated by extraction industries.

10.3. Globalization is linked closely with:
A. the self-sufficiency model of development.
B. a low level of HDI and high GII.
C. the Rostow model of international trade.
D. a low GEM and high GII.
E. investment from the IMF and the World Bank.

10.4. Sustainable development seeks to:
A. improve human and environmental conditions today in order to provide for future generations.
B. promote global extraction of resources to fund development in the poorest countries.
C. continue current productions rates with depleting resources.
D. implement controls on birth rates to cause global populations to not exceed 25 billion.
E. prevent a global collapse of the world's leading manufacturing corporations.

10.5. Small loans to individuals in developing countries to promote personal/family development is known as:
A. microfinance.
B. debt-to-development program.
C. sustainable development.
D. individual monetary finance (IMF).
E. microbusiness.

10.6. Which region has the lowest GII numbers?
A. South Asia
B. East Asia
C. South America
D. Western Europe
E. Central Africa

10.7. Which of these U.S. regions continues to experience inequality since 1950?
A. Maritime Northeast
B. Northern Midwest
C. Pacific Northwest
D. Central South
E. Alaska and Hawaii

10.8. Which of the following is on the periphery limiting the locational benefit of development?
A. Thailand
B. South Africa
C. Portugal
D. Iran
E. Indonesia

10.9. The share of the GNI from the primary sector:
A. has decreased in developing countries but remains higher than in developed countries.
B. is increasing for developed countries.
C. has increased for developing countries due to global climate disasters.
D. has become stagnant with no growth into the secondary sector due to lack of foreign investment.
E. has increased because of more women entering the workforce in developing countries.

10.10. Promoting safe and sustainable farming methods and working conditions is part of the business practices associated with _____.
A. microfinancing
B. Human Development Index
C. Sustainable Development Goals
D. fair trade
E. international trade

Free Response

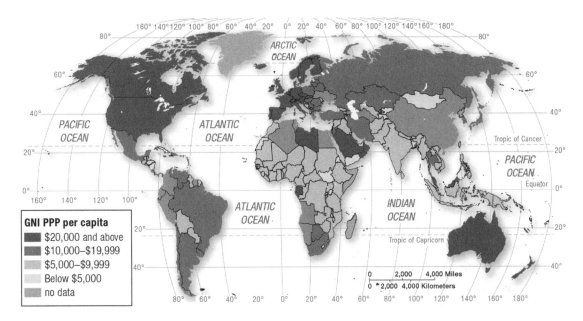

Figure 10-1 GNI per capita PPP, 2017

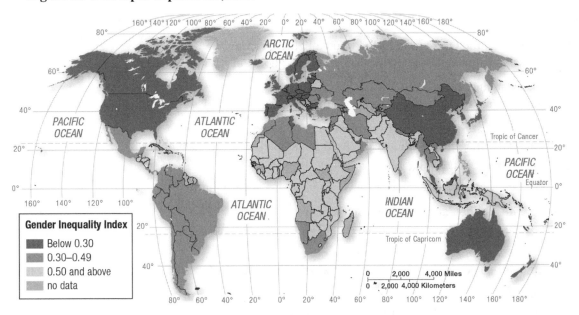

Figure 10-2 Gender Inequality Index,

Using the maps above, answer the following free response question:

1. Identify the regions with the highest income and lowest inequality index.

2. Explain the correlation between income and inequality.

3. Identify one country where this correlation does not hold true.

On the Web

www.masteringgeography.com

www.hdr.undp.org/en/statistics/

www.cgdev.org/section/initiatives/_active/cdi/

www.sustainabledevelopment.un.org/

www.blogs.worldbank.org/opendata/introducing-online-guide-world-development-indicators-new-way-discover-data-development

www.unesco.org/new/en/education/themes/leading-the-international-agenda/efareport/statistics/efa-development-index/

www.hdr.undp.org/en/statistics/gii/

www.countryeconomy.com/hdi

www.as-coa.org/articles/infographic-how-latin-america-ranks-human-development-index

www.globalvolunteers.org/global-role-of-women/

www.unwomen.org/en/digital-library/world-survey-on-the-role-of-women-in-development

www.brookings.edu/topic/global-development/

www.sdg-tracker.org/

www.ourworldindata.org/economic-growth

TED Talks

Steven Johnson, How the Ghost Map Helped End a Killer Disease
www.ted.com/talks/lang/eng/steven_johnson_tours_the_ghost_map.html

Parag Khanna, Mapping the Future of Countries
www.ted.com/talks/parag_khanna_maps_the_future_of_countries.html

Hans Rosling, The Best Stats You've Ever Seen
www.ted.com/talks/hans_rosling_shows_the_best_stats_you_ve_ever_seen.html

Hans Rosling, New Insights on Poverty
www.ted.com/talks/hans_rosling_reveals_new_insights_on_poverty.html

Hans Rosling, Global Population Growth, Box by Box
www.ted.com/talks/hans_rosling_on_global_population_growth.html

Hans Rosling, Asia's Rise—How and When
www.ted.com/talks/hans_rosling_asia_s_rise_how_and_when.html

Ngozi Okonjo-Iweala, Aid versus Trade
www.ted.com/talks/ngozi_okonjo_iweala_on_aid_versus_trade.html

Bono, My Wish: Three Actions for Africa
www.ted.com/talks/bono_s_call_to_action_for_africa.html

Bill Gates, Mosquitos, Malaria and Education
www.ted.com/talks/bill_gates_unplugged.html

Rethinking Poverty theme page: Development, Population, Migration
www.ted.com/themes/rethinking_poverty.html

Key Figures

Figure 10-2 Human Development Index (HDI), 2018
Figure 10-3 Development Regions
Figure 10-4 GNI per Capita PPP, 2017
Figure 10-5 GNI by Region
Figure 10-6 Economic Structure
Figure 10-7 Productivity
Figure 10-8 Mean Years of Schooling, 2018
Figure 10-9 Expected Years of Schooling
Figure 10-11 Literacy Rate, 2016
Figure 10-12 Life Expectancy at Birth, 2018
Figure 10-16 IHDI by Country, 2018
Figure 10-18 Core & Periphery: North-South Divide
Figure 10-19 Core & Periphery: North Polar Projection
Figure 10-25 Inequality within the United States
Figure 10-28 Gender Inequality Index, 2018
Figure 10-30 Gender Development Index, 2018
Figure 10-31 Trend in Gender Inequality
Figure 10-33 Women in the National Legislature
Figure 10-35 Gender Differences in Secondary School
Figure 10-37 Trend in Maternal Mortality Rate, 1990-2015
Figure 10-36 Adolescent Fertility Rate, 2018
Figure 10-43 International Trade as a Percentage of GDP
Figure 10-46 GDP per Capita Change in India
Figure 10-47 Growth in FDI
Figure 10-48 Sources and Destinations of FDI
Figure 10-50 World Bank Loans, 2017
Figure 10-52 Developing Country Debt as a Percentage of GNI
Figure 10-58 HDI Change by Region
Table 10-1 U.N. Sustainable Development Goals

AP® Human Geography

Unit 7: Industrial and Economic Development Patterns & Processes

Topic	APHG Topic No. Title	Suggested Skills	Enduring Understandings	Learning Objective	Big Ideas
10.1.1; 10.1.2	7.3: Measures of Development	3.F: Explain possible limitations of the data provided.	SPS-7: Industrialization, past and present, has facilitated improvements in standards of living, but it has also contributed to geographically uneven development.	SPS-7.C: Describe social and economic measures of development.	BI-3: Spatial Processes and Societal Change
10.1.2	7.6: Trade and the World Economy	5.B: Explain spatial relationships across various geographic scales using geographic concepts, processes, models, or theories.	PSO-7: Economic and social development happen at different times and rates in different places.	PSO-7.A: Explain causes and geographic consequences of recent economic changes, such as the increase in international trade, deindustrialization, and growing interdependence in the world economy.	BI-1: Patterns and Spatial Organization
10.1.3; 10.1.4; 10.2.1	7.3: Measures of Development	3.F: Explain possible limitations of the data provided.	SPS-7: Industrialization, past and present, has facilitated improvements in standards of living, but it has also contributed to geographically uneven development.	SPS-7.C: Describe social and economic measures of development.	BI-3: Spatial Processes and Societal Change
10.2.1; 10.2.2	7.2: Economic Sectors and Patterns	2.B: Explain spatial relationships in a specified context or region of the world, using geographic concepts, processes,	SPS-7: Industrialization, past and present, has facilitated improvements in standards of living, but it has also contributed to geographically uneven development.	SPS-7.B: Explain the spatial patterns of industrial production and development.	BI-3: Spatial Processes and Societal Change

		models, or theories.			
10.2.3; 10.2.4; 10.2.5	7.3: Measures of Development	3.F: Explain possible limitations of the data provided.	SPS-7: Industrialization, past and present, has facilitated improvements in standards of living, but it has also contributed to geographically uneven development.	SPS-7.C: Describe social and economic measures of development.	BI-3: Spatial Processes and Societal Change
10.2.4; 10.2.5	7.4: Women and Economic Development	3.D: Compare patterns and trends in maps and in quantitative and geospatial data to draw conclusions.	SPS-7: Industrialization, past and present, has facilitated improvements in standards of living, but it has also contributed to geographically uneven development.	SPS-7.D: Explain how and to what extent changes in economic development have contributed to gender parity.	BI-3: Spatial Processes and Societal Change
10.3.1; 10.3.2; 10.3.3; 10.3.4	7.5: Theories of Development	1.E: Explain the strengths, weaknesses, and limitations of different geographic models and theories in a specified context.	SPS-7: Industrialization, past and present, has facilitated improvements in standards of living, but it has also contributed to geographically uneven development.	SPS-7.E: Explain different theories of economic and social development.	BI-3: Spatial Processes and Societal Change
10.3.3	7.4: Women and Economic Development	3.D: Compare patterns and trends in maps and in quantitative and geospatial data to draw conclusions.	SPS-7: Industrialization, past and present, has facilitated improvements in standards of living, but it has also contributed to geographically uneven development.	SPS-7.D: Explain how and to what extent changes in economic development have contributed to gender parity.	BI-3: Spatial Processes and Societal Change
10.4.1; 10.4.2	7.6: Trade and the World Economy	5.B: Explain spatial relationships across various geographic scales using	PSO-7: Economic and social development happen at different times and rates in different places.	PSO-7.A: Explain causes and geographic consequences of recent economic changes,	BI-1: Patterns and Spatial Organization

		geographic concepts, processes, models, or theories.		such as the increase in international trade, deindustrialization, and growing interdependence in the world economy.	
10.4.1	7.8: Sustainable Development	5.D: Explain the degree to which a geographic concept, process, model, or theory effectively explains geographic effects and across various geographic scales.	IMP-7: Environmental problems stemming from industrialization may be remedied through sustainable development strategies.	IMP-7.A: Explain how sustainability principles relate to and impact industrialization and spatial development.	BI-2: Impacts and Interactions

Source: College Board AP Human Geography Course Description, effective Fall 2019

FRQ's From College Board

2001 FRQ #1
2004 FRQ #1
2006 FRQ #2
2007 FRQ #3
2008 FRQ #3
2013 FRQ #1
2014 FRQ #1
2016 FRQ #1

Chapter

11 Industry & Energy

Where Is Industry Distributed?

This chapter addresses the distribution of industrial regions and the factors related to the site and situation of manufacturing locations. The locational considerations for industries are based on the location of the consumer market and the accessibility of necessary resources. More recently, industry has diffused from developed countries to developing countries and into nontraditional locations especially through the operation of transnational corporations. Industrial development is challenged with resource availability, distribution, and sustainable usage.

Learning Outcome 11.1.1: Summarize the causes of the Industrial Revolution.
The Industrial Revolution was stimulated by the use of technology to gradually change the way goods were manufactured resulting in the transformation of social, economic, and political innovations.

Learning Outcome 11.1.2: Describe the locations of the three principal industrial regions.
Most of the world's industry is clustered in the three regions of Europe, North America, and East Asia and centered around accessible bulk transportation places, sources of raw materials, or market areas.

Learning Outcome 11.1.3: Analyze the three types of site factors.
The three site factors are land, labor, and capital.

Learning Outcome 11.1.4: Explain why some industries locate near their inputs.
A location near sources of inputs is optimal for bulk-reducing industries. Industries that extract a large amount of minerals tend to be bulk-reducing industries.

Learning Outcome 11.1.5: Explain why some industries locate near markets.
Bulk-gaining industries, single-market manufacturers, motor vehicles, and perishable products companies tend to locate near markets.

Learning Outcome 11.1.6: Explain why industries use different modes of transportation.
Trucks are most often used for short-distance delivery, trains for longer trips within a region, ships for ocean crossings, and planes for very high-value packages. Some firms locate near break-of-bulk points, where goods are transferred between modes of transportation.

The modern Industrial Revolution began in the mid-1700s in northern England and southern Scotland because of the combination of entrepreneurs, capital, raw materials, and available labor. Prior to the Industrial Revolution, small-scale manufacturing was home based and known as the **cottage industry**. The Industrial Revolution resulted in major changes for the iron and steel industry, coal mining, transportation, textiles, chemicals, and food processing. The Industrial Revolution has changed social, political, and economic systems, diffusing ideas and processes across the globe for more than 200 years.

The use of iron to make tools was transformed with the extraction of coal and the development of canals and railroads to move coal and iron ore to manufacturing areas and finished goods to consumer markets. Access to flowing water and the development chemicals to dye cotton transformed the textile industry with the use of laborsaving machines. More labor became available from the early 1800s when fewer people were needed to produce raw food materials and to develop sterilized canned food to feed factory workers. Coal, petroleum, and natural gas provided the energy to develop more efficient manufacturing processes at higher temperatures. These fossil fuels for industrial development have led to current efforts to create more sustainable development and a reduction in the use of nonrenewable energy sources in exchange for renewable energy sources.

Europe, North America, and East Asia are the three principal industrial regions. China, Germany, Japan, and the United States account for almost one-half of the world's industrial output. The other leading industrial producers are Brazil, Russia, and India. Today, Brazil, Russia, India, and China are known as the **BRIC** countries and account for more than 25 percent of global GDP, (globalsherpa.org/bric-countries-brics/).

Western Europe has major industrialization regions in Britain, the Rhine-Ruhr Valley, the mid-Rhine, and northern Italy. The United Kingdom is the oldest of these industrial regions, and with the decline of traditional industry, it was able to attract high-tech industries in the late twentieth century. The Rhine-Ruhr is an important source of coal and iron deposits predominately for steel making. The mid-Rhine region includes parts of Germany and France. It is an important region for diversified industries because of its proximity to large consumer markets and available skilled labor. The Po valley of northern Italy began with **textile** manufacturing developed from the available water supply and low labor costs. Northeastern Spain was Western Europe's fastest growing industrial area in the late-twentieth century, especially in the motor-vehicle industry.

The oldest industrial areas in Eastern Europe are in the central industrial district, which is centered on Moscow, and the St. Petersburg industrial district, which was one of Russia's early nodes of industrial development. Other industrial areas in Eastern Europe include the Volga industrial district, particularly important for petroleum and natural gas, and the Ural industrial district, which has become a main source of raw materials but lacks energy sources. The Kuznetsk is Russia's most important industrial region east of the Ural Mountains. Outside of Russia, there are important industrial regions in the Donetsk Basin, Eastern Ukraine, and Silesia region of Poland and Czechia (formerly known as the Czech Republic).

North America became a major industrial region later than Europe. Textiles were important in the United States by 1860. Access to inland waters was important for moving raw materials but also for harnessing power sources in the Eastern United States, an area which became an excellent location for the manufacture of textiles and food processing. These areas included New England, the Middle Atlantic, the Mohawk Valley, and the Pittsburgh-Lake Erie region. The development of settlements inland from the coast running from Georgia to Boston, along the fall line, illustrates the importance of the integration of the physical environment in the beginning of modern industrialization. The Western Great Lakes have also become important, especially because of the dominance of Chicago as a market center. Southern California is the leading U.S. industrial area outside of the Northeast. Canada's most important industrial area is in southeastern Ontario, benefiting from its location on the St. Lawrence Seaway and the availability of cheap hydroelectric power.

East Asia has become a major industrial region since the end of World War II and the 1950s. Japan rapidly industrialized by providing consumer goods for the global market, especially high-quality electronic products. South Korea, Taiwan, and China industrialized and entered the global market by mass-producing goods at a low cost as a result of lower labor costs. China is the world's largest manufacturer of textiles and apparel, steel, and many household products. It also has the world's largest supply of low-cost labor and the world's largest market for many consumer products.

Site factors include labor, land, and capital. **Labor-intensive industries** are those where the highest percentage of expenses is the cost of employees, such as in textile and apparel production. Land, which includes natural resources, is a major site factor. City sites offer proximity to a large supply of labor, as well as to sources of capital. More recently, factories are locating in suburban and rural locations because land is less expensive and proximity to highways is more important now. There are also important environmental factors. For example, aluminum producers locate near dams to take advantage of hydroelectric power. The availability of capital is critical to the location of high-tech industries such as those in California's Silicon Valley. The distribution of industries in developing countries is largely dependent on the ability to borrow money. The emerging industrial leaders are the BRIC countries. Brazil, Russia, India, and China are expected to be the leading industrial bloc in the twenty-first century as a result of their large labor force and abundant natural resources needed for industrial manufacturing facilitated by a global trade network.

In some developed countries, industry remains in traditional regions because of skilled labor and rapid delivery to market for just-in-time delivery. The **Fordist** approach, named for Henry Ford, traditionally assigned each worker a specific task in mass production industry. **Post-Fordist production** has recently become the norm in developed countries. It is flexible production with skilled workers characterized by teams working together, problem solving through consensus, and factory workers being treated alike regardless of their level.

Situation factors involve decisions about industrial location that attempt to minimize transportation costs by considering the location of the source of raw materials and the distance to the market(s). If the cost of transporting the inputs is greater than the cost of transporting the finished product, the best plant location is nearer to the inputs. Otherwise, the best location for the factory will be closer to the consumers.

The North American copper industry is a good example of locating near the source of the raw material. Copper concentration is a **bulk-reducing industry**; the final product weighs less than the inputs as the ore is extracted from waste rock known as gangue. Two-thirds of U.S. copper is mined in Arizona, so most of the concentration mills and smelters are also in Arizona. The manufacturing of products using copper is a bulk-gaining industry and the foundries are located near large market areas. To review, bulk-reducing industries occur near the source of the ore. Once the mineral is extracted, it is then shipped to the manufacturing location and combined with other products. Thus, the bulk-gaining of the final product occurs at the market location.

The location of **bulk-gaining industries** is determined largely by the market because they gain volume or weight during production. Most drink-bottling industries are examples of bulk-gaining industries; empty cans or bottles are brought to the bottler, filled, gaining weight, and shipped to consumers.

Single-market manufacturers are specialized, with only one or two customers, such as manufacturers of motor vehicle parts. These manufacturers tend to cluster around their customers—the carmaker's assembly plant. Today, many of the vehicle parts for Toyota and Ford are manufactured in maquiladoras in Mexico under the North American Free Trade Agreement (NAFTA) and transported by truck to San Antonio or Dallas for assembly into new cars. This expands the spatial distribution between the manufacturing location and the assembly plants. Perishable-product industries such as fresh food and newspapers will usually locate near their markets.

Transportation costs will decline with distance because loading and unloading costs are the greatest. The major modes of transportation are ship, rail, truck, and air. A **break-of-bulk point** is a place where goods are transferred from one mode of transportation to another for distribution elsewhere. Distance that goods are transported factors into the price that consumers must pay. Goods shipped by airplanes have the highest transportation cost, are typically more expensive, and have the highest urgency for delivery. Trains transport large amounts of heavy bulk goods that do not have an urgency for delivery. Trucks are for short-haul delivery at the lowest cost. Ships are attractive for transportation across oceans. With the development of product distribution centers near major markets, trucks are the main transportation source for **just-in-time delivery** of inputs to manufactures for production. The cost savings occur with the reduction of bulk storage of inventory.

Key Issues Revisited

11.1. Where Is Industry Distributed?

- The three principal industrial regions are Europe, North America, and East Asia.

- Factories try to identify a location where location costs are minimized.

- Situation factors involve the cost of transporting both inputs into the factory and products from the factory to the consumer.

- Three site factors—land, labor, and capital—control the cost of doing business at a location.

Review Questions

11.1.1. One of the major catalysts for the Industrial Revolution in England was:
A. Adam Smith's *Wealth of a Nation.*
B. James Watt's steam engine.
C. Henry Ford's assembly line.
D. Horace Greeley's "manifest destiny."
E. Steve Job's microprocessor.

11.1.2. Canada's most important industrial area is:
A. Southeastern Ontario.
B. The Mohawk Valley.
C. Lake Michigan.
D. The Western Great Lakes.
E. The Prairie Provinces.

11.1.3. Which are site factors related to the cost of production?
A. Site and situation
B. Land, labor, and capital
C. Transportation and production
D. Distribution, production, and labor
E. Market, resources, and mechanization

11.1.4. Situational factors related to the location of a factory are based on:
A. cost of transporting either the raw material or the finished product.
B. the environmental impact of production.
C. available source of labor.
D. just-in-time access to markets.
E. access to raw materials.

11.1.5 Which of the following is a bulk-gaining industry located near the market?
A. Cheese
B. Beverage bottling
C. Copper ore
D. Uranium
E. Pet food manufacturer

11.1.6. Which method will be most expensive for a cross-continental U.S. delivery?
A. Direct rail from Salt Lake City, Utah, to Pittsburgh, Pennsylvania
B. Truck to airport in Los Angeles, flight to Boston, truck to manufacturer
C. Ship from New York port to New Orleans port
D. Truck from Denver to New York
E. Just-in-time delivery by air and truck

KEY ISSUE 2

Why Do Industries Face Energy Challenges?

Learning Outcome 11.2.1: Identify the principal sources of energy supply and demand.

Fossil fuels are the predominate source of energy. Demand for energy comes from industries, transportation, homes, and commercial businesses.

Learning Outcome 11.2.2: Describe the distribution of fossil fuel production and reserves.

Fossil fuel formation and distribution is the result of the geologic history and condition of the planet 350–365 million years ago.

Learning Outcome 11.2.3: Analyze changing patterns of oil trade and demand.

The developed countries are the largest supplier of fossil fuels but also demand more energy than they produce.

Learning Outcome 11.2.4: Evaluate possible future options for fossil fuels.
Reserves of fossil fuels are dependent on geologic history and the climatic conditions at that time. Reserves are classified as proven, potential, and unconventional.

Learning Outcome 11.2.5: Describe the distribution of nuclear energy and challenges in using it.
One kilogram of enriched uranium can be used to generate nuclear energy and produce more than 2 million times the energy of 1 kilogram of coal. Forty percent of electricity in many European countries is generated from nuclear power.

Learning Outcome 11.2.6: Identify alternative sources of energy and challenges to using them.
Renewable energy sources are dependent on the environmental and geologic conditions of a place to harness them as a dependable resource replacement.

Learning Outcome 11.2.7: Compare passive and active solar energy.
Passive solar energy uses building construction design to capture energy without storing or converting the energy. Active solar energy collects and converts solar energy with photovoltaic cells.

Demand for energy today differs between developed and developing countries. Since 2006, the developing countries have been the largest consumers of energy used for industry and domestic consumption. However, these statistics include China, South Korea, Russia, and Japan, which are also home to some of the most developed cities and leaders in the global market for manufacturing. China is now the single largest consumer of energy used to fuel the country's vast manufacturing complex. Industries use petroleum and natural gas for energy and use coal for generating electricity. Transportation uses petroleum and, in some cases, electricity to operate older public transportation systems. The demand for energy for commercial and home consumption use fossil fuels, either as electricity generated from coal and oil or as natural gas for heating and cooling systems. The challenge today comes from the control and price setting of many known reserves by OPEC limiting the accessibility of some developing countries to purchase sufficient amounts of fuel.

According to the U.S. Energy Information Administration, the United States generated about 4.18 trillion kilowatt hours of electricity in 2018. About 63 percent of the electricity generated was from fossil fuels (coal, natural gas, and petroleum). The U.S. EIA lists the major energy sources and the percentage of total U.S. electricity generation in 2018:

Coal = 27%

Natural gas = 35%

Nuclear = 19%

Hydropower = 7%

Other renewables = 17%

     Biomass = 1.5%

     Geothermal = 0.4%

     Solar = 1.6%

     Wind = 6.6%

Petroleum = 1%

Other gases = <1%

Source: www.eia.gov/tools/faqs/faq.cfm?id=427&t=3

Coal, natural gas, and petroleum are the fossil fuels that run industries, provide electricity for homes and businesses, and allow for access to the globalized world. China, the United States, Russia, Germany, Poland, Venezuela, South Africa, India, and Australia have the main reserves of coal. The availability of coal, like all fossil fuels, is a factor in the geologic history of the land. Places with coal deposits were shallow swamp or marsh areas when the planet had a tropical hot climate with high sea levels between 300 and 365 million years ago during the Paleozoic and Mesozoic eras. Petroleum and natural gas sources date back as early as 600 million years ago. Land areas that are sources of gas and oil were at one time under water in shallow seas at various times over the past millenniums. Russia and the United States are the leading countries for both natural gas and oil and Saudi Arabia for oil. Much of these resources are the result of the Interior Seaway (Figure 11-1 (below)) that extended from the Arctic deep into the landmasses for almost 150 million years, and at its height during the Cretaceous period contained abundant sea and land plants and animals. Over time, the decaying plants and animals were buried, and through continued heat, pressure, and time, oil and gas were formed, trapped in the layers of sedimentary bedrock.

In North America, the Interior Seaway extended to the Gulf of Mexico through the high plains and Great Plains of the United States, the prairie provinces of Canada, and along the entire Rocky Mountain range, which had not formed at this time. Referring to Figure 11-44 in the textbook, note that natural gas fields in the United States correspond to the Interior Seaway and higher sea levels that existed prior to the beginning of the Ice Age and demise of the dinosaurs 65 million years ago. Evidence of the origin of the relationship between fossil fuel deposits and ancient plant and animal deposits is most readily observed from the fossilized remains of primordial species in areas of known deposits. These fossilized remains have even been found in Antarctica, which at this time was not located in the polar location that it is today.

Ultimately, the wealth in fossil fuel resources that divide countries between the "haves and have-nots" was determined when the earliest dinosaurs roamed the planet, well before humans inhabited the planet. The countries that have fossil fuels experienced significant areas of life, both marine and terrestrial, at a time when the planet was warm and wet. Countries and areas without these resources were areas that did not exist at the time or were not areas with significant amounts of plant and animal life.

Figure 11-1 Extent of the Interior Seaway in North America

Source: United States Geologic Survey

Access to future sources of fossil fuels is dependent on technology to know where it is located and to reach the resources. Thus, the continued use of fossil fuels is dependent on financial resources to conduct research and development to access the potential reserves. A **proven reserve** is a field that is known. At current rates of consumption, the proven reserves of coal will last 130 years, and one-fourth of those reserves are in the United States with the remaining amounts in Russia and China. At current rates of consumption, proven reserves of natural gas are expected to last 56 years and petroleum proven reserves would last 55 years.

Potential reserves are reserves that probably exist in an area but are not currently extracted due to demand, cost of extraction, or current market value. Until it is drilled and used, it remains a potential reserve. Potential reserves also include smaller reserves and remote locations where extraction is costly, such as in areas offshore of northern Alaska or the deep-sea bed.

Access to potential and proven reserves is dependent on demand and economic costs. Extracting oil from the tar sands in the Athabasca region of Alberta, Canada, Russia, and Venezuela is an expensive process of heating sandy soils to extract the tar known as bitumen and processing this into a usable fuel source. The bitumen extracted in Alberta is shipped by pipeline to refineries in, for example, Port Arthur, Texas; Romeoville, Illinois; Toledo, Ohio; and Salt Lake City, Utah among other places. Some of the bitumen is sent to tank farms where the bitumen is blended with lighter crude oil and shipped out to other refineries around the United States.

Hydraulic fracturing is another means of extracting natural gas trapped in rock layers. Drilling mud and water is forced into the rock layers under intense pressure to break and release the gas that is then captured and shipped to processing facilities. Fracking, as it is known, is used in proven areas of Texas, Oklahoma, and West Virginia; however, this process is also dependent on the cost of extraction and the profitability of the gas.

Europe and the United States import more than half of their petroleum needs, while Japan imports more than 90 percent. Of the U.S. petroleum imported, 70–80 percent is crude oil, with 40 percent coming from Canada and 10 percent from Saudi Arabia in 2018. It is less expensive for the United States to import petroleum through trade arrangements than to drill in proven reserves. Improvements in energy usage, alternative energy sources, and a shift in the global manufacturing market have led to a decline in the demand of petroleum resources. An increasing demand for petroleum products is occurring in developing countries, particularly China and India, as they experience even more growth in the global manufacturing market.

Nuclear power is an alternative energy source that can produce more than 2 million times the amount of energy as the same amount of coal. From another perspective, the fission of about 1 pound of uranium fuel releases the same amount of energy as burning 50 tons of coal. Additionally, coal plants emit more than 7 million tons of carbon dioxide into the atmosphere, contributing to global climate change and the greenhouse effect.

Comparison: for 1 year	**Nuclear power:** *producing 1,000 megawatts of energy*	**Coal-fired power:** *producing 1,000 megawatts of energy*
Fuel requirement	30 tons enriched uranium from 75,000 tons of ore produces 60 tons of uranium, which runs a nuclear power plant for 2 years	2–3 million tons of coal is required for 1 year
Carbon dioxide emissions	No CO_2 in production; production of CO_2 in mining and transportation	Emits more than 7 million tons of CO_2 into the atmosphere contributing to global climate change and the greenhouse effect.
Sulfur dioxide and other emissions	Produces no acid-forming pollutants or particulates	Emits more than 300,000 tons of sulfur dioxide, particulates, causing acid rain and air pollution
Radioactivity	Releases low levels of radioactive waste gas	Radioactive compounds in coal releases 100 times more radioactive particles
Solid waste	Produces 250 tons of radioactive wastes requiring safe storage and disposal	Produces about 600,000 tons of ash for disposal
Accidents	Minor emissions of radioactivity; catastrophic releases lead to radiation sickness, deaths, cancers, and long-lasting environmental contamination	Potential coal mining accidents, fatalities, and fire

Figure 11-2

Source: Richard T. Wright, *Environmental Science, 10th ed.* (Upper Saddle River, NJ: Pearson, 2008).

Globally, there are 440 operating nuclear plants and another 28 under construction. Nuclear power is responsible for 79 percent of all electricity in France and 50 percent in Belgium, Sweden, and Ukraine. There are 60 commercially operating nuclear power plants with 98 nuclear reactors in 30 U.S. states (www.eia.gov). There are 103 nuclear power plants operating in the United States, predominately in the eastern states, generating 20 percent of the U.S. electrical power.

Of the developed nations, only France and Japan are fully committed to nuclear programs. The challenge to using nuclear power as an alternative energy source is safe disposal of spent fuel rods and the high cost of power plant construction. Due to the cost of construction, extraction, and movement of uranium, safety procedures, highly skilled training, and waste disposal, nuclear power is more expensive to generate electricity than coal-burning plants. Waste disposal presents a challenge because there is not an adequate and safe permanent waste storage acceptable to the local population or regulatory agencies.

Fossil fuels are nonrenewable energy sources. Nuclear power is also considered nonrenewable because of the use of uranium-235, which is a rare mineral and the energy is not readily replenished. Renewable energy resources cannot be depleted through consumption.

In the eighteenth century, falling water moved paddle wheels that drove machinery to grind grains, process lumber, and create more energy; it also helped introduce the Industrial Revolution in areas where water fell from natural elevations. Today, energy from hydroelectric power is proportionate to the height of the water behind the dam creating pressure and the volume of water flowing through channels. The flowing water turns the turbines conducting electricity in the generator, which is a coil of wire that rotates in a magnetic field as it is rotated. In the United States, 6.7 percent of electrical power is generated from hydroelectric dams. Globally, hydroelectric power provides 17 percent of the electrical power and is the most common form of renewable energy.

The benefits of hydroelectric dams include flood control, source for irrigation, and recreational and tourist opportunities. However, the trade-offs have to be considered, too. The flooding of farmland, physical features, or ancient towns as with the Three Gorges Dam (2006), in China's Yangtze River, displaced population (40–80 million in the last 50 years), restricted animal and fish migrations, and changed the sediment and nutrient supplies downstream. At times, dams can cause drought and water restrictions downstream as a way to maintain reservoir levels to create electricity.

Wind energy is another renewable and sustainable energy source. The United States ranks third in production of energy from wind power behind Germany and Spain. Wind-generated power is second to solar-produced power due to subsidies and targets for the reduction in the use of fossil fuels. Wind produces 1.3 percent of the global electricity demand and in Denmark supplies more than 20 percent of the electricity demands. The American Wind Energy Association estimates that wind power has the potential to meet the demands of the entire United States. However, there are some concerns. Wind power is dependent on blowing wind; therefore, it is necessary to store the energy generated for periods with no wind. Additionally, windmills can be a visual nuisance to a landscape for some, and lastly, windmills are hazardous to birds along migratory routes.

Renewable energy sources obtained from biomass, hydrogen fuels, geothermal, tidal, and ocean thermal energy conversion are other sources of alternative energy. Of these, geothermal energy contributes the largest share of energy production on a global scale. In 2013, the U.S. Energy Information Administration reported that 20 countries, including the United States, generated a total of about seventy billion kWh of electricity from geothermal energy.

Philippines is the second-largest geothermal power producer after the United States, at about 11 billion kWh of electricity, which equaled approximately 27 percent of Philippine's total power generation. Iceland was the seventh-largest producer at about 5 billion kWh of electricity and has the second-largest share of its total electricity generation from geothermal energy at 30 percent. Kenya produces 51 percent of its energy from geothermal sources. The largest facility in the United States is outside of San Francisco and produces 74 percent of the electricity of California.

Currently, the carbon footprint remains from the construction costs of materials, transportation, and continued dependence on conventional fossil fuel energy production in times when alternative resources are not an option for electricity production.

About half of the sun's energy reaches the Earth's surface with 30 percent reflected and 20 percent absorbed by the atmosphere. Solar energy is a renewable and sustainable source of energy. The sun can generate 700 megawatts of power to an area of 390 square miles. Another way to understand this is that about 40 minutes of sunlight is equal to a year's usage of fossil fuels. Passive solar energy uses south-facing windows and dark surfaces to capture heat and light. Active solar energy captures the light energy in photovoltaic cells, which converts the light energy into electrical energy, or indirectly converts light to heat energy and then to electricity. The main problem for active solar use is the inconsistency from seasonal changes, latitude, and atmospheric conditions without storage. The obstacle to widespread usage is because of the inconsistency of availability, the cost of installation, storage, and the inverter, which changes the direct current from the photovoltaic cell to the alternate electricity current compatible with the appliances operated in households. However, the costs factors are decreasing.

Key Issues Revisited

11.2. Why Do Industries Face Resource Challenges?

- Supplies of coal, natural gas, and petroleum are not uniformly distributed.
- Industries, transportation, residential, and commercial activities are the four major consumers of energy.
- Hydroelectricity, wind, nuclear, solar, and geothermal are alternative energy sources.

Review Questions

11.2.1. Which region of the world has the highest per capita energy consumption?
A. Vietnam
B. India
C. Germany
D. Brazil
E. China

11.2.2. Which countries are the major producers of petroleum and natural gas?
A. Russia and the United States
B. China and the United States
C. Saudi Arabia and Brazil
D. Canada and Norway
E. Iran and Saudi Arabia

11.2.3. Which country is the only one with proven reserves in coal, natural gas, and petroleum?
A. Canada
B. Russia
C. India
D. Qatar
E. Venezuela

11.2.4. Mining Canada's oil sands and hydraulic fracturing have:
A. increased the proven reserves.
B. increased potential reserves.
C. increased natural gas dependency on Venezuela.
D. decreased proven reserves.
E. decreased potential reserves.

11.2.5. Which region of the United States generates more than 20 percent of its power from nuclear energy?
A. Gulf Coast
B. Great Plains
C. Northeast
D. Interior west
E. Pacific West Coast

11.2.6. Which country is the largest producer of geothermal energy?
A. United States
B. Indonesia
C. Iceland
D. Italy
E. New Zealand

11.2.7. What is used to bring electricity to remote areas in developing countries?
A. Hydroelectric dams
B. Nuclear power
C. Coal and charcoal
D. Photovoltaic cells
E. Wind turbines

KEY ISSUE 3

Why Do Industries Face Pollution Challenges?

Learning Outcome 11.3.1: Describe causes and effects of air pollution at local, regional, and global scales.
Air pollution is caused from factories, power plants, combustion engines, and motor vehicles.

Learning Outcome 11.3.2: Compare and contrast point sources and nonpoint sources of water pollution.
Point-source pollution originates from a specific place, such as a pipe, generated principally by factories and sewage disposal. Nonpoint sources are generated primarily by agricultural runoff.

Learning Outcome 11.3.3: Describe principal strategies for reducing solid waste pollution.
Strategies to reduce solid waste include reduce, reuse, and recycle materials.

Learning Outcome 11.3.4a: Explain the concept of recycling.
Recycling and remanufacturing are ways to ensure a more sustainable environment.

Learning Outcome 11.3.4b: Explain the concepts of remanufacturing.
Recycling and remanufacturing are ways to ensure a more sustainable environment.

Air, water, and land remove and disperse waste, but **pollution** will occur when more waste is added than a resource can accommodate. **Air pollution** is a concentration of trace substances at a greater level than occurring in average air. The burning of fossil fuels generates most air pollution. Air pollution may contribute to global warming because of the **greenhouse effect**, which is when carbon dioxide traps some of the radiation emitted by Earth's surface. The **ozone** layer of Earth's atmosphere absorbs dangerous ultraviolet (UV) rays from the sun but is threatened by pollutants called **chlorofluorocarbons (CFCs)**.

Pollution in the form of tiny droplets of sulfuric acid and nitric acid, formed as a result of the emission of burning fossil fuels, returns to Earth's surface as **acid deposition**. When dissolved in water, the acids may fall as **acid precipitation**, which damages lakes and agricultural land in regions of heavy industrial development. In the United States, the area that experiences the greatest impact of acid deposition runs from the Southern Great Lakes across the Ohio valley to upstate New York. Urban areas are also centers of concentrated pollution from industrial emissions and the high density of vehicles.

Urban air pollution consists of carbon monoxide, hydrocarbons, and particulates. In the presence of sunlight, this forms **photochemical smog**, which contributes to unhealthy living conditions. According to the World Health Organization and reported in the World Economic Forum, air pollution has risen 8 percent globally in the last five years, causing 3 million premature deaths and making it one of the greatest environmental risks to human health. Additionally, the latest urban air quality data reveals that 98 percent of cities with over 100,000 inhabitants in low- and middle-income countries do not meet WHO air quality guidelines. Among megacities (urban areas with over 10 million inhabitants), Delhi and Cairo had the highest levels of urban air pollution.

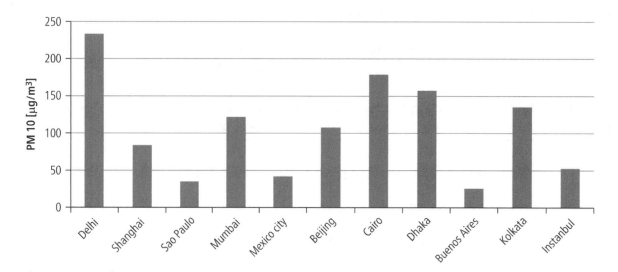

Figure 11-3 Air Pollution levels

Source: World Health Organization

Most water pollution is generated by water-using industries, municipal sewage, and agriculture. Polluted water can harm aquatic plants and animals. It also causes waterborne diseases such as cholera, typhoid, and dysentery, especially in developing countries that suffer from poor sanitation and untreated water. Dead zones or hypoxic areas in lakes, ponds, bays, and open waters have developed with the increase of nitrogen and phosphorus nutrients from agricultural runoff and waste treatment plants. The wastewater decomposition depletes the oxygen in the water, causing fish kills. The increase in nutrients causes algal blooms, also depleting oxygen levels in the water essential for aquatic life in a process known as eutrophication. Water pollution is classified by its origin. If the source is a specific location, then it is a **point-source pollution**, and if it is from a large area, it is considered **nonpoint-source pollution**. Treated wastewater from a municipal sewage processing plant is point-source pollution.

Paper products constitute the largest percentage, 35 percent, of municipal solid waste in the United States. Figure 11-4 (below) illustrates the composition of U.S. municipal solid-waste composition.

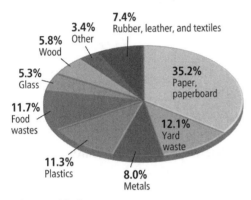

Figure 11-4

Source: Richard T. Wright, *Environmental Science, 10th ed.* (Upper Saddle River, NJ: Pearson, 2008), p. 466.

Most of this waste is disposed of in **sanitary landfills**. The number of landfills in the United States has declined by three-fourths since 1990; there are now a smaller number of larger regional landfills. Incineration reduces the bulk of trash by about three-fourths, but burning releases toxins into the air. Landfills can cause environmental problems with groundwater contamination from leachate, methane production, incomplete decomposition, and settling. As a result of these environmental hazards, the Environmental Protection Agency enacted the Resource Conservation and Recovery Act (RCRA) in 1976 to establish regulatory measures to manage solid-waste disposal. As a result of RCRA, landfills must be managed to prevent contamination of groundwater, capture and monitor methane production, and maintain the structural integrity of the land. The disposal of hazardous waste is also guided by federal mandates. Hazardous waste is buried deep in the ground through deep-well injection into salt domes, contained in excavated surface depressions where the wastes are drained and held, or maintained in contained hazardous waste landfills.

Several practices and programs have been established to reduce solid waste pollution. The program of "reduce, reuse, and recycle" is targeted toward domestic waste. To reduce the amount of solid waste, industry is redesigning, manufacturing, or using other materials to reduce the amount of trash generated by consumers. Recycling plastics, paper, rubber, metals, and glass creates less waste in the landfill and reuses the components by recycling the original product. Ultimately, the goal is a system of integrated waste management for recycling, source reduction, and landfill performance.

Key Issues Revisited

11.3. Why Do Industries Face Pollution Challenges?

- Air pollution can occur at global, regional, and local scales.

- Water pollution is classified as point-source and nonpoint-source based on its source.

- The agricultural industry has the heaviest demand for water.

- Solid waste is either transported to landfills or incinerated.

- Recycling and remanufacturing are industrial sustainable methods.

Review Questions

11.3.1. Which country has a higher concentration of particulate matter?
A. Canada
B. Australia
C. Brazil
D. France
E. China

11.3.2. What accounts for the shrinking of the Aral Sea?
A. A sinkhole causing the water to drain through the sea floor
B. Increased evaporation due to climate change
C. Implementation of a hydroelectric dam using the water for electricity generation
D. Diversion of the sources of water for irrigation of cotton crops
E. Extended decades of drought

11.3.3. Solid waste in the United States is:
A. burned in open pits outside of town.
B. burned in massive furnaces where the heat is used to generate electricity.
C. dumped off of barges into the depths of the oceans.
D. collected by trucks and disposed in sanitary landfills.
E. recycled and repurposed for less developed countries.

11.3.4. What practices are used in industry to promote sustainable industrial processes?
A. Using only repurposed machinery
B. Recycling and remanufacturing of new parts
C. Restrictive production and processing
D. Reducing fossil fuels in energy production
E. Global manufacturing

KEY ISSUE 4

Why Are Industries Changing Locations?

Learning Outcome 11.4.1: Explain reasons for the emergence of new concentrations of industries.
Some jobs have been transferred to low-wage countries as part of the new international division of labor. The BRIC countries (Brazil, Russia, India, and China) are expected to be the top industrial powers by the middle of the twenty-first century.

Learning Outcome 11.4.2: Explain the distribution of clothing production.
The clothing industry is a labor-intensive industry. Three steps in production are spinning, weaving, and sewing. Most spinning and weaving occur in low-wage countries, but some sewing occurs in developed countries near consumers.

Learning Outcome 11.4.3: Summarize changes in the distribution of steel production.
Steel production has traditionally been located near the sources of the key inputs: coal and iron ore. Some steel production, especially mini mills, is now located near the markets since the primary input is scrap metal. Industries that extract a large amount of minerals tend to be bulk-reducing industries.

Learning Outcome 11.4.4: Explain industrial location changes within developed regions.
Industry is moving from the North to the South within the United States. Europe is experiencing a similar north-to-south and eastern labor shift into convergence regions. Lower labor costs and absence of unions are major factors in the migration.

The growth of new industrial regions in the world is based on labor costs and access to emerging markets. The historic industrial regions of Western Europe and the Northeast United States now make up less than 45 percent of the global manufacturing market. As industry has declined in developed countries, it has increased in developing countries. In 1980, 80 percent of the world's steel was produced in developed countries. According to Deloitte's Global Manufacturing Competitiveness Index, Asia, and in particular China, India, Korea, and Japan, is the most competitive location for manufacturing and is expected to hold this title for at least the next five years. The United States is among the most competitive countries but is expected to lose some of its importance in the long term. The cost of labor is changing the spatial organization of industry around the world. This is particularly true of the textile and apparel industry. In the twentieth century, production in the United States moved from the Northeast to the Southeast to take advantage of cheaper wages. More recently, the apparel industry has located in Latin America, China, and other Asian countries. Now, the United States imports more than 75 percent of its clothing needs. This is one part of the **new international division of labor**. Industrial jobs are transferring to developing countries largely as a result of transnational corporations' search for low-cost labor. **Transnational corporations** are **outsourcing**, turning over much of the responsibility for production to independent suppliers. Outsourcing to save labor and manufacturing costs is in contrast to the traditional business practice of **vertical integration**, where all aspects of production are controlled by one company.

China is the leading new industrial center in the world because of its low labor costs and vast consumer market. Mexico and Brazil are the leading industrial centers in Latin America, with manufacturing clustered near large cities such as Mexico City and Sao Paulo. Since the 1980s, manufacturing in Mexico has moved north to take advantage of the U.S. market, and **maquiladora** plants have been established close to the U.S. border. Maquiladoras, which assemble U.S. parts and ship the finished product back to the United States, have benefited from the **North American Free Trade Agreement (NAFTA)**. NAFTA has eliminated restrictions on the flow of materials and products between the United States and Mexico. Mexican labor wages are higher than China's, but the lower shipping costs make Mexico the third largest trading partner for the United States in 2016 according to the U.S. Department of Commerce. Canada is the largest trading partner with the United States, accounting for 15.3 percent of total trade, while China is second with 14.8 percent.

Textile manufacturing is a bulk-gaining industry dependent on low-skill and low-cost labor. The spinning, weaving, and assembly of material a make textile products are typically completed in developing countries because of lower labor costs.

Today, the U.S. steel industry is located near major markets in mini mills. It has become a **foot-loose industry**, which can locate virtually anywhere because the main input is scrap metal and is available almost everywhere. Currently, the U.S. steel industry takes advantage of **agglomeration economies**, or sharing of services with other companies that are available at major markets. The agglomeration of companies can lead to the development of **ancillary activities** that surround and support large-scale industry. This will result in continued growth, which is called **cumulative causation**. **Deglomeration** occurs when a firm leaves an agglomerated region to start in a distant, new place. However, according to Alfred **Weber's theory of industrial location** or **least-cost theory**, firms will locate where they can minimize transportation and labor costs as well as take advantage of agglomeration economies.

Within regions in developed countries, industry has relocated to urban peripheries and rural areas from central city locations. At the interregional level, manufacturing has moved toward the South and West in the United States. Historically, industrial growth has been encouraged in the South by government policies to reduce regional disparities. Southern states have enacted **right-to-work laws** that require factories to maintain an "open shop" and prohibit a "closed shop." In a closed shop, everyone who works in the factory has to join the union. Thus, southern right-to-work laws have made it much more difficult for unions to organize, collect dues, and bargain. States that have passed these laws are called **right-to-work states**.

In Western Europe, government policies and those of the European Union have also encouraged industry to move from traditional industrial centers in northwestern Europe toward Southern and Eastern Europe. For example, Spain's textile and motor-vehicle manufacturing industries have grown substantially since its admission to the European Union in 1986. The European Union provides financial incentives to move industrial operations into lower-income areas of Eastern and Southern Europe, in particular Poland, Czechia, Hungary, and Slovakia. These central European countries provide a skilled workforce, lower labor costs, and close proximity to Western European markets.

Key Issues Revisited

11.4. Why Are Industries Changing Locations?

- New industrial regions are able to attract some industries, especially because of low wage rates.

- Traditional industrial regions have been able to offer manufacturers skilled workers and proximity to customers demanding just-in-time delivery.

Review Questions

11.4.1. The transfer of jobs in industrial manufacturing to developing regions is known as:
A. outsourcing.
B. vertical integration.
C. new international division of labor.
D. maquiladoras.
E. right to work.

11.4.2. Some industries expand their production to developing countries to :
A. be closer to the market for their goods.
B. be able to use less-skilled low-cost labor.
C. reduce transportation costs after manufacturing.
D. take advantage of free trade relationships.
E. focus on development strategies in developing economies.

11.4.3. What has caused the shift in the location of steel producers?
A. It is important to be closer to the market in China.
B. There is a lack of resources in historical production areas.
C. Focus in construction materials in markets has shifted to sustainable practices.
D. Labor and shipping costs of iron ore and coal have decreased.
E. Tariff restrictions on imported steel have increased.

11.4.4. What is one of the main reasons that industry in the United States has shifted production?
A. To move to states with closed shops
B. To move closer to low-skilled labor
C. To operate in right-to-work states
D. To seek better climate and recreation for company managers
E. To be closer to raw materials

Key Terms

Acid deposition
Acid precipitation
Agglomeration economies
Ancillary activities
Break-of-bulk point*
Bulk-gaining industry
Bulk-reducing industry
Carbon monoxide
Chlorofluorocarbons (CFCs)
Climate Change*
Cottage industry*
Deglomeration
Demand
Environmental sustainability*
Foot-loose industry
Fordist*
Geothermal energy
Global warming
Greenhouse effect
Hazardous waste
Hydrocarbons
Hydroelectric power
Industrial Revolution*
Just-in-time delivery*
Labor-intensive industry

Least-cost theory*
Maquiladora
Municipal landfill
New international division of labor
Non-point source pollution*
Non-renewable resource*
North American Free Trade Agreement
  (NAFTA)
Outsourcing*
Particulates
Photochemical smog
Point-source pollution*
Post-Fordist production*
Recycle
Remanufacturing
Renewable resource
Right-to-work laws
Right-to-work states
Sanitary landfill
Site factors*
Situation factors*
Solar power
Sweatshops
Textile
Transnational corporation*
Vertical integration

* Term is in 2019 College Board Curriculum & Exam Description.

Source: College Board AP Human Geography Course Description, effective Fall 2019

Think Like a Geographer Activities

Design an infographic major company to investigate, display, and evaluate the factors for site and situation for that company's location. Determine the labor, capital, and land characteristics and evaluate the transportation costs for the materials and distribution to market.

Quick Quiz

11.1. Industrial areas developed:
A. on vast open plains.
B. along rivers and coastal areas.
C. interior areas near markets.
D. in well-developed cities.
E. near airports.

11.2. Which is not a renewable energy source?
A. Geothermal
B. Hydroelectric
C. Solar
D. Wind
E. Biomass

11.3. How does heavy manufacturing contribute to the greenhouse effect?
A. Carbon dioxide, produced from burning fossil fuels, binds with water vapor, eventually trapping heat from escaping the Earth's surface.
B. The production of chlorofluorocarbons from manufacturing erodes the ozone layer, allowing more solar rays to heat the surface.
C. Sulfur and nitrogen oxides bind with water to create acids that prevent snow and ice from forming on the surface.
D. Carbon produced from manufacturing enriches the soil, causing extreme plant growth during warm periods on the planet.
E. Heavy manufacturing does not contribute to the greenhouse effect.

11.4. Why would an industry choose to locate in a traditional region, like the northeastern United States?
A. Availability of cheap labor and transportation
B. Availability of cheap land and unskilled labor
C. Availability of skilled labor and the ability to deliver to the market
D. Availability of cheap land and the ability to deliver to the market
E. Availability of cheap labor and the ability to deliver to the market

11.5. Where is the future growth in manufacturing expected to concentrate?
A. China, Mexico, Indonesia, and Vietnam
B. South Africa, Argentina, Vietnam, and India
C. Bangladesh, Romania, Indonesia, and Cambodia
D. Chile, Ireland, Rwanda, and Belize
E. Brazil, Russia, India, and China

11.6. What are the world's three principal industrial regions?
A. Europe, North America, and East Asia
B. Europe, East Asia, and South Asia
C. Europe, North America, and Japan
D. Europe, North America, and Oceania
E. Europe, Oceania, and East Asia

11.7. Which fossil fuel is predicted to increase in development and production in the next 20 years?
A. Petroleum
B. Coal
C. Natural gas
D. Uranium
E. Tar sands

11.8. Why are just-in-time products important for industries?
A. They can be stockpiled and used just in the nick of time.
B. They are not perishable so they may be used anytime.
C. They are delivered to the factory right when they are going to be used.
D. They are put on container ships because there is no hurry as to when they will be used.
E. They are used in cottage industries at any time they are needed.

11.9. What explains the growth of manufacturing and industry in Central Europe?
A. Low-wage and low-skilled labor and proximity to Western European markets
B. Access to inland waterways and ports
C. Well-educated population that speaks multiple European languages
D. Source area for mineral resources, reducing transportation costs
E. Large unemployed population willing to work for low wages

11.10. Before corporations began outsourcing production to developing countries, they controlled all aspects of the production process known as:
A. new international division of labor.
B. vertical integration.
C. fair trade.
D. industrial relocation.
E. integrated manufacturing.

11.11. The two largest flows of petroleum from their source to their destination are:
A. Saudi Arabia to India and Iraq to India.
B. Mexico to the United States and Iraq to Europe.
C. Nigeria to Europe and Iraq to China.
D. Canada to the United States and Russia to Europe.
E. China to Australia and Saudi Arabia to Japan.

Free Response

Sustainable development integrates economic development with environmental sustainability.

1. Define sustainable development.

2. Explain how each industry below has focused on sustainable development.
    a. Agriculture
    b. Energy
    c. Textile manufacturing

3. Identify and provide an example of each:
    a. Recycling
    b. Reducing
    c. Reuse/remanufacturing

On the Web

www.pearsonmylabandmastering.com/northamerica/masteringgeography/
www.businessdictionary.com/definition/industrial-sector.html
www.victorianweb.org/technology/ir/irchron.html
www.eh-resources.org/timeline/timeline_industrial.html
www.wisegeek.org/what-is-outsourcing.htm
www.ed.ted.com/lessons/how-containerization-shaped-the-modern-world
www.globalsherpa.org/bric-countries-brics/#
www.gapminder.org/dollar-street/matrix
www.vox.com/2018/4/6/17206230/china-trade-belt-road-economy
PBS-America Revealed 2/4 Nation on the Move: www.youtu.be/B-Ff_sE5Lgc
PBS-America Revealed 3/4 Electric Nation: www.youtu.be/7t2vzk7YAt0
PBS-America Revealed 4/4 Made in the USA: www.youtu.be/pK0lWEywbrg
What Is Sustainable Development?: www.youtu.be/_ofmAGaMfkA
How Algae Could Change The Fossil Fuel Industry: www.youtu.be/yCNkmi7VE0I
Factory City: EUPA. Documentary China labors and the largest factory in the world: www.youtu.be/xMm-YMO5H7o

TED Talks

Ngozi Okonjo-Iweala, Aid versus Trade:
www.ted.com/talks/ngozi_okonjo_iweala_on_aid_versus_trade.html
Hans Rosling, The Best Stats You've Ever Seen:
www.ted.com/talks/hans_rosling_shows_the_best_stats_you_ve_ever_seen.html
Ngozi Okonjo-Iweala, Want to Help Africa? Do Business Here :
www.ted.com/talks/ngozi_okonjo_iweala_on_doing_business_in_africa.html
Bono, My Wish: Three Actions for Africa:
www.ted.com/talks/bono_s_call_to_action_for_africa.html
Hans Rosling, Global Population Growth, Box by Box:
www.ted.com/talks/hans_rosling_on_global_population_growth/up-next
Parag Khanna, Mapping the Future of Countries:
www.ted.com/talks/parag_khanna_maps_the_future_of_countries/up-next
Hans Rosling, Asia's Rise—How and When:
www.ted.com/talks/hans_rosling_asia_s_rise_how_and_when/up-next

Key Figures

Figure 11-3 Diffusion of the Industrial Revolution
Figure 11-4 Industrial Output, 2017
Figure 11-5 Europe's Industrial Areas
Figure 11-6 North America's Industrial Areas
Figure 11-14 Distribution of Copper Production
Figure 11-16 Distribution of Minerals
Figure 11-19 Motor Vehicle Production
Figure 11-20 Changing Distribution of North American Assembly Plants

AP® Human Geography Outline of Industrialization and Economic Development

Unit 5: Agriculture and Rural Land-Use Patterns and Processes

Topic	APHG Topic No. Title	Suggested Skills	Enduring Understandings	Learning Objective	Big Ideas
11.1.1; 11.1.2	7.1: The Industrial Revolution	4.D: Compare patterns and trends in sources to draw conclusions.	SPS-7: Industrialization, past and present, has facilitated improvements in standards of living, but it has also contributed to geographically uneven development.	SPS-7.A: Explain how the Industrial Revolution facilitated the growth and diffusion of industrialization.	BI-3: Spatial Processes and Societal Change
11.1.3; 11.1.4; 11.1.5; 11.1.6	7.2: Economic Sectors and Patterns	2.B: Explain spatial relationships in a specified context or region of the world, using geographic concepts, processes, models, or theories.	SPS-7: Industrialization, past and present, has facilitated improvements in standards of living, but it has also contributed to geographically uneven development.	SPS-7.B: Explain the spatial patterns of industrial production and development.	BI-3: Spatial Processes and Societal Change
11.2.1; 11.2.2; 11.2.3; 11.2.4; 11.2.5; 11.2.6; 11.2.7	7.3: Measures of Development	3.F: Explain possible limitations of the data provided.	SPS-7: Industrialization, past and present, has facilitated improvements in standards of living, but it has also contributed to geographically uneven development.	SPS-7.C: Describe social and economic measures of development.	BI-3: Spatial Processes and Societal Change
11.3.1; 11.3.2; 11.3.3; 11.3.4	7.8: Sustainable Development	5.D: Explain the degree to which a geographic concept, process, model, or theory effectively explains geographic effects across various geographic scales.	IMP-7: Environmental problems stemming from industrialization may be remedied through sustainable development strategies.	IMP-7.A: Explain how sustainability principles relate to and impact industrialization and spatial development.	BI-2: Impacts and Interactions

11.4.1; 11.4.2; 11.4.3; 11.4.4	7.6: Trade and the World Economy	5.B: Explain spatial relationships across various geographic scales using geographic concepts, processes, models, or theories.	PSO-7: Economic and social development happen at different times and rates in different places.	PSO-7.A: Explain causes and geographic consequences of recent economic changes, such as the increase in international trade, deindustrialization, and growing interdependence in the world economy.	BI-1: Patterns and Spatial Organization

Source: College Board AP Human Geography Course Description, effective Fall 2019

FRQ's From College Board

2001 FRQ #1
2004 FRQ #1
2006 FRQ #2
2007 FRQ #3
2008 FRQ #3
2013 FRQ #1
2014 FRQ #1
2016 FRQ #1
2019 FRQ #1 set 2

Chapter

12 Services & Settlements

Where Are Services Distributed?

In more developed countries, most workers are employed in the **tertiary sector** of the economy, which is the provision of goods and services. There is a close relationship between services and settlements; most services are clustered in settlements. They are also clustered in more developed countries because that is where people are more likely to be able to buy services, rather than developing countries. Within more developed countries, business services locate in large settlements, which are also the key markets. The focus of the AP Human Geography curriculum is how economic development differs among places and reasons for this difference. Characteristics of more developed economies in comparison to less developed include aspects of the population, industry, resource access, and global situation.

Learning Outcome 12.1.1: Describe the three types of services.
Three types of services are consumer, business, and public. Jobs are growing in the service sector rather than in agriculture and industry.

In North America, three-quarters of employees work in the service sector. There are three types of services: consumer services, business services, and public services.

Consumer services provide services to individual consumers and include retail services and personal services. Retail and wholesale services include about 15 percent of all jobs in the United States and provide goods for sale to consumers. Other consumer services include education services, health services, and leisure and hospitality services.

Business services include financial services, professional services, transportation, and information services; they diffuse and distribute services to help other businesses.

Public services, which include governmental services at various levels, provide security and protection for citizens and businesses. Ten percent of U.S. jobs are in the public sector with one-sixth working for the federal government, one-fourth for a state government, and three-fifths for local governments.

All the growth in employment in the United States between 1972 and 2019 has been in the service sector, as employment in primary and secondary sector activities has declined. Within business services, jobs expanded most rapidly in professional services. The most rapid increase within consumer services has been in the provision of health care. There have been other large increases in education, entertainment, and recreation.

Settlements probably originated to provide consumer and public services. Business services came later.

There have been major urban settlements in different parts of the world since ancient times, including Mesopotamia, Greece, and Rome. In ancient Greece, **city-states** such as Athens and Sparta emerged. These included the city and surrounding countryside or hinterland. Athens made major contributions to the development of culture, philosophy, and other elements of Western civilization. This shows that urban settlements have been distinguished from rural ones not only by public services but also by a concentration of consumer services, especially cultural activities. Cities in the Roman world, especially Rome, were important centers of administration, trade, culture, and a host of other services.

Key Issues Revisited

12.1. Where Are Services Distributed?

- Consumer (including retail, health, education, and leisure), business (including financial, professional, and management), and public (including federal, state, and local) are the three types of services that can be found distributed in society.

- Services originated in rural settlements, and the earliest services were primarily personal and public.

Review Questions

12.1.1. What is the fastest growing business service?
A. Transportation
B. Professional services
C. Financial services
D. Retirement services
E. Recreational services

12.1.2. What part of the consumer service industry has not seen an increase in the number of jobs?
A. Education
B. Health care
C. Government
D. Retail
E. Entertainment

KEY ISSUE 2

Where Are Consumer Services Distributed?

Learning Outcome 12.2.1: Explain the concepts of market area, range, and threshold.
The market area is the area surrounding a service from which customers are attracted. The range is the maximum distance people are willing to travel to use a service. The threshold is the minimum number of people needed to support a service.

Learning Outcome 12.2.2: Describe the distribution of different-sized settlements.
Larger settlements provide consumer services that have larger thresholds, ranges, and market areas. In many developed countries, settlements follow a regular hierarchy.

Learning Outcome 12.2.3: Explain how to use threshold and range to find the optimal location for a service.
The gravity model predicts that the optimal location of a service is directly related to the number of people in the area and inversely related to the distance people must travel to access it.

Learning Outcome 12.2.4: Give examples of consumer services that do not have a fixed location.
Periodic markets provide a collection of individual vendors that offer foods and services in a location on specified days. Sharing services utilize smartphone access to secure services at the customer's location.

Consumer services are generally provided in a regular pattern based on size of settlements, with larger settlements offering more than smaller ones.

Central place theory provides a framework for looking at the relationship among settlements of different sizes, especially their ability to provide various goods and services. It was developed by Walter Christaller in the 1930s and was based on his studies of settlement patterns in southern Germany. A service will have a **market area** or **hinterland** of potential customers. Each urban settlement will have a market area, assuming that people will get services from the nearest settlement. The **range** is the maximum distance that people are willing to travel for a service, and the **threshold** is the minimum number of people needed to support a service. Retailers and other service providers will use these concepts to analyze the potential market area. Determining the profitability of a location and optimal location within a market is called **market-area analysis**. Services and settlements are hierarchical, and larger settlements will provide consumer services that have larger thresholds, ranges, and market areas than smaller settlements. Central place theory shows market areas in more developed countries as a series of hexagons of various sizes. The **gravity model** predicts that the best location for a service is a location that is directly related to the number of people in the area and inversely related to the distance that people must travel for it. A place with more people will have more potential customers, and people who are further away from a service are less likely to use it. Christaller identified four different levels of market area and seven different settlement sizes. Since this is a theory, he made certain assumptions that may or may not be true in reality, such as equal ease of transportation in all directions, and that people would always get a service from the nearest available market.

Geographers have observed that, in many more developed countries, there is sometimes a regular hierarchy of settlements from largest to smallest. This is the **rank size rule**, where a country's *n*th-largest settlement is 1/*n*th the population of the largest settlement. So the second largest city would be half the size of the largest. Developing countries as well as some European countries follow the primate city rule rather than the rank-size rule. A **primate city** is at least twice the population size of the next largest city and is the financial, political, and frequently the cultural center of the country.

In more developed and developing countries, periodic markets are set up to provide consumer goods. These markets are typically in accessible parking lots and intersections of major transportation routes, but most importantly, they do not have daily operations or fixed commercial structures. These are collections or individual vendors who offer goods and services in a specific location one or two times a week. Periodic markets support the needs of sparse populations and low income area where the purchasing power is too low to support full-time retailing. In urban areas, periodic markets offer residents fresh food brought in from the countryside in the form of farmer's markets and flea markets. The frequency of periodic markets varies by culture and location. Sharing services have evolved with the use of smart phones and immediate connections. These car, food, and delivery services are completely dependent on access to an independent contractor connected through the latest in GPS and electronic communication. This is a shift from the building-based operations that initially developed in a postindustrial society.

Key Issues Revisited

12.2. Where Are Consumer Services Distributed?

- Central place theory determines the most profitable location for a consumer service.

- A central place is surrounded by a market area that has a range and a threshold.

- Urban settlements are centers for consumer and business services.

Review Questions

12.2.1. A market area is a good example of a:
A. vernacular region.
B. formal region.
C. hierarchical region.
D. functional region.
E. sphere of influence.

12.2.2. When plotted on logarithmic paper, states whose cities follow the rank size rule will show cities in a:
A. hexagonal shape.
B. circular shape.
C. square shape.
D. triangular shape.
E. straight line.

12.2.3. Which model predicts that the optimal location of a service is directly related to the number of people in the area and inversely related to the distance people must travel to access it?
A. Periodic model
B. Threshold model
C. Gravity model
D. Attraction model
E. Central place model

12.2.4. What would be an example of a periodic market in a developed country?
A. Weekly flea market
B. Farmer's market each Thursday on the town square
C. Grocery store with seasonal local fruits and vegetables
D. Cottage industries
E. Selling items online

KEY ISSUE 3

Where Are Business Services Distributed?

Learning Outcome 12.3.1: Explain the clustering of business services in global cities.
Global cities (or world cities) are the centers for finance, business operations, and professional services.

Learning Outcome 12.3.2: Describe two types of business services in developing countries.
Some small countries offer offshore financial services, which attract investors because of low taxes and extreme privacy. Developing countries also specialize in back-office operations, also called business process outsourcing.

Learning Outcome 12.3.3: Explain the concept of economic base.
The economic base is made up of basic and non-basic businesses. Basic businesses generate income from outside of the settlement.

Modern world cities offer business services, especially financial services. They also have retail services with huge market areas, such as leisure and cultural services of national importance. London presents more plays than the rest of Britain combined. World cities are also centers of national and international power. New York is the headquarters of the United Nations, and Brussels is one of the headquarters of the European Union.

Geographers have identified four levels of cities. These are global or world cities, command and control centers, specialized producer-service centers, and dependent centers. A combination of factors is used to identify and rank global cities, including economic factors including the number of headquarters for multinational corporations, financial institutions, and law firms; political factors including the number of foreign consulates and embassies, and international organizations; cultural factors including performing arts, media outlets, sports facilities, and educational institutions; and advanced infrastructure, communications, and transportation networks.

London, New York, and Tokyo are at the top of the hierarchy of world cities and are considered alpha++ cities because they provide many services in the global economy. Global cities are divided according to their economic, political, cultural, and infrastructural factors using the levels alpha, beta, and gamma. There are also second- and third-tier world cities. Some major corporations and banks have their headquarters in second-tier or major world cities. Third-tier world cities are called secondary world cities.

Command and control centers contain the headquarters of large corporations and concentrations of a variety of business services. There are regional centers like Atlanta and Boston and subregional centers such as Charlotte and Des Moines. Specialized producer-service centers have management, as well as research and development activities associated with specific industries. Detroit is a specialized producer-service center specializing in motor vehicles. As the term suggests, dependent centers depend on decisions made in world cities for their economic well-being. They provide relatively unskilled jobs. San Diego is an industrial and military dependent center.

In the global economy, developing countries specialize in two distinctive types of business services—**offshore financial services** and back-office functions. Small countries, often islands and microstates, offer offshore financial services. These offshore centers provide tax-free or lower taxes for companies and privacy from disclosure. Back-office functions include processing insurance claims, payroll management, transcription work, and other routine clerical work. Some developing countries have attracted **back offices** because of low wages and the ability to speak English.

Basic (sector) industries are exported mainly to consumers outside a settlement and constitute that community's **economic base.** These industries employ a large percentage of a community's workforce. **Nonbasic (sector) industries** are usually consumed within that community. The growth of a community's economy that results from its basic and non-basic industries is called the **multiplier effect**. Basic industries are vital to the economic health of a settlement, as these are the industries that are bringing revenue into the community. Nonbasic industries are generating revenue but simply shifting it from one to another in the same community. The concept of basic industries originally referred to the secondary sector of the economy, such as manufacturing, but in a **postindustrial society** such as the United States, they are now more likely to be in the service sector.

Cities develop agglomerations of businesses that are supported by research, education, and related support industries. As a result of this concentration, the skilled labor and professional population is not distributed uniformly among cities or across a country. Cities have to attract these industries and make the place appealing to competition from other places trying to lure the same workforce. Ultimately, cities become specialized in different economic activities; for example, Houston is known for the oil and gas industry and medical research industries and Seattle for ship building and aircraft equipment and design.

Key Issue Revisited

12.3. Where Are Business Services Distributed?

- Business services cluster in global cities.

- Developing countries provide offshore financial services and business process outsourcing.

- Cities specialize in the provision of particular services; the specialized services constitute a community's economic base.

Review Questions

12.3.1. Global cities typically offer _____.
A. corporate offices
B. theaters
C. libraries
D. sporting events
E. all of these

12.3.2. Which of the following is an example of a business process outsourcing function?
A. Spinning wool into thread
B. Setting up periodic markets
C. Managing technical inquiries for personal computer operations
D. Negotiating trade for large manufacturing companies
E. Teaching English as a second language

12.3.3. What is the economic base?
A. Exports of goods to customers outside the settlement
B. Businesses that support customers within the settlement
C. Operations management and technical support for Amazon
D. Business centers clustered in global cities
E. Permanent markets for home-produced goods

KEY ISSUE 4

Why Do Services Cluster in Settlements?

Learning Outcome 12.4.1: Compare clustered and dispersed rural settlements.
A clustered rural settlement is an agricultural-based settlement in which houses are close together. A dispersed rural settlement has isolated individual farms.

Learning Outcome 12.4.2: Identify important prehistoric and ancient urban settlements.
Urban settlements may have originated in Southwest Asia, or they may have originated in multiple hearths. Few people lived in urban settlements until modern times.

Learning Outcome 12.4.3: Describe two dimensions of urbanization.
Urbanization involves an increase in the percentage of people living in urban settlements. More developed countries have higher percentages of urban residents than do developing countries. Urbanization also involves an increase in size of settlements. Most very large settlements are in developing countries.

Learning Outcome 12.4.4: Identify the location of the largest and fastest-growing urban settlements.
A **megacity** is an urban settlement with a total population in excess of 10 million people. A **metacity** has a population of more than 20 million people.

A large percentage of the world's population still practices agriculture and lives in rural settlements. In **clustered rural settlements**, families live close to one another and fields surround houses and farm buildings. In **dispersed rural settlements**, farmers live on individual farms and are more isolated from their neighbors.

Circular rural settlements consist of a central open space surrounded by buildings. The medieval German Gewandorf settlements and East African Maasai villages are examples of circular settlements. Linear rural settlements are clustered along transportation routes like roads or rivers. In North America, most linear settlements can be traced to the original French long lot or seigneurial pattern.

Dispersed rural settlements are associated with more recent agricultural settlements in the more developed world. In some European countries, clustered patterns were converted into dispersed settlements. The rural **enclosure movement** that accompanied the Industrial Revolution in Britain is a good example of this transition. It provided greater efficiency in an agricultural world that relied on fewer farmers.

The arrangement of these settlements was based on providing security, support, or access to transportation arteries.

Urbanization is the process by which the population of cities grows, both in *numbers* and *percentage*. The early settlements, dating back almost 10,000 years, were established as centers for religion, trade, military protection, and the need to provide services to the surrounding populations. The early settlements expanded as trade areas to provide a continual source of surplus food and to accommodate trade with people in the hinterlands.

Today in more developed countries, about three-fourths of the people live in urban areas, compared to about two-fifths in developing countries, although urbanization in Latin America is comparable to more developed countries. In more developed countries, the process of urbanization that began around 1800 has largely ended because the percentage living in urban areas cannot increase much more. The percentage living in cities in developing countries in recent years has increased because of rural to urban migration. Eight of the ten most populous cities in the world are currently in developing countries.

The population of urban settlements exceeded that of rural settlements for the first time in human history in 2008. In the 1930s, Louis Wirth observed major differences between urban and rural residents. He defined a **city** as a permanent settlement that has three characteristics—large size, high population, and socially heterogeneous people. In the urban world, most relationships are contractual and employment is more highly specialized than in rural settlements. In more developed countries, social distinctions between urban and rural residents have become more blurred than in developing countries because the majority of people in a more developed country now live in urban areas. The development level of a country affects the percentage of people living in urban settlements. Over 79 percent of the population in developed countries lives in urban areas compared to 50 percent in developing countries. In more developed countries, increased urbanization is the result of evolving industrialization and the growth of tertiary sector businesses, as well as the decline in the need of labor in the agricultural sectors.

In addition to Tokyo, only Seoul and New York City are among the 10 largest cities in the world and are the only cities in this list of more developed countries. Forty-one of the fifty largest urban areas are in developing countries and 97 of the top 100 fastest-growing urban areas are also in developing countries. Additionally, many of these cities are in the tropics and subtropics (see the following table). In the past, the growth of cities was associated with development; however, growth today is associated with rural to urban migration, even though there might not be jobs available. In addition, natural increase rates contribute to growing urban populations. There are 37 **megacities**, each with a population of 10 million people. Eleven of the megacities are also metacities with more than 20 million people.

The Largest Cities in the World

Rank	City	Country	Population	Location	Development level
1	Shanghai	China	24,153,000	subtropics	Developing
2	Beijing	China	18,590,000	continental	Developing
3	Karachi	Pakistan	18,000,000	subtropics	Developing
4	Istanbul	Turkey	14,657,000	subtropics	Developing
5	Dhaka	Bangladesh	14,543,000	tropics	Developing
6	Tokyo	Japan	13,617,000	subtropics	More Developed
7	Moscow	Russia	13,197,596	continental	More Developed
8	Manila	Philippines	12,877,000	tropics	Developing
9	Tianjin	China	12,784,000	subtropics	Developing
10	Mumbai	India	12,400,000	tropics	Developing
11	Sao Paulo	Brazil	12,038,000	tropics	Developing
12	Shenzhen	China	11,908,000	tropics	Developing
13	Guangzhou	China	11,548,000	tropics	Developing
14	Delhi	India	11,035,000	subtropics	Developing
15	Wuhan	China	10,608,000	subtropics	Developing
16	Lahore	Pakistan	10,355,000	subtropics	Developing
17	Seoul	South Korea	10,290,000	temperate	Developing
18	Chengdu	China	10,152,000	temperate	Developing
19	Kinshasa	Congo D.R.	10,125,000	tropics	Developing
20	Lima	Peru	9,752,000	tropics	Developing

www.worldatlas.com/articles/the-10-largest-cities-in-the-world.html

Key Issue Revisited

12.4.1 Why Do Services Cluster in Settlements?

- Settlements are either rural or urban, with a pattern of rural areas clustered or dispersed.

- More developed countries have higher percentages of urban residents, but developing countries have most of the very large cities.

Review Questions

12.4.1. The French long-lot system is an example of a:
A. circular rural settlement.
B. linear rural settlement.
C. city structure outside North America.
D. colonial city.
E. dispersed service settlement.

12.4.2. The earliest settlements may have been established to:
A. establish governments.
B. establish and preserve burial grounds.
C. create protection from invading forces.
D. create a place for periodic markets to remain permanent.
E. create business centers.

12.4.3. What percentage of the world's population lives in urban settlements?
A. 6%
B. 30%
C. 45%
D. 54%
E. 75%

12.4.4. Where are the majority of the fastest-growing cities?
A. Europe
B. North America
C. Asia
D. Australia
E. Africa

Key Terms

Back offices
Business services
Basic (sector) industries
Central place theory*
Christaller*
City*
City-state
Clustered rural settlement*
Consumer services
Dispersed rural settlement*
Economic base
Enclosure movement
Gravity model*
Hinterland

Market-area analysis
Megacity*
Metacity*
Multiplier effect*
Nonbasic (sector) industries
Offshore financial services
Periodic markets
Postindustrial society
Primate city*
Public services
Range
Rank-size rule*
Service settlement*
Threshold
Urbanization

* Term is in 2019 College Board Curriculum & Exam Description.

Source: College Board AP Human Geography Course Description, effective Fall 2019

Think Like a Geographer Activities

Using a blank world map of countries, locate and label all of the cities with over 10 million inhabitants. On the same map, draw in the climate regions and natural hazard potentials for each of these areas. Determine what risks and hazards face the population of these areas. Discuss how development levels in these countries will affect the cities and population if a potential hazard becomes an event creating a natural disaster.

Quick Quiz

12.1. What is the fastest-growing consumer service?
A. Urban construction
B. Urban farming
C. Hydroponic agriculture
D. Health care
E. Health food restaurants

12.2. The area surrounding a service from which customers are attracted is the _____.
A. catchment
B. hinterland
C. market area
D. service area
E. zone of accessibility

12.3. What is the oldest documented prehistoric urban settlement found in present-day Iraq?
A. Baghdad
B. Babylon
C. Ur
D. Memphis
E. Alexandria

12.4. What is the maximum distance people are willing to travel to use a service?
A. Range
B. Threshold
C. Distance decay
D. Zone of accessibility
E. Gravity model

12.5. What is the minimum number of people needed to support a service?
A. Rank-size rule
B. Multiplier effect
C. Consumer sector
D. Economic base
E. Threshold

12.6. An area with a substantial amount of low-income residents and poor access to a grocery store is known as a _____.
A. food desert
B. poverty island
C. minority enclave
D. neglected neighborhood
E. central city

12.7. Most of the world's major urban areas are found in _____.
A. central city
B. the developing world
C. the more developed world
D. Southern Hemisphere
E. Africa

12.8. Where are circular rural settlements most commonly found?
A. Ontario
B. Tanzania
C. Vermont
D. United Kingdom
E. Greece

12.9. A market center for the exchange of goods and services by people attracted from the surrounding area is a _____.
A. megaregion
B. central place
C. settlement
D. market area
E. hinterland

12.10. Why do companies engage in outsourcing part of their labor needs to other countries?
A. They have many highly skilled workers available to work.
B. Labor wages are low and they can speak English.
C. Workers are willing to live in on-site dormitories.
D. Workers are willing to travel to other countries to work.
E. Workers can switch between many languages to work in call centers.

Free Response

Evaluate the situational factors of major retail businesses that appeal to different economic levels—for example, Dollar General, Target, and Macy's. Using a major city map, plot the locations of the different businesses using a color-coded legend. Evaluate the locations to determine the range and threshold of the stores. You can do this same exercise with restaurants—for example, McDonald's to Maggiano's Little Italy.

On the Web

www.pearsonmylabandmastering.com/northamerica/masteringgeography/
www.businessdictionary.com/definition/services.html
www.geography.about.com/od/urbaneconomicgeography/a/sectorseconomy.htm
www.geography.about.com/od/urbaneconomicgeography/a/centralplace.htm
www.nationalgeographic.org/topics/ap-human-geography-cities/
www.nytimes.com/projects/census/2010/explorer.html
www.citylab.com/equity/2016/06/mapping-6000-years-of-urban-settlements-yale/486173/
www.citylab.com/life/2015/03/sorry-london-new-york-is-the-worlds-most-economically-powerful-city/386315/
www.citylab.com/life/2012/05/americas-most-powerful-global-cities/1904/
www.theguardian.com/cities/2015/feb/16/whats-the-oldest-city-in-the-world
www.citylab.com/life/2012/10/global-cities-offer-most-opportunity/3551/

TED Talks

Derek Sivers, Weird, or just different?
www.ted.com/talks/derek_sivers_weird_or_just_different.html
Eric Sanders, New York—Before the City:
www.ted.com/talks/eric_sanderson_pictures_new_york_before_the_city.html
Carolyn Steel, How Food Shapes Our Cities:
www.ted.com/talks/carolyn_steel_how_food_shapes_our_cities.html
Stewart Brand, What Squatter Cities Can Teach Us:
www.ted.com/talks/stewart_brand_on_squatter_cities.html
Robert Neuwirth, The Hidden World of Shadow Cities:
www.ted.com/talks/robert_neuwirth_on_our_shadow_cities.html
Majora Carter, Greening the Ghetto:
www.ted.com/talks/majora_carter_s_tale_of_urban_renewal.html
The Power of Cities theme page Urban, Development:
www.ted.com/themes/the_power_of_cities.html
James H Kunstler, The Ghastly Tragedy of the Suburbs:
www.ted.com/talks/james_howard_kunstler_dissects_suburbia.html

Key Figures

Figure 12-1 U.S. Employment by Sector, 2017
Figure 12-5 U.S. Megaregions
Figure 12-6 Why Geographers Use Hexagons to Delineate Market Areas
Figure 12-10 Central Place Theory
Figure 12-16 U.S. Food Deserts
Figure 12-23 Global Cities
Figure 12-24 Global Cities in North America
Figure 12-25 Offshore Financial Service Centers
Figure 12-28 Economic Base of Selected U.S. Communities
Figure 12-31 Clustered Circular Rural Settlement
Figure 12-32 Clustered Linear Rural Settlement
Figure 12-34 Dispersed Rural Settlement: United States
Figure 12-35 Rural Settlement: United Kingdom
Figure 12-36 Largest Urban Settlements Through History
Figure 12-37 Largest Urban Settlements before 350 B.C.E.
Figure 12-38 Largest Urban Settlements 350 B.C.E.–1750 C.E.
Figure 12-40 Percentage Living in Urban Settlements
Figure 12-42 Metacities and Megacities
Figure 12-45 World's 100 Fastest-Growing Urban Settlements

AP® Human Geography Outline of Industrialization and Economic Development
Unit 7: Industrial and Economic Development Patterns and Processes

Topic	APHG No. Title	Suggested Skills	Enduring Understandings	Learning Objectives	Big Ideas
12.1.1	7.6: Trade and the World Economy	5.B: Explain spatial relationships across various geographic scales using geographic concepts, processes, models, or theories.	PSO-7: Economic and social development happen at different times and rates in different places.	PSO-7.A: Explain causes and geographic consequences of recent economic changes, such as the increase in international trade, deindustrialization, and growing interdependence in the world economy.	BI-1: Patterns and Spatial Organization
12.2.1; 12.2.2; 12.2.3	6.4: The Size and Distribution of Cities	2.C: Explain a likely outcome in a geographic scenario using geographic concepts, processes, models, or theories.	PSO-6: The presence and growth of cities vary across geographical locations because of physical geography and resources.	PSO-6.C: Identify the different urban concepts such as hierarchy, interdependence, relative size, and spacing that are useful for explaining the distribution, size, and interaction of cities.	BI-1: Patterns and Spatial Organization
12.2.4	7.2: Economic Sectors and Patterns	2.B: Explain spatial relationships in a specified context or region of the world, using geographic concepts, processes, models, or theories.	SPS-7: Industrialization, past and present, has facilitated improvements in standards of living, but it has also contributed to geographically uneven development.	SPS-7.B: Explain the spatial patterns of industrial production and development.	BI-3: Spatial Processes and Societal Change
12.3.1; 12.3.2; 12.3.3	7.6: Trade and the World Economy	5.B: Explain spatial relationships across various geographic scales using geographic concepts, processes, models, or theories.	PSO-7: Economic and social development happen at different times and rates in different places.	PSO-7.A: Explain causes and geographic consequences of recent economic changes, such as the increase in international trade, deindustrialization, and growing interdependence in the world economy.	BI-1: Patterns and Spatial Organization

12.4.1	5.2: Settlement Patterns and Survey Methods	1.D: Describe a relevant geographic concept, process, model, or theory in a specified context.	PSO-5: Availability of resources and cultural practices influence agricultural practices and land-use patterns.	PSO-5.B: Identify different rural settlement patterns and methods of surveying rural settlements.	BI-1: Patterns and Spatial Organization
12.4.2; *12.4.3;* *12.4.4*	6.1: The Origin and Influences of Urbanization	2.D: Explain the significance of geographic similarities and differences among different locations and/or at different times.	PSO-6: The presence and growth of cities vary across geographical locations because of physical geography and resources.	PSO-6.A: Explain the processes that initiate and drive urbanization and suburbanization.	BI-1: Patterns and Spatial Organization

Source: College Board AP Human Geography Course Description, effective Fall 2019

FRQ's From College Board

2001 FRQ #2
2002 FRQ #3
2003 FRQ #1
2004 FRQ #3
2005 FRQ #3
2009 FRQ #2
2011 FRQ #1
2013 FRQ #3

Chapter

13 Urban Patterns

Why Are Cities Challenging to Define?

Urban geographers are concerned with the global distribution of urban settlements as well as the distribution of people and activities within urban areas. This chapter begins by addressing why services cluster downtown. The chapter then examines models that have been developed to help explain the internal structure of urban areas in North America and elsewhere. The distinctive problems of inner cities and suburbs are also considered.

Learning Outcome 13.1.1: Compare various definitions of urban settlements.
The central city is part of the urban area, which is then part of the metropolitan statistical area. Smaller areas are inclusive in a micropolitan statistical area.

Learning Outcome 13.1.2: Describe the distinctive features of the central business district (CBD).
The central business district contains a large percentage of an urban area's public, business, and consumer services. Offices cluster in the CBD to take advantage of its accessibility. Retail services, as well as manufacturers and residents, are less likely than in the past to be in the CBD.

Learning Outcome 13.1.3: Describe the use of vertical space in the CBD and the exclusion of some land uses.
A CBD is characterized by an extensive underground city of services and utilities, as well as high-rise buildings. Outside North America, CBDs may have more consumer services and fewer high-rise offices. As a result of high land costs, manufacturing operations have moved out to areas away from the city and near newer shipping facilities. New residents and new residential buildings have developed in the CBD, replacing the older abandoned warehouse districts.

A **central city** is an urban area that is legally incorporated by state charter with defined borders and a **municipal** government. The central city has expanded from the growth of population and shifting of economic activities to the market locations and labor sources. The area extending out from the city and its suburbs is the **urban area**. An **urbanized area** is an urban area with a least 50,000 inhabitants and an **urban cluster** is an urban area with a population from 2,500 to 50,000 inhabitants. It is estimated that 30 percent of the U.S. population live in a central city and its suburbs, and 40 percent live in smaller surrounding jurisdictions in one of the 486 urbanized areas. Another 10 percent live in one of the 3,087 urban clusters.

The U.S. Census Department defines a larger functional area of a settlement as a **metropolitan statistical area (MSA)**. An MSA is an urban area with 50,000 people; it includes the county and the surrounding counties with a high density population, and a large percentage of workers commute into the central city. Smaller urban areas are defined as **micropolitan statistical areas** and include urbanized areas between 10,000 and 50,000 people, the county, and surrounding counties. There are 541 micropolitan statistical areas, which contain about 9 percent of the U.S. population. Some U.S. cities have experienced a decline in their population in the central city while experiencing a growth in the suburbs and extending urban areas.

The **central business district (CBD)** is the center of a city where services have traditionally clustered. The CBD occupies less than 1 percent of the urban land area. Three types of retail services have concentrated in the center because they require accessibility. These include services with a high threshold, those with a long range, and those that serve people who work in the center. A large department store is a service with a high threshold. Retail services with a high range are specialized shops that are patronized infrequently. Both of these types of services have moved in large numbers to suburban locations in recent years. Retailers survive in some CBDs if they combine retailing with recreational activities. This has become a reality in Boston, Baltimore, Philadelphia, and San Francisco. Services that cater to people working in the CBD have remained in this location and have actually expanded, especially where CBDs have been revitalized. Business services such as advertising and banking have also remained clustered in the CBD. Additionally, public services are located in the CBD. The public services include city, county, and state agencies such as city hall and the courts. Other public services frequently include convention centers, sports facilities and unique restaurants, bars, and hotels.

Land costs in the CBD are very high because of competition for accessibility. Thus, land use is more intensive in the CBD, and some activities are excluded from the center because of the high cost of space. The built character is more vertical than other parts of urban areas, both above and below ground. Infrastructure, including transportation and utilities, typically run underground. Skyscrapers give the central city its distinctive image. Washington, D.C., is the only large U.S. CBD that does not have skyscrapers because no building is allowed to be higher than the U.S. Capitol dome.

High rents and land shortages have excluded industrial and residential activities from the CBDs of North American cities. Many industries have moved to suburban areas or smaller neighboring towns because land is less expensive. Residents have also moved away from CBDs. Pull factors have lured them to the suburbs; the crime and poverty of central cities have acted as a push factor. In the twenty-first century, the population of many U.S. CBDs has increased, largely as a result of urban renewal. "Empty nesters" and young professionals are particularly attracted to downtown living. Professional offices cluster into the CBD with related service and support industries, which also attracts the employees to residences in the changing CBD.

European CBDs are visibly very different because they have tried to preserve their historic cores by limiting high-rise buildings. More people live downtown outside North America, but renovation is more expensive and does not always produce enough space to meet the demand. As a result, rents are much higher in the center of European cities than in U.S. cities.

Key Issue Revisited

13. 1. Why Are Cities Challenging to Define?

- The CBD has few manufacturers and residents.

- Business, public, and some consumer services cluster in the CBD.

- North American CBDs utilize vertical space above and below ground level to minimize square footage on a city block.

Review Questions

13.1.1. The oldest area of a city would be found in:
A. the zone of transition.
B. the industrial zone.
C. the CBD.
D. the zone of gentrification.
E. the suburbs.

13.1.2. In cities outside the United States, more people live in :
A. the agricultural zone.
B. the manufacturing zone.
C. the suburbs.
D. rural areas.
E. the CBD.

13.1.3. Why are industrial and residential activities discouraged in the CBD?
A. Low labor cost and unskilled labor
B. Low retail threshold and poor accessibility
C. High land rent and land shortage
D. Poor visibility and lack of services
E. Lack of land available for new industries

KEY ISSUE 2

Where Are People Distributed in Urban Areas?

Learning Outcome 13.2.1: Describe the models of internal structure of urban areas.
According to the concentric zone model, a city grows outward in rings. According to the sector model, a city grows along transportation corridors. According to the multiple nuclei model, a city grows around several nodes.

Learning Outcome 13.2.2: Analyze how the three models help explain where people live.
According to the concentric zone model, housing is newer in outer rings than in inner rings. In the sector model, wealthier people live in different corridors than do poorer people. In the multiple nuclei model, different ethnic groups cluster around various nodes.

Learning Outcome 13.2.3: Relate the models of urban structure to European urban areas.
European cities have a different mix of land uses than those in North America as a result of their medieval past.

Learning Outcome 13.2.4: Describe patterns in precolonial and colonial cities.
Many cities in developing countries are shaped by colonial powers. Since gaining their independence, developing countries have seen cities grow rapidly. In some countries, colonial powers built a new city next to the existing one. In other countries, the colonists destroyed precolonial cities. In both cases, European colonial policies left a lasting impact.

Learning Outcome 13.2.5: Understand how the three models of urban structure describe patterns in cities in developing countries.
The concentric zone model is applied most frequently to explain growth in developing countries. Other models are sector development and the multiple nuclei model.

Learning Outcome 13.2.6: Describe stages of development and apply urban models to Mexico City.
Mexico City is an example of precolonial, colonial, and postcolonial development. Spanish colonists built Mexico City on the destroyed Aztec city of Tenochtitlan, designing it in the Spanish colonial style. After independence, Mexico City was relatively small, but it grew rapidly in the twentieth century, influenced in part by physical factors such as elevation.

Three different models developed at the University of Chicago explain the internal spatial organization of the urban environment. The urban models were first applied only to U.S. cities, specifically Chicago, as they developed through the Industrial Revolution and changing modes of transportation. The concentric zone and sector models are specific to transportation access and income. The multiple nuclei model focuses on the agglomeration of businesses and settlement patterns based on socioeconomic status. The **concentric zone model** was developed in 1923 by Burgess and applies to cities that have concentric rings of development emanating outward from a core or **CBD**. The ring immediately outside the CBD is a **zone of transition,** containing industry and poorer-quality housing. The rings each contain different kinds of urban land use, and residences become more affluent further away from the CBD and can afford adequate transportation into the city core. The underlying sociological concepts of invasion and succession help to explain how people move away from the city center as they become wealthier and are prepared to commute further.

The **sector model** was developed in 1939 by Hoyt, who saw the city developing as a series of sectors rather than rings. He believed that certain areas of the city might be more attractive for various activities because of environmental factors. The sectors often followed transportation lines. Areas of the city that developed for certain types of businesses pulled workers toward those areas for access. Heavy manufacturing, animal processing, and transportation services concentrated on and became sectors for those types of industries connecting neighborhoods dominated by the workers.

The **multiple nuclei model** was developed in 1945 by Harris and Ullman. They believed that cities lack one central core and instead have numerous **nodes** of business and cultural activities. Although dated, these models help geographers to understand where different people live in an urban area and why they live there. Nodes of business and consumer services called **edge cities** have developed around or near the existing freeway intersections. Edge cities have grown from rural or outer suburbs that were originally primarily residential and governed as part of a surrounding county. These business areas are accessed by cars and typically have more commercial traffic coming in to work and shop than residential traffic. Cities in more developed as well as developing countries exhibit characteristics of these models, **but no one city matches any model perfectly**.

North American cities are increasingly following a structure that Harris calls the **peripheral model**. The peripheral model consists of an inner city surrounded by growing suburbs that combine residential and business areas and is tied together by a beltway or ring road. The metropolitan areas of the northeastern United States now form one continuous urban complex or **megalopolis** (from the

Greek word meaning great city), which extends from Boston to south of Washington, D.C., and is referred to as the Boswash corridor.

In order to apply the urban models to reality, accurate data must be available. In the United States, that information is available from the U.S. Census Bureau, which has divided urban areas into **census tracts** that are essentially urban neighborhoods. They provide information about the characteristics of residents living in each tract. Social scientists can compare the distributions of characteristics and create an overall picture of where different people live. This kind of study is known as **social area analysis**.

These three models were developed to describe the spatial distribution of social classes in the urban United States. European CBDs have a different pattern of land usage because of their medieval origins. European cities have a higher density of residences in the CBD, in part due to the concentration of consumer services and cultural activities as well as traditional churches, squares, parks, and government facilities. In European cities, wealthier people tend to live closer to the CBD, and there is more suburban poverty. In developing countries, the poor are also accommodated in the suburbs, whereas the wealthier live near the center of cities. European colonial policies left a heavy mark on the development of cities in developing countries.

Islamic cities, such as Mecca, were laid out surrounding a religious core. They have mosques and a **bazaar** or marketplace at their center with walls guarding the perimeter. In the outer rings, there were secular businesses and quarters laid out for Jews, Christians, and foreigners. Some features of these cities were adaptations to the hot and dry physical environment.

In Asia, Africa, and Latin America, cities combine elements of native culture, colonial rule, religion, industry, and poverty. During the period of colonialism, the foreign rulers left their cultural footprint on the landscape of their colonies. Some colonial powers built a new city next to the precolonial city or destroyed the precolonial city and replaced it with a city designed for and by the colonial power; examples of this are Mexico City and Saigon.

The Spanish cities in Latin America were built according to the Law of the Indies, implemented in 1573. The law outlined how colonial cities were to be constructed with a street plan centered on a central plaza where the church is located. The city's residential patterns are based on one's role in the community. Griffin and Ford developed a model of a **Latin American city**, which shows the wealthy living close to the CBD along the wide spine leading to the central plaza and the core area of the city. Cities such as San Antonio, San Diego, Albuquerque, and Santa Fe, in the southwestern United States and Florida which were developed during Mexican or Spanish control of the land, have remnants of the Latin American model. The Latin American city model may no longer be accurate or current; the wealthy also live in the outskirts of the city and the poor have squatter settlements within the CBD.

Industrial sectors radiate out from the CBD, and the poorest live on the urban fringe in **squatter settlements** known as **informal settlements**. Squatter settlements are known by a variety of names such as *barrios, barriadas,* and *favelas* in Latin America, *bidonvilles* in North Africa, and *bustees* in India. The Global Development Research Center defines a squatter settlement as a residential area in an urban locality inhabited by the very poor who have no access to tenured land of their own, and hence "squat on vacant land, either private or public," or has not been built according to building codes. These squatter or informal settlements frequently lack services, sanitation, transportation into the city, and satisfactory housing. Kibera in Nairobi, Kenya, is the largest slum area in Africa and one of the largest in the world with about 250,000 residents. Attention to the conditions of living in these squatter settlements is the focus of the United Nations development programs, nongovernmental organizations, and governments of some of the settlements. Providing adequate water supplies, sanitary conditions, police presence, and access to public transportation into city centers for work is the focus of several local and national governments in order to improve the living conditions for millions of people.

Key Issue Revisited

13.2. Where Are People Distributed in Urban Areas?

- The concentric zone, sector, and multiple nuclei models help explain where various groups of people live in urban areas.

- These models provide a framework for understanding the distribution of social and economic groups within urban areas.

- Cities in Europe, Latin America, Africa, and Asia reflect a colonial influence.

- Some developing countries have large populations residing in informal settlements.

Review Questions

13.2.1. Outlying areas that function as consumer and business centers are known as:
A. squatter settlements.
B. edge cities.
C. suburbs.
D. villages.
E. boroughs.

13.2.2. Urban areas in the United States are divided by:
A. the Department of Homeland Security.
B. the Department of Urban Planning.
C. the Census Bureau.
D. the Population Reference Bureau.
E. the World Health Organization.

13.2.3. What is not normally found in a CBD in Europe?
A. Industrial factories
B. Cathedral
C. Large numbers of residences
D. Royal palaces
E. Public squares and private gardens

13.2.4. A precolonial Muslim city was laid out around:
A. a palace and armory.
B. a mosque and a Medinah.
C. a cathedral and a plaza.
D. public squares and private gardens.
E. citadel and an inner city.

13.2.5. What is the name for a squatter settlement in Latin America?
A. Kampongs
B. Barong-barong
C. Barriadas and favelas
D. The hood and the ghetto
E. Bustees

13.2.6. Prior to the arrival of the Spanish, what was the center of the Aztec Empire?
A. Quetzalcoatl
B. Zocalo
C. Tenochtitlan
D. Mexico City
E. Chapultepec

KEY ISSUE 3

Why Do Urban Areas Expand?

> **Learning Outcome 13.3.1: Explain the process of suburban growth.**
>
> Local government in the United States is extremely fragmented because of the difficulty in annexing suburban jurisdictions.
>
> **Learning Outcome 13.3.2: Describe suburban sprawl.**
>
> In the past, cities expanded their land area to encompass outlying areas, but now they are surrounded by independent suburban jurisdictions. Suburban sprawl has been documented to be costly.
>
> **Learning Outcome 13.3.3: Explain ways in which suburbs are segregated.**
>
> Suburbs are segregated according to social class and land uses.
>
> **Learning Outcome 13.3.4: Describe the strategies to reduce the impact of motor vehicles in urban areas.**
>
> Motor vehicles take up a lot of space in cities, including streets, freeways, and parking areas. Some cities control the number of vehicles that can enter the center of the city.
>
> **Learning Outcome 13.3.5: Describe the benefits and drawbacks of public transport.**
>
> Public transit, such as subways and buses, are more suited than private cars to move large numbers of people into and out of the CBD. New investment in public transit has occurred in a number of U.S. cities, though less extensively than in other countries.

As a result of the continued growth of the city and increased migration from rural to urban centers, the suburbs grew extensively with the Industrial Revolution as support areas for workers. A **suburb** is a residential or commercial area located within the urban area but outside of the central city. Today, 50 percent of Americans live in suburbs. Suburbs are appealing because they offer larger amounts of space for home ownership, parking spaces, space for parks and playgrounds, and protection from high crime areas and noisy traffic. Suburban living grew rapidly as incomes rose allowing people to buy larger living spaces on less expensive land further away from the city. Suburban living also required personal transportation.

Annexation is the process of legally adding land area to a city. In the United States, most surrounding suburban lands have their own jurisdictions and want to remain legally independent of the central city. Instead of annexing peripheral areas, cities are now surrounded by suburbs. As a result, several definitions have been created to characterize cities and their suburbs. In the 1930s, Louis Wirth, an urban geographer, defined a **city** as a permanent settlement that has a large size, high population density, and socially heterogeneous people. Urban settlements today can be physically defined by legal boundary, as continuously built-up area, and as a functional area. Virtually, all countries have a political system that recognizes cities as legal entities with fixed boundaries.

Many urban regional problems cannot be easily solved because of the fragmentation of local government. There are 6,953 governmental jurisdictions in Illinois and 90,056 throughout the United States. Most U.S. metropolitan areas have a **council of governments**, consisting of representatives of the various local governments that can do some planning for the entire area. There are two kinds of metropolitan-wide governments. A **federation system** of government combines the various municipalities of a metropolitan area into a single government. Toronto, Ontario, has a federation system. Some U.S. cities have consolidated city and county governments. Indianapolis and Miami are both examples of **consolidations**. Other governmental entities include utility districts, school districts, library, health districts, and transportation districts.

Several U.S. states are passing legislation and regulations called **smart growth**; it limits suburban sprawl and preserves farmland on the urban periphery. Maryland has done an especially good job in this area. The idea behind smart growth is to allow cities to annex only lands that are included in urban growth areas and avoid extending urban sprawl into viable farmlands.

In North American urban areas, the further one gets from the center of the city, the greater the decline in population density. This is called the **density gradient**. The number of houses per unit area of land will decline with distance from the center city. In North American and European cities in recent years, the density gradient has leveled out as more people have moved to the suburbs. **Suburban sprawl** has increased at the expense of agricultural land, and it results in the need for costly infrastructure. Several British cities are surrounded by **greenbelts**, or rings of open space, to prevent suburban sprawl.

Zoning ordinances, which prevent the mixing of land uses, has resulted in segregated residential suburbs. Suburbs now reflect two types of segregation: segregation of social classes and segregation of land use. Residents are separated from industrial and service activities, and poorer residents are excluded from certain areas because of the cost, size, or location of housing. North American suburbs are no longer just areas of residential growth. Businesses have moved to the suburbs. Retailing has become concentrated in suburban malls. Factories and offices have also moved to suburbia. If they don't require face-to-face contact, they can take advantage of the lower rents in the suburbs. Suburban communities create zoning restrictions, which limit low income and minorities out of fear of the effect on property values. Zoning laws can restrict land use, number of residents, access into a community, means of transportation allowed, and types of construction on properties.

Suburban locations of businesses have created a challenge for the businesses as well as for unskilled or low-skilled workers. Businesses move out to the suburban areas to pay less for land expenses or rent. However, many of these businesses, in particular shopping malls, are dependent on low-skilled sales workers. Many of these workers do not live in suburban areas but are part of the central city workforce living in less expensive areas. The problem that exists is that the business management can afford transportation to get to the suburban location, but frequentlyl, the low-skilled worker is dependent on public transportation that typically does not extend to the suburban locations. This imbalance of the access to available labor and work locations is known as a spatial mismatch. This imbalance contributes to the number of unemployed urban labor and job availability in the suburban areas.

Suburban sprawl has resulted in an increased dependence on transportation, especially motor vehicles in the United States. The peak hours for commuting have the heaviest flow of commuters into the CBD in the morning and out to the suburbs in the evening. Public transportation is much more important in most European and Japanese cities. Public transportation in the form of rapid transit is becoming more common in U.S. cities, although it is still not recognized as a key utility that needs to be subsidized. In the United States, public transportation is used primarily for commuting into and out of the CBD. In most cities outside of the megalopolises of Washington-Boston, San Francisco, and Chicago, public transport is minimal at best. Commuting to work alone accounts for 76 percent of commuting workers into the CBD. The growth of the suburbs depended on having a car for commuting and developed without accessibility to public transport or the infrastructure to implement it.

Since 1972, several cities have built entirely new subway systems to move people around the cities. The initiative to develop new subway or light rail systems was propelled by demands to meet new environmental emissions standards, combat long commutes in heavily congested traffic, and to make commuting more affordable with the rising cost of fuel. Despite recent success in developing public transportation in many larger cities, the fares do not cover operating costs, and as ridership declines, expenses rise and fares are increased, once again creating an accessibility challenge for low-income workers.

Improvements in transportation have changed the structure of the urban area. Urban areas are better suited to public transportation than individual motor vehicles because of the large number of people who need to be moved efficiently and effectively. Public transportation is less expensive, more environmentally friendly, and more time efficient. Only 2 percent of trips in the United States are by public transport or school bus. Geographer John Borchert classified five eras of U.S. urban development resulting from changing transportation systems corresponding to changing industrial development and the growth of cities. Understanding how the city is changing with increased development is a study in change over time, with a temporal and spatial perspective. The epochs as defined by Borchert are as follows.

Sail-Wagon Epoch, 1790–1830: Coastal locations were dependent on ocean-going wind-powered ships and pedestrian mobility. Major cities were focused on trade with European countries.

Iron Horse Epoch, 1830–1870: The use of steam engines was to move inland along waterways with steam-powered ships and steam-powered railroads accessing inland areas and emerging settlements. The growth of New York, Chicago, Detroit, and Pittsburgh were all tied to their location and role in the production of power and movement of goods.

Steel Rail Epoch, 1870–1920: The use of long-haul rail lines connected cities to the rural areas. The rail lines brought goods and supplies into the market and manufacturing areas of the city as the older cities begin to develop into sectors. Cities experience the development of agglomeration centers in the emerging sectors of the city focusing on heavy manufacturing, in particular, steel production.

Auto-Air-Amenity Epoch, 1920–1970: Shaped by the combustion engine, cities expand from long-distance travel between distant urban centers. Cities expanded out beyond earlier suburbs dependent on the car for access. This period experienced a shift to white-collar jobs and a declining blue-collar manufacturing industrial development. Less expensive amenities were available in the growing suburbs forming nodal centers. Distance away from the CBD was based on the ability to afford the transportation and the new housing. Areas that were slow to grow because of climate and accessibility took advantage of the changing technology to manage the climate. The growth of the Sun Belt began.

Satellite-Electronic-Jet Propulsion, 1970–present: This current era is characterized by global communication and transportation. This is the age of telecommuting, outsourcing, and demand for amenities by workers in the work and living space. The demand for faster and better and more modern drives the influence of technology on the urban landscape.

Strategies to reduce the impact of motor vehicles in urban areas include using technology to operate vehicles, reducing the human error of operation, and increased funding for cities to develop public transportation systems that facilitate ease of movement with efficiency and direct access.

Key Issue Revisited

13.3. Why Do Urban Areas Expand?

- U.S. cities annex surrounding lands to expand, but this has become less common. The suburban lifestyle attracts many people.

- Transportation improvements, notably the railroad in the nineteenth century and the automobile in the twentieth century, have facilitated urban sprawl.

- Suburbs are often segregated by social class and land-use activities.

- Suburban sprawl uses land that requires infrastructure investment to create accessibility to the CBD.

Review Questions

13.3.1. The largest increase in population within U.S. cities has occurred in:
A. the CBD.
B. rural areas.
C. the zone of transition.
D. the manufacturing zone.
E. the suburbs.

13.3.2. The only megalopolis in the United States extends from:
A. San Francisco to San Diego.
B. Dallas to Chicago.
C. Chicago to Pittsburgh including Detroit and Toronto.
D. Washington, D.C., to Miami including Atlanta.
E. Boston to Washington, D.C.

13.3.3. The set of laws that limit the permitted uses of land and density of development in a community is
A. zoning ordinances.:
B. redlining.
C. suburbanization ordinances.
D. Borchert laws.
E. smart growth ordinances.

13.3.4. Which area experiences a greater use of public transport?
A. South Texas-Gulf Coast
B. Pacific Northwest
C. Midwest
D. Southeast
E. Northeast

13.3.5. Public transit is challenged by:
A. high volume of riders and late schedules.
B. low ridership and high operating costs.
C. abuse of equipment and high rates of crime.
D. disconnect amog population areas of the urban area.
E. inability to access public transit in suburban areas.

KEY ISSUE 4

Why Might Cities Be More Sustainable?

Learning Outcome 13.4.1: Summarize social challenges faced by many cities.
Inner cities have concentrations of very poor people, considered to belong to an underclass, some of whom are homeless. A culture of poverty traps some poor people in the inner cities.

Learning Outcome 13.4.2: Describe the process of gentrification.
The older housing in the inner city can deteriorate through processes of filtering and redlining. Massive public housing projects were once constructed for poor people, but many of them have been demolished. Some cities have experienced gentrification, in which higher-income people move in and renovate previously deteriorated neighborhoods.

Learning Outcome 13.4.3: Consider alternative methods for addressing traffic congestion.
Commuting efforts are designed to reduce congestion and improve mobility in the urban area. Various forms of fees can reduce demand, such as tolls or permit charges.

Learning Outcome 13.4.4: Describe changes in vehicles and the impact of the changes on cities.
The future sustainability of cities depends on how transportation is managed.

Learning Outcome 13.4.5: Apply geography's five basic concepts to cities.
A city is a unique place at the center of the economic activity of a region that changes the scale of relationships with other places through cultural, political, and economic connections.

There are numerous inner-city social problems. There is a disproportionate share of residents considered an underclass because they are trapped in a cycle of economic and social problems. Many lack the necessary job skills for even the most basic jobs, and there are more than 3 million homeless people in the United States today. This culture of poverty leads to various crimes, including drug use, gangs, and other criminal activities. Additionally, cities have large numbers of homeless residents due to lack of affordable housing, lack of income, and mental health issues. According to the National Alliance to End Homelessness, there are 552,830 people homeless on any given night as of 2018. The prevalence of drugs, crime, and lack of adequate services compound the problems in an inner city.

Food deserts have begun to emerge in major cities, which compounds the problems of the underclass as they do not have accessibility to healthy foods because they lack transportation and the ability to go to a local supermarket. A **food desert** is a spatial area where obtaining fresh fruits and vegetables is not possible without access to an automobile. Typically, food deserts develop in declining neighborhoods where grocery stores cannot survive because the threshold of consumers is insufficient to maintain business. Available workers and crime are often cited as reasons for adequate food stores to survive as well. The presence of food deserts helps explain poor health and dietary complications. Food deserts have given rise to community gardens started by urban activists to clean up abandoned lands and respond to the lack of quality food.

Figure 13-1

Source: Norm Christensen and Lissa Leege, *The Environment and You, 2nd ed.* (Upper Saddle River, NJ: Pearson, 2016), 17.

Urban decline continues to challenge the central city as vacant houses and abandoned lands increase and those who can leave the areas do, causing further decline. One of the major physical problems is **filtering**, which is when houses are subdivided and occupied by successive waves of lower-income people. It can lead to total abandonment. As a result of filtering, inner-city neighborhoods have rapidly declining populations. **Redlining** is when banks draw lines on a map to identify areas where they will refuse to loan money, although the Community Reinvestment Act has essentially made this illegal.

Most inner-city residents cannot pay the taxes that are necessary to provide public services. A city has two choices to close the gap between the cost of services and the funding available from taxes. It can reduce services and/or raise tax revenues. Federal government contributions have helped, but these have declined substantially since the 1980s. The percentage of the budgets of the 50 largest U.S. cities supplied by the federal government declined to 6 percent from 1990 and 2000. Some state governments have increased financial assistance to cities.

A major cause of the recession that began in 2008 was the collapse in the housing market, primarily in the inner city. Compounding the problem, housing prices have fallen in the United States and other more developed countries since their peak in 2006.

Governments at various levels have put together grants to help the revitalization of inner-city neighborhoods. This process is called **urban renewal**. Substandard inner-city housing has been demolished and replaced with **public housing** for low-income people. Many of the public high-rise projects built during the 1950s and 1960s have since been demolished because they were considered unsafe. More recently, the trend has been to renovate deteriorating inner-city houses and former factories so that they will appeal to middle-class people. This process is known as **gentrification**. Gentrification involves repurposing older buildings, particularly with historic architecture. These buildings are usually refurbished and repaired, the space reapportioned into offices, modern apartment style housing, or eclectic markets for urban consumers. Gentrifying older buildings and building new structures is an ongoing process in urban areas as part of urban renewal. The purpose of urban renewal is to bring residents with money back into a central city and create a unique shopping and housing areas. Bringing residents back into the urban center also helps with the ongoing environmental challenges of air quality and mobility.

Sustainable development of cities to make them better places to live today and in the future has become the focus of many cities in the United States and Europe. Urban planners recognize that continued growth of cities can only be economically, environmentally, and socially sustainable if combined with smart growth. Urban planning for a sustainable future is known as **new urbanism**. New urbanism is based on the following basic tenets:

Promote Compact Communities	Planners encourage compact developments within the natural landscape with abundant green space, however, not dense high-rise development.
Mix land uses	Mix of residential, commercial, and public land that creates a sense of community and minimizes transportation needs
Create a range of housing opportunities and choices	Through promoting the urban village in which multi-family and singl-family housing is mixed with shops, cafes, and public transit, tax incentives are provided to ensure accessible lower income housing.
Foster communities that provide a sense of place	Sustainable cities promote the development of unique environments creating a social context of an area and of the city.
Conserve open space, farmland, natural beauty, and critical environmental areas	Purchasing the development rights in open spaces around and outside the developed area but allowing farming and forest management to continue on the land
Strengthen existing communities first	Urban infill focuses on the development and restoration of undeveloped or abandoned building lots. By strengthening existing communities, cities can grow and evolve through gradual change.
Provide a variety of transportation choices	Create transit-oriented development to halt the urban sprawl caused by building more roads for more cars.
Create walkable neighborhoods	Pedestrian oriented neighborhoods promote human well-being and a sense of community and access to public transportation options.
Make development decisions predictable, fair, and cost-effective	Decision making should be open to the public and consider social, economic, cultural, and environmental needs.
Encourage community collaboration in development decisions	Public support and participation empowers the community and resolves criticism and conflict to reach the intended goals.

Source: Norm Christensen and Lissa Leege, *The Environment and You, 2nd ed.* (Upper Saddle River, NJ: Pearson, 2016), 530–531

Key Issues Revisited

13.4. Why Might Cities Be More Sustainable?

- Inner-city residential areas have physical problems because of older, deteriorating houses.

- Inner-city residential areas have social problems as a result of a high percentage of low-income households who live in a culture of poverty.

- Inner-city residential areas have economic problems stemming from a gap between demand for services and supply of local tax revenue.

Review Questions

13.4.1. The process of limiting investment monies in declining inner-city housing areas is known as:
A. filtering.
B. redlining.
C. gentrification.
D. smart growth.
E. community restructuring.

13.4.2. The trend in public housing is:
A. to build dense high-rise facilities on abandoned lands.
B. to distribute within gentrified and urban redevelopment areas that blend into the area.
C. to relocate the urban poor to suburbs to fill low-skilled jobs in suburban malls.
D. to convert old apartments into large, multifamily apartment style communities with services to meet their needs.
E. to eliminate all public housing.

13.4.3. The biggest challenge for inner-city residents is:
A. access to low-skill, service industry jobs more frequently located in the suburbs.
B. loss of property by rapidly spreading ideas of gentrification.
C. shift in urban areas to retail and leisure services in old industrial neighborhoods.
D. destruction of transportation routes through the inner city.
E. elimination of cars and urban transport in the inner city.

13.4.4. Urban planning for a sustainable city of the future is known as:
A. smart growth.
B. urban renewal.
C. gentrification.
D. urbanology.
E. new urbanism.

Key Terms

African city model*
Annexation
Census tract*
Central Business District (CBD)
Central city
City*
Combined Statistical Area (CSA)
Concentric zone model*
Consolidations
Council of government
Density gradient
Edge city*
Filtering
Food desert
Gentrification
Ghetto
Greenbelt*
Islamic city
Latin American city*
Megalopolis*
Metropolitan Statistical Area (MSA)

Micropolitan statistical area
Multiple nuclei model*
New Urbanism*
Nodes
Peripheral model*
Public housing
Redlining*
Sector model*
Smart growth*
Social area analysis
Southeast Asia model*
Sprawl*
Squatter settlements*
Statistical area (PCSA)
Sustainable Development*
Urban geography*
Urban renewal*
Urbanization*
Urbanized area
Zone of transition
Zoning ordinance*

* Term is in 2019 College Board Curriculum & Exam Description.

Source: College Board AP Human Geography Course Description, effective Fall 2019

Think Like a Geographer Activities

Investigate what your city is doing to develop a sustainable city. Develop a photographic essay illustrating the area in the past and how it looks today. Document the statistical change of the area including demographics, median income, tax base, services, green space, and average housing cost.

Quick Quiz

13.1. An example of a retailer with a high threshold would be a (an):
A. department store.
B. office supply store.
C. shore repair shop.
D. dry cleaners.
E. rapid photocopying store.

13.2. One common characteristic of all three models of urbanization is that:
A. none of them include the suburbs.
B. the CBD is always in the middle.
C. high-class housing is always near heavy industry.
D. working-class homes were located farthest from the CBD.
E. immigrants live in single-family dwellings.

13.3. The underground CBD would include all but which of the following?
A. Garage
B. Loading dock
C. Sewer
D. Pedestrian passages
E. All of these would be found in an underground CBD.

13.4. An example of vertical geography is:
A. Mt. Everest.
B. terracing rice paddies.
C. a skyscraper.
D. a subway train.
E. a monument.

13.5. All of the following are ways governments try to reduce the demand to use congested roads EXCEPT:
A. tolls.
B. congestion charges.
C. permits.
D. bans on autos.
E. subsidized fuel charges.

Free Response

Define gentrification and urban renewal.

Explain why gentrification might be an alternative to suburban sprawl.

Identify examples of how cities are engaged in smart growth objectives.

Investigate ways that cities are trying to bring people back into the urban center.

On the Web

www.masteringgeography.com

www.stats.oecd.org/glossary/detail.asp?ID=2819

www.visibleearth.nasa.gov/view

www.geography.about.com/od/urbaneconomicgeography/a/Urban-Geography-Models.htm

www.nrdc.org/resources/runaway-american-dream-case-smart-growth-america

www.unhabitat.org/documents/SOWC10/R4.pdf

www.gdrc.org

www.gdrc.org/uem/define-squatter.html

www.news.nationalpost.com/2012/02/11/canada-as-immigration-booms-ethnic-enclaves-swell-and-segregate/

www.theatlanticcities.com/neighborhoods/2013/03/class-divided-cities-houston-edition/4850/

www.economist.com/news/united-states/21644164-gentrification-good-poor-bring-hipsters

www.youtube.com/watch?v=nTAlOxqKYNo#action=share

World Bank Harnessing Urbanization for Growth and Poverty Alleviation

www.youtu.be/XGIvVXVmnss **Urbanization's Cost in China**

www.youtu.be/Z2sj3k2Z544 **The Shocking Urbanization of or Planet is Accelerating**

www.youtu.be/7QWAXWhtSCQ **Urbanization: Who's Afraid of the Big Bad City**
www.youtu.be/eFboV2m1yuw **Megacities Reflect Growing Urbanization Trend**
www.youtu.be/NxFnwu7pSTg **BBC One - Andrew Marr's Megacities, Cities on the Edge**
www.youtube.com/watch?v=0ULzxD3w_c8 **The World's Megacities**

TED Talks

James H Kunstler, The Ghastly Tragedy of the Suburbs:
www.ted.com/talks/james_howard_kunstler_dissects_suburbia.html
Derek Sivers, Weird, or Just Different?
www.ted.com/talks/derek_sivers_weird_or_just_different.html
Eric Sanders, New York—Before the City:
www.ted.com/talks/eric_sanderson_pictures_new_york_before_the_city.html
Carolyn Steel, How Food Shapes Our Cities:
www.ted.com/talks/carolyn_steel_how_food_shapes_our_cities.html
Stewart Brand, What Squatter Cities Can Teach Us:
www.ted.com/talks/stewart_brand_on_squatter_cities.html
Robert Neuwirth, The Hidden World of Shadow Cities:
www.ted.com/talks/robert_neuwirth_on_our_shadow_cities.html
Majora Carter, Greening the Ghetto:
www.ted.com/talks/majora_carter_s_tale_of_urban_renewal.html
The Power of Cities theme page Urban, Development:
www.ted.com/themes/the_power_of_cities.html

Key Figures

Figure 13-9 Concentric Zone Model
Figure 13-11 Sector Model
Figure 13-14 Multiple-Nuclei Model
Figure 13-16 Galactic (Peripheral) Model
Figure 13-38 Model of Latin American City
Figure 13-40 Multiple Nuclei Model Applied to Cities in Developing Countries
Figure 13-62 Transportation Epochs

AP® Human Geography Outline of Cities and Urban Land Use

AP® Human Geography Outline of Industrialization and Economic Development

Unit 6: Cities and Urban Land-Use Patterns and Processes

Topic	APHG Topic No. Title	Suggested Skills	Enduring Understandings	Learning Objective	Big Ideas
13.1.1	6.9: Urban Data	3.E: Explain what maps or data imply or illustrate about geographic principles, processes, and outcomes.	MP-6: The attitudes and values of a population, as well as the balance of power within that population, are reflected in the built landscape.	IMP-6.E: Explain how qualitative and quantitative data are used to show the causes and effects of geographic change within urban areas.	BI-2: Impacts and Interactions
13.1.2; 13.1.3	6.7: Infrastructure	3.C: Explain patterns and trends in maps and in quantitative and geospatial data to draw conclusions.	IMP-6: The attitudes and values of a population, as well as the balance of power within that population, are reflected in the built landscape.	IMP-6.B: Explain how a city's infrastructure relates to local politics, society, and the environment.	BI-2: Impacts and Interactions
13.2.1; 13.2.2; 13.2.3; 13.2.4; 13.2.5; 13.2.6	6.5: The Internal Structure of Cities	1.E: Explain the strengths, weaknesses, and limitations of different geographic models and theories in a specified context.	PSO-6: The presence and growth of cities vary across geographical locations because of physical geography and resources.	PSO-6.D: Explain the internal structure of cities using various models and theories.	BI-1: Patterns and Spatial Organization
13.3.1; 13.2.2	6.6: Density and Land Use	3.D: Compare patterns and trends in maps and in quantitative and geospatial data to draw conclusions.	IMP-6: The attitudes and values of a population, as well as the balance of power within that population, are reflected in the built landscape.	IMP-6.A: Explain how low-, medium-, and high-density housing characteristics represent different patterns of residential land use.	BI-2: Impacts and Interactions

13.3.3	6.10: Challenges of Urban Changes	4.E: Explain how maps, images, and landscapes illustrate or relate to geographic principles, processes, and outcomes.	SPS-6: Urban areas face unique economic, political, cultural, and environmental challenges.	SPS-6.A: Explain causes and effects of geographic change within urban areas.	BI-3: Spatial Processes and Societal Change
13.3.4; 13.3.5; 13.4.1; 13.4.4	6.11: Challenges of Urban Sustainability	2.D: Explain the significance of geographic similarities and differences among different locations and/or at different times.	SPS-6: Urban areas face unique economic, political, cultural, and environmental challenges.	SPS-6.B: Describe the effectiveness of different attempts to address urban sustainability challenges.	BI-3: Spatial Processes and Societal Change
13.4.2; 13.4.3	6.10: Challenges of Urban Changes	4.E: Explain how maps, images, and landscapes illustrate or relate to geographic principles, processes, and outcomes.	SPS-6: Urban areas face unique economic, political, cultural, and environmental challenges.	SPS-6.A: Explain causes and effects of geographic change within urban areas.	BI-3: Spatial Processes and Societal Change

Source: College Board AP Human Geography Course Description, effective Fall 2019

FRQ's From College Board

2001 FRQ #2
2002 FRQ #3
2003 FRQ #1
2004 FRQ #3
2005 FRQ #3
2009 FRQ #2
2011 FRQ #1
2013 FRQ #3
2017 FRQ #1
2018 FRQ #2
2019 FRQ #1 set 1
2019 FRQ #2 set 2

AP Human Geography Practice Test 1

Multiple-Choice Section: You have 60 minutes to answer these questions.

Directions: *Choose the one alternative that best completes the statement or answers the question.*

1. Situation identifies a place by its:
A. absolute location.
B. mathematical location on Earth's surface.
C. location relative to other places.
D. unique physical characteristics.
E. nominal location.

2. The concept that the distribution of one phenomenon is related to the location of another phenomena is:
A. regional analysis.
B. spatial analysis.
C. spatial association.
D. spatial distribution.
E. relative location.

3. What is an important feature with significant future implication of the world's population?
A. It is increasing more slowly than in the past.
B. There are more people alive in the world now than at any time in the past.
C. Death rates are significantly higher than in the past.
D. People are uniformly distributed across Earth.
E. The most rapid growth is occurring in the developing world.

4. Physiological density is the number of:
A. acres of farmland.
B. farmers per area of farmland.
C. people per area of land.
D. people per area suitable for agriculture.
E. people living in a given nation-state.

5. India and the United Kingdom have approximately the same arithmetic density. From this, we can conclude that the two countries have the same:
A. level of output per farmer.
B. number of people per area of land suitable for agriculture.
C. pressure placed by people on the land to produce food.
D. number of people per area of land.
E. all of the above.

6. The medical revolution has been characterized by:
A. the invention of new medical technologies.
B. diffusion of medical practices.
C. the elimination of traditional causes of death in developing countries.
D. longer life expectancies in the developing world.
E. all of the above.

7. Countries with the lowest natural increase are in which stage of the demographic transition?
A. Stage 1
B. Stage 2
C. Stage 3
D. Stage 4
E. Stages 1 and 2

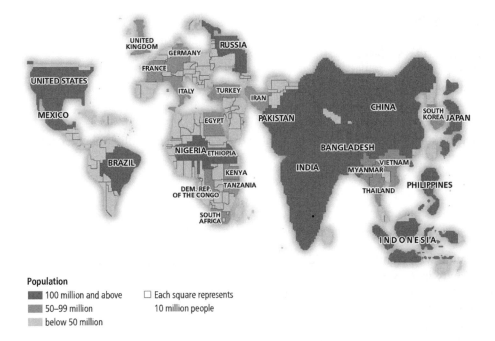

Population
■ 100 million and above
■ 50–99 million
☐ below 50 million

☐ Each square represents
10 million people

8. The accompanying map, which displays countries according to population size rather than land area, is a:
A. cartogram map.
B. isopop map.
C. choropleth map.
D. political map.
E. isosize map.

9. Thomas Malthus concluded that:
A. population increased geometrically while food production increased arithmetically.
B. the world's rate of population increase was lower than the available food supplies.
C. moral restraint was producing lower crude birth rates.
D. population growth was outpacing available resources in every country.
E. technology would increase food production and support the rising population.

10. Which push factor explains why most people migrate?
A. Economic opportunities
B. Environmental degradation
C. Political extremism
D. Religious discrimination
E. Social isolation

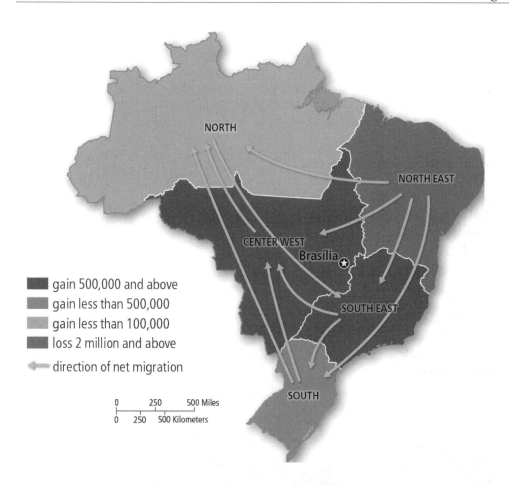

gain 500,000 and above
gain less than 500,000
gain less than 100,000
loss 2 million and above
direction of net migration

11. The accompanying map shows which type of migration?
A. Intraurban
B. International
C. Interregional
D. Intraregional
E. Interurban

12. Many Asians are currently migrating to the United States through the process of :
A. political asylum.
B. brain drain.
C. chain migration.
D. illegal immigration.
E. brain drain followed by chain migration.

13. Counterurbanization is:
A. the move from the urban core to suburban areas.
B. largely international migration.
C. increased migration to rural areas and small towns.
D. the trend of the elderly retiring to rural locations.
E. mostly intraurban.

14. Folk cultures are spread primarily by:
A. contagious diffusion.
B. remote diffusion.
C. relocation diffusion.
D. stimulus diffusion.
E. hierarchical diffusion.

15. The current distribution of soccer demonstrates that :
A. a folk custom can become part of a popular culture.
B. all sports are examples of folk culture.
C. television has infused all sports into popular culture.
D. American football is also an example of a folk culture.
E. most popular cultures began as obscure folk cultures.

16. One significant impact of popular culture is to :
A. create a more varied and less uniform landscape.
B. prevent the diffusion of folk culture.
C. limit access to electronic media.
D. modify the physical environment.
E. create a homogeneous landscape.

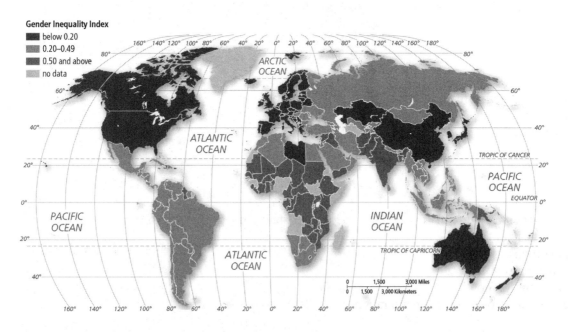

17. Which of the following is shown by the accompanying Gender Inequality (GII) Index map?
A. There is least inequality in Europe.
B. There is most inequality in Asia.
C. There is least inequality in Latin America.
D. The highest GII numbers are in sub-Saharan Africa.
E. Both A and D are true.

18. Critics and defenders of sustainable development both agree that:
A. definitions of resources change drastically and unpredictably over time.
B. the world has only 11.4 billion hectares of biologically productive land.
C. less international cooperation is needed to reduce the gap between developed and developing countries.
D. more international cooperation is needed to reduce the gap between developed and developing countries.
E. the world will reach a population ceiling before the end of the next century.

19. A group of languages that share a common ancestor before recorded history is a :
A. dialect.
B. language branch.
C. language tree.
D. language group.
E. language family.

20. A creole language is:
A. extinct.
B. endangered.
C. an isolated language family.
D. a possible prehistoric super family.
E. a mix of indigenous and colonial languages.

21. What is the relationship between culture, religion, and the physical environment?
A. Some religions derive meaningful events from the physical environment.
B. Religious ideas may be responsible for some of the changes people make in the physical environment.
C. Religion is still an important source of identification for some distinct cultural groups.
D. The origin of most religions is associated with specific places.
E. All of the above are true.

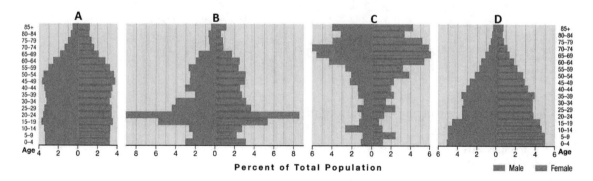

22. Which of the following is a true statement about the population pyramids shown here?
A. The highest dependency populations are in C and D.
B. A and C has the largest percentage of elderly population.
C. Pyramid B reflects the population of a country with guest workers.
D. Pyramid D is the most developed of all of the places.
E. Pyramid C is reflective of anti-natalist policies.

23. The world's largest universalizing religion is:
A. Buddhism.
B. Christianity.
C. Judaism.
D. Islam.
E. Hinduism.

24. The world's largest ethnic religion is :
A. Judaism.
B. Daoism.
C. Hinduism.
D. Shintoism.
E. Confucianism.

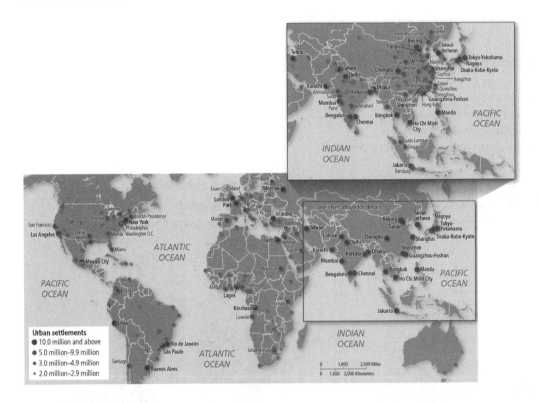

25. According to the accompanying map, most of the world's largest urban settlements are in:
A. the Southern Hemisphere.
B. East Asia, especially China and Japan.
C. North America.
D. Western Europe.
E. South Asia, especially India.

26. Iceland is the best example of a nation-state because:
A. nearly all Icelanders speak Icelandic and live in Iceland.
B. Iceland is part of the European Union.
C. it is a pure democracy.
D. it is located far enough away to avoid conquest by other peoples.
E. all of the above.

27. Balkanization refers to:
A. the creation of nation-states in southeastern Europe.
B. a small state inhabited by many ethnic groups.
C. a small geographic area that cannot successfully be organized into states.
D. the breakdown of a state due to conflicts among nationalities.
E. ethnic cleansing.

28. What is the principal strategy to reduce solid waste pollution?
A. Increase combustion of waste.
B. Dump it in the ocean.
C. Reduce, reuse, recycle.
D. Bury it in underground caves.
E. Expel it out to space.

ETHNICITIES IN WESTERN ASIA

29. Which of the following can be supported from the accompanying map?
A. Armenia is primarily a homogeneous state.
B. Syria is a Shi'ite Arab state.
C. Most Kurds in western Asia live in northern Iran.
D. Turkey is primarily a homogenous state.
E. Enclaves of Armenians are in Iran.

30. The process when a group forcibly removes another group is called:
A. war.
B. apartheid.
C. racism.
D. ethnic cleansing.
E. genocide.

31. One example of a multinational state is ?
A. United Kingdom.
B. Greenland.
C. Austria.
D. Iceland.
E. Republic of Korea.

32. An area organized into an independent political unit is a:
A. colony.
B. sphere of influence.
C. state.
D. protectorate.
E. satellite.

33. The United Nations Law of the Seas (UNCLOS), recognizes ocean boundaries by:
A. designating all oceans as the "high seas" with no state control allowed.
B. giving some countries exclusive control of international waters.
C. standardizing the territorial limits for most countries at 200 nautical miles.
D. standardizing the territorial limits for most countries at 12 nautical miles.
E. allowing landlocked countries to claim rights to some international waters.

34. The gerrymandered map of Congressional District No. 3 in Maryland illustrates:
A. the redrawing of political boundaries to provide more electoral equality.
B. the redrawing of legislative boundaries in most European countries.
C. methods of creating electoral districts that are still legal in the United States.
D. the redrawing of political boundaries by a bipartisan commission.
E. the redrawing of legislative boundaries to benefit the party in power.

35. A fragmented state presents a challenge to political control because:
A. the distribution of goods and services are disrupted.
B. parts of the population is located inside of other states.
C. the peninsular extension is influenced by neighboring states and populations.
D. it is difficult to effectively manage the islands from a central location.
E. the state does not cross enough lines of latitude to have a diverse agricultural supply.

36. The Human Development Index:
A. measures the level of development of a country.
B. considers development to be a function of a decent standard of living.
C. considers development to be a function of a long and healthy life.
D. considers development to be a function of access to education.
E. all of the above.

37. An example of a primary sector activity is:
A. education.
B. manufacturing.
C. mining.
D. retailing.
E. the processing of raw materials.

38. Which is NOT a characteristic of less developed countries?
A. Higher crude birth rates
B. Low infant mortalities
C. Higher percentage of children under age 15
D. Lower percentage of elderly
E. Lower life expectancy

39. According to Rostow's development model, the process of development begins when:
A. a high percentage of national wealth is allocated to nonproductive activities.
B. an elite group initiates innovative activities.
C. take-off industries achieve technical advances.
D. workers become more skilled and specialized.
E. the economy shifts from production of heavy industry to consumer goods.

40. In contrast to the international trade approach, the self-sufficiency approach to development:
A. begins when an elite group initiates innovative activities.
B. results in uneven resource development.
C. suffers from market stagnation.
D. spreads investment through all sectors of the economy.
E. calls for a country to identify its unique economic assets.

41. Which of the following is not a renewable alternative energy?
A. Hydroelectric power
B. Solar energy
C. Geothermal energy
D. Nuclear power
E. Wind power

42. The main features that distinguish commercial agriculture from subsistence agriculture include all of the following except:
A. whether the product is consumed on or off the farm.
B. whether crops are grown, or animals are raised.
C. the percentage of farmers in the labor force.
D. the use of machinery.
E. farm size.

43. The form of subsistence agriculture that feeds the largest number of people in the developing world is:
A. intensive subsistence.
B. shifting cultivation.
C. pastoral nomadism.
D. dairy farming.
E. plantation farming.

44. Pastoral nomadism is most commonly found in which climate region?
A. Humid low-latitude
B. Dry/arid regions
C. Warm mid-latitude
D. Cold mid-latitude
E. Marine west coast

45. According to von Thünen's model, a commercial farmer is most concerned with which of these costs?
A. Cost of the land
B. Cost of transporting output to market
C. Value of yield per hectare
D. All of the above
E. A and B only

46. Unlike most other types of agriculture, plantation agriculture is:
A. part of agribusiness.
B. a form of subsistence agriculture found in developed countries.
C. a form of commercial agriculture found in developing countries.
D. practiced in much of the world's high-latitude climates.
E. usually situated in densely settled locations.

47. Compared to the United States, people with socioeconomic problems in European cities are more likely to be:
A. clustered in inner-city neighborhoods.
B. dispersed throughout the city.
C. clustered in remote suburbs.
D. distributed uniformly throughout the urban area.
E. concentrated in central locations.

48. Copper production is a bulk-reducing industry because:
A. the mills are near the mines.
B. the final product has a much higher value per weight.
C. refineries import most material from other countries.
D. copper ore is low-grade.
E. it involves several steps.

49. Maquiladoras:
A. are factories in Mexico near the U.S. border.
B. have become more important since the North American Free Trade Agreement eliminated international trade barriers in the region.
C. take advantage of much lower labor costs in Mexico.
D. are factories built by U.S. companies.
E. all of the above are true.

50. A company that uses more than one mode of transport will often locate near:
A. break-of-bulk points.
B. consumers.
C. raw material.
D. major urban areas.
E. their sources of inputs.

Toxic waste chemical
release (pounds)
● 100 million and above
● 10–99 million
○ 2–10 million

51. The accompanying map of toxic chemical release sites shows:
A. that most sites are located in the western United States.
B. that toxic waste in the United States is a much bigger problem today than it was 20 years ago.
C. that most sites are located in Georgia.
D. that the largest sites are in the western United States.
E. that the largest sites are mines in Ohio.

52. The Central Business District attracts services primarily because of its:
A. geographical size compared to the rest of the urban land area.
B. high land costs.
C. more intensive land use.
D. construction of skyscrapers.
E. accessibility.

53. According to the sector model, the best housing is located in:
A. sectors throughout the urban area.
B. an outer ring surrounding the city.
C. nodes near universities and parks.
D. renovated inner-city neighborhoods.
E. a corridor from downtown to the edge of the city.

54. Rural settlements differ from urban settlements primarily according to which type of activity?
A. Cultural
B. Economic
C. Political
D. Religious
E. Social

55. Historically, linear rural settlements were developed primarily because of:
A. collective land ownership.
B. the need for common grazing land.
C. inheritance laws.
D. the need for access to a river or other means of communication.
E. the need for defense.

56. The most significant anticipated benefit of the enclosure movement in Great Britain was to:
A. destroy traditional village life.
B. provide labor for the factory system.
C. replace abandoned villages with new farmsteads.
D. stimulate urbanization.
E. promote agricultural efficiency.

57. In the United States, which of the following definitions of a city covers the largest land area?
A. Central business district
B. Central city
C. Suburban area
D. Metropolitan statistical area
E. Urban cluster

58. The maximum distance people are willing to travel for a service is the:
A. hinterland.
B. range.
C. threshold.
D. market area.
E. friction of distance.

59. According to the gravity model, the potential use of a service at a location is related:
A. directly to population and inversely to distance.
B. directly to distance and inversely to population.
C. directly to both population and distance.
D. inversely to both distance and population.
E. to none of the above.

60. If a country's largest city has 1,000,000 inhabitants and the second largest city has 200,000 inhabitants, the country follows what distribution?
A. Central place theory
B. Economic base
C. The primate city rule
D. The rank-size rule
E. The gravity model

End of the multiple-choice section of the practice test.

Free Response Questions

Directions: *Answer each of the three free response questions in 75 minutes or less.*

1. Density is defined as the frequency with which something exists within a given unit of area. Population density is the number of humans living within an area.
    A. Define arithmetic density
    B. Define agricultural density.
    C. Define physiological density
    D. Explain how agricultural density is related to development.
    E. Explain how carrying capacity is related to measurements of density
    F. Compare the pattern of physiological density in more developed and less developed countries.

2. A state is an area organized into a political unit and ruled by an established government that has control over its internal and foreign affairs. Some national governments are better able than others to provide the leadership needed to promote peace and prosperity. In contrast, a corrupt repressive government embroiled in wars is less able to respond effectively to economic challenges.

Types of Regimes

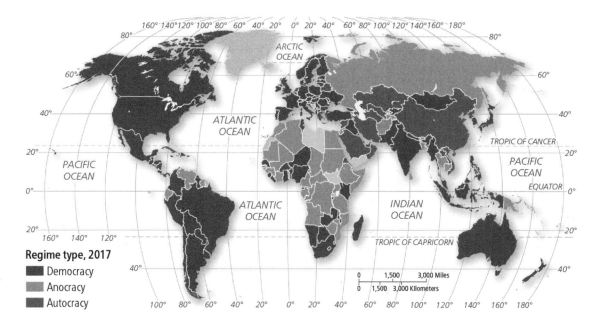

Regime type, 2017
■ Democracy
■ Anocracy
■ Autocracy

A. Define an Autocratic government
B. Define an Anocratic government
C. Define a Democratic government
D. Identify which region of the world has the most autocratic regimes.
E. Explain why the region identified has the most autocratic regimes.
F. Explain how devolution factors lead to a failed state.

3.

Figure W   **Figure X**   **Figure Y**

A. Identify the urban land use model in figure W
B. Identify the urban land use model in figure X
C. Identify the urban land use model in figure Y
D. Compare two differences between the models.
E. Explain how Latin American cities differ in their historical design from the concentric zone model.

AP Human Geography Practice Test 2

Multiple-Choice Section: You have 60 minutes to answer these questions.

Directions: *Choose the one alternative that best completes the statement or answers the question.*

1. A map is:
A. a scale model of the real world.
B. a very accurate model of the real world.
C. an artistic fabrication of the real world.
D. a method of scientific inquiry used to explain the real world.
E. an ancient explanation of the cosmos.

2. Which of these is an disadvantage of a Mercator projection map?
A. The shape is distorted very little.
B. Landmasses at the poles are very accurate.
C. It is very useful to display information across the oceans.
D. The eastern and western hemispheres are separated.
E. It was developed using GIS technology.

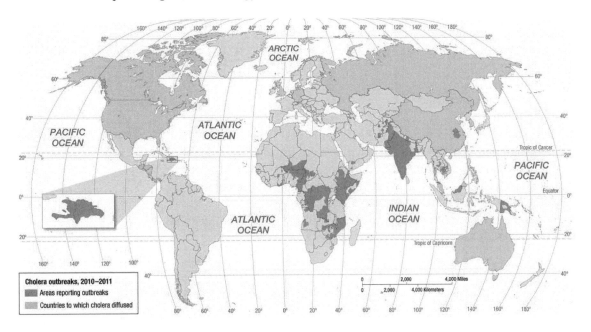

3. Which of the following statements is supported by the accompanying map?
A. Countries reporting cholera in recent years are found primarily in sub-Saharan Africa.
B. Some countries, especially in the developed world, have reported imported cholera cases.
C. Cholera is not a major health concern in South America.
D. Countries reporting cholera in recent years are found primarily in South Asia.
E. All of the preceding statements are supported by the map.

4. The most common measure of population change in a country is determined by looking at:
A. crude birth rate, crude death rate, and total fertility rate.
B. crude birth rate, total fertility rate, and life expectancy.
C. crude birth rate, crude death rate, and natural increase rate.
D. natural increase rate, life expectancy, and infant mortality rate.
E. life expectancy, infant mortality rate, and total fertility rate.

5. The dependency ratio shows demographers:
A. the number of males per hundred females in the total population.
B. the number of people too young or too old to work.
C. the number of babies born per 1,000 people.
D. the number of children over 15 years old.
E. the number of women between the ages of 15–49.

6. According to Wilbur Zelinsky's migration transition, in which stage on the demographic transition model is international migration and internal migration likely to occur?
A. Stage 4 for international and stage 2 for internal migration
B. Stage 2 for international and stage 3 for internal migration
C. Stage 3 for international and stage 2 for internal migration
D. Stage 2 for international and stage 1 for internal migration
E. No correlation exists between migration and the demographic transition model.

7. An intervening obstacle to migration would be:
A. U.S. quota laws.
B. family reunification.
C. brain drain.
D. transportation improvements.
E. chain migration.

8. Why are geographers particularly interested in studying the differences in dialects?
A. They reflect distinctive features of the environments in which groups live.
B. They are a reflection of the influence of globalization on folk cultures.
C. They show how folk cultures affect popular culture.
D. They predict what type of products can successfully be marketed in an area.
E. They are generally confined to English.

9. In which U.S. state would you find the greatest clustering of Asian Americans?
A. Hawaii
B. Mississippi
C. Texas
D. Maryland
E. Alabama

10. Of the following, the best example of an ethnic group divided among many countries are the:
A. croats.
B. serbs.
C. kurds.
D. turks.
E. druze.

11. The earliest sovereign states that comprised a town, together with the surrounding countryside, were known as:
A. nation-states.
B. nations.
C. countries.
D. colonies.
E. city-states.

12. Which of these states has a unitary system of government?
A. France
B. Russia
C. The United States
D. Brazil
E. India

13. The Human Development Index (HDI) includes which of the following factors in order to determine a country's level of development?
A. GDP, literacy rate, total fertility rate, educational level
B. GDP, life expectancy, total fertility rate, literacy rate
C. GDP, life expectancy, literacy rate, educational level
D. GDP, literacy rate, educational level, net emigration
E. GDP, life expectancy, educational level, net emigration

14. In what region of the world is the HDI significantly lower because females do not have access to educational opportunities?
A. Central Asia
B. Southwest Asia
C. Latin America
D. Southeast Asia
E. Oceania

15. Shifting cultivation takes place mainly:
A. in the tropics.
B. in the high latitudes.
C. in arid regions.
D. in rugged mountains.
E. in the temperate zone.

16. The accompanying map shows forced migration after World War II. Which of the following statements is true about these migrations?
A. The largest migration streams were from eastern to western Europe.
B. There were important migration streams from northern to southern Europe.
C. Most of this migration was mandated by the United Nations.
D. Many people moved to Scandinavia.
E. Large numbers of people left the Balkans after World War II.

17. One of the main characteristics of mixed crop and livestock farming is:
A. the effort to grow crops is not uniform throughout the year.
B. most crops grown are for human consumption.
C. it is generally referred to as truck farming.
D. crops are fed to animals rather than consumed by humans.
E. the farm must be closer to the market because the products are highly perishable.

18. Some commercial farms are converting to sustainable agriculture, which is distinguished by:
A. sensitive land management.
B. better integration of crops and livestock.
C. limited chemicals.
D. ridge tillage.
E. all of the above.

19. The process of limiting suburbs and preserving agricultural land is known as:
A. redlining.
B. smart growth.
C. suburbanization.
D. gentrification.
E. sprawl.

20. The type(s) of distortion that can occur on a map of the world is/are:
A. shapes appear more elongated than they really are.
B. distance between two points may become more increased or decreased.
C. the relative size of areas might be altered.
D. direction from one place to another can be distorted.
E. all of the above.

21. The four ways geographers use to identify a location on Earth are:
A. place name, site, situation, and grid coordinates.
B. toponym, relative location, grid coordinates, and place names.
C. relative location, site, situation, and grid coordinates.
D. grid coordinates, postal address, site, and situation.
E. postal address, grid coordinates, place name, and site.

22. The cultural traits most often looked at in identifying a culture's location and global distribution are:
A. language, religion, and ethnicity.
B. language, religion, and GNP.
C. language, ethnicity, and literacy rate.
D. language, ethnicity, and GNP.
E. religion, ethnicity, and literacy rate.

23. Which demographic measure most affects the doubling time of a country?
A. Natural increase rate
B. Total fertility rate
C. Infant mortality rate
D. Literacy rate
E. Life expectancy

24. Identity with a group who share the cultural traditions of a particular hearth is:
A. race.
B. ethnicity.
C. nationality.
D. multinationalism.
E. self-determination.

25. Which country shape could potentially suffer the most from isolation?
A. Compact
B. Prompted
C. Fragmented
D. Elongated
E. Perforated

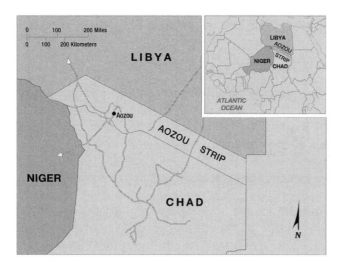

26. The boundary between Chad and Libya, shown on the accompanying map, is an example of a:
A. physical boundary.
B. cultural boundary.
C. ethnic boundary.
D. geometric boundary.
E. language boundary.

27. The process of redrawing legislative boundaries is:
A. blockbusting.
B. redlining.
C. segregation.
D. desegregation.
E. gerrymandering.

28. According to the Human Development Index (HDI), the lowest-ranking countries in the world would be found in which region?
A. Central Asia
B. Sub-Saharan Africa
C. South Asia
D. Latin America
E. Southeast Asia

29. A characteristic of commercial gardening and fruit farming is:
A. the effort to grow crops is not uniform throughout the year.
B. most crops grown are for human consumption.
C. it is generally referred to as truck farming.
D. crops are fed to animals rather than consumed by humans.
E. the farm must be closer to the market because the products are highly perishable.

30. The earliest crops were first domesticated in which agricultural hearth?
A. Southwest Asia
B. East Asia
C. Sub-Saharan Africa
D. Latin America
E. All of the above

31. When geographers look at urban settlements, they often refer to a functional area with a county containing a city, where a large percentage of workers are employed as a:
A. city.
B. county seat.
C. micropolitan area.
D. metropolitan statistical area.
E. census tract.

32. According to the peripheral model, an inner city, and the surrounding suburbs are tied together by:
A. a ring road.
B. interstate highways.
C. a system of walking paths.
D. major rail links.
E. a bus route.

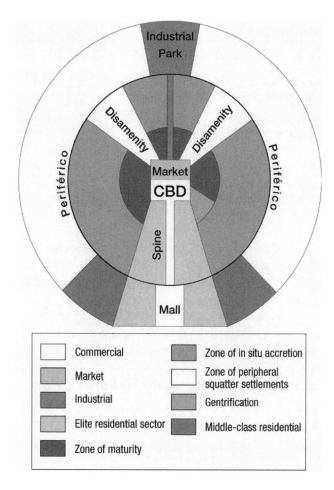

33. Why is the model of a Latin American city shown here different from models of American cities?
A. It doesn't have a central business district.
B. It shows that different types of people live in distinctive parts of the city.
C. It is a simplification of urban reality.
D. Poorer people live on the outskirts of the urban area while the spine area includes the affluent
E. It has a gentrification zone.

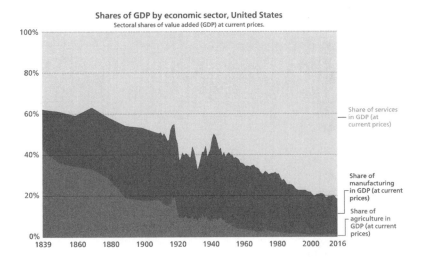

Several highly developed countries have deindustrialized and are transitioning to a postindustrial economy. **Referring to the map above answer questions #34 to #36.**

34. Which economic sector becomes dominant when a country deindustrializes and restructures from an industrial to a postindustrial economy?
A. Primary sector of mining and agriculture
B. Secondary sector of manufacturing
C. Tertiary sector of services
D. Quaternary sector of information technology, media, and research and development
E. Quinary sector of leading government and business decision-making operations

35. Which statement about the share of the GDP from the economic sectors in the United States is correct?
A. In 2016, the share of the GDP from agriculture was 1 percent, and the service sector had 82 percent.
B. The war years between 1917 and 1950 did not affect the manufacturing sector.
C. There is no longer an agricultural sector in the United States.
D. The manufacturing sector has been expanding since 1980.
E. All of these are correct.

36. Which conclusion is supported by the trends in the graph?
A. International migration is drawn to the United State to work in research and development.
B. Rural to urban migration follows with the decline in the agricultural sector.
C. Urban areas have shifted from manufacturing to service industries.
D. The service sector is very valuable to the continued development of the United States.
E. All of these are correct statements.

37. How have transnational companies in postindustrial economies optimized costs?
A. They use recycled and repurposed components in the production process.
B. They have supported the use of tariffs to cause the consumer to support the increase in costs.
C. They have allocated production to low-wage countries through outsourcing.
D. They use a relocation plan that allows for just-in-time delivery.
E. They sponsor low-wage, unskilled workers for needed worker visas that bind the worker to the company or face deportation back to their home country.

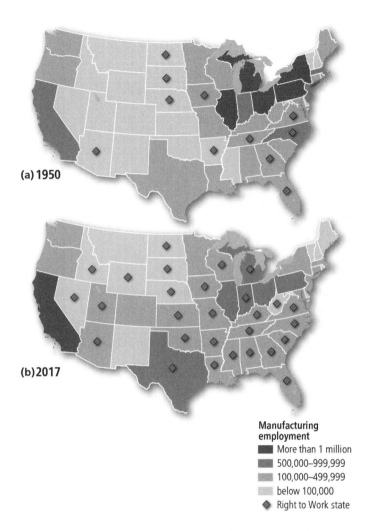

(a) 1950

(b) 2017

Manufacturing employment
- More than 1 million
- 500,000–999,999
- 100,000–499,999
- below 100,000
- ◆ Right to Work state

Using the map of Changing Distribution of U.S. Industry answer #38.

38. How has industrial manufacturing changed since 1950?
A. The Midwest region does not have manufacturing industries.
B. Right to work states do not have the growth in manufacturing that closed shop states do.
C. Industry has declined in the Northeast and increased in the South and West.
D. A shift in industrial production from the Southeast to the Great Lakes region has occurred since 1950.
E. More than 1 million people work in industrial manufacturing in Texas.

39. What is one way in which the roles of women in the paid labor force of developed countries change as a result of the transition to a postindustrial economy?
A. Women hold jobs in agriculture to support the family.
B. In developed countries, more then 50 percent of women work full-time jobs outside the home.
C. Manufacturing and skilled labor jobs decline as more women enter the workforce.
D. Sub-Saharan Africa has above 60 percent of women working outside of the home.
E. High maternal mortality rates discourage women from working outside of the home in less-developed countries.

40. Which of the following is an example of point-source pollution?
A. Fertilizer and pesticide runoff from agricultural fields along the Mississippi River
B. Wastewater treatment pipes running into discharge channels
C. Acid rain carried over forested areas
D. Dead zones in water systems from algal blooms
E. Contamination of the Aral Sea

41. What is a brownfield?
A. Remnants of a colonial past
B. Commons areas used in central areas of a city or town
C. Fields that have turned brown for overuse of fertilizers and pesticides
D. Former industrial sites that are typically abandoned
E. Neglected urban garden projects

42. Where do the largest number of international migrants reside?
A. Saudi Arabia
B. Germany
C. Turkey
D. United States
E. Australia

43. The galactic city model:
A. is a modification of the multiple nuclei model.
B. results from large urban areas in-filling toward each other.
C. reflects the growth of suburbs with nodes of consumer and business services around the edges.
D. is a modification of the sector model.
E. A and C are both true.

44. A food desert exists if:
A. the distance to the nearest grocery store is greater than 1 mile in an urban area.
B. the preferred type of food can only be grown in sand.
C. there are no fruits and vegetables available.
D. grocery stores will only accept cash for food products.
E. the number of people in an area exceed the amount of food supplies carried in the local grocery stores.

45. Why do food deserts exist in urban areas within developed countries?
A. Urban areas have large areas of low-income populations without car transportation.
B. Grocery businesses must carry a large inventory and sell most of it quickly to make money.
C. With the growth of suburban communities, grocery stores moved out to the suburbs, abandoning the people left in the city.
D. Grocery stores are not able to sell enough fresh foods, resulting in providing more processed prepackaged foods.
E. Grocery stores cannot afford to remain in business due to high crime rates in the urban areas.

46. A metacity has 20 million people. Which of the 11 metacities are in a developed country?
A. Los Angeles, Chicago, New York
B. London, Paris, Rome
C. New Delhi, Jakarta, Cairo
D. Tokyo, Seoul, New York
E. Osaka, Nagoya, Guangzhou

47. Four of the fastestgrowing urban settlements are in developed countries and three are in the United States. Which three U.S. cities are among the fastest-growing urban settlements in the world?
A. Beihai, China; Ghaziabad, India; Sana'a, Yemen
B. Las Vegas, Nevada; Austin, Texas; Atlanta, Georgia
C. Phoenix, Arizona; El Paso, Texas; Kansas City, Kansas
D. Hong Kong; Ho Chi Minh City, Bangkok
E. New Orleans, Louisiana; St. Louis, Missouri; Seattle, Washington

48. An urbanized area with a population of at least 50,000 encompasses the county within which the city is located and the adjacent counties with a high population density and a large percentage of residents working in the central city's county is the definition of:
A. a micropolitan statistical area.
B. a metropolitan statistical area.
C. a combined statistical area.
D. a megalopolis.
E. an urban area.

49. Which of the following countries has the lowest Gender Inequality Index rating?
A. Iceland
B. Mongolia
C. Jordan
D. Mexico
E. South Africa

50. Which of the following is the largest and most populated "non-self-governing territory"?
A. Hong Kong
B. Western Sahara
C. Puerto Rico
D. Greenland
E. French Polynesia

51. Using any map projection, there will always be some distortion because:
A. a map has to depict the curved surface of the three-dimensional earth on a two-dimensional sheet of paper
B. equivalent projections must be distinguished from conformal ones
C. some spatial phenomena are not tangible or visible
D. the map scale is changed
E. cartographers use different techniques to depict the Earth's surface

52. The single greatest health disparity between developed and developing nations is the:
A. birth rate
B. death rate
C. infant mortality rate
D. maternal mortality rate
E. gender equity

53. Globally, life expectancy increases and alterations to birth and death rates can be attributed to:
A. population growth
B. political policies regarding birth rates
C. modern medicine and improved sanitation
D. religious differences
E. laws granting women's rights

54. The present-day spatial distribution of Buddhism is best described as:
A. China, Tibet, Siberia, Korea
B. Central Asia, China, Southeast Asia
C. Southeast Asia, Tibet, China, Mongolia, Japan
D. Tibet, India, Middle East, Japan
E. France, England, Italy, United States

55. The pattern of international commodity flows in primary commodities is from:
A. produced or extracted in less developed countries and sent to markets in less developed countries
B. b. resources are extracted where they can be, manufactured where transportation costs are lower and sent to markets in need of the products.
C. produced or extracted in more developed countries and sent to markets in less developed countries
D. produced or extracted in more developed countries and sent to markets in more developed countries
E. resources are extracted where they can be, manufactured where low labor costs exist and sent to markets in more developed countries.

PREDOMINANT CHURCH AFFILIATION BY COUNTY, 2000

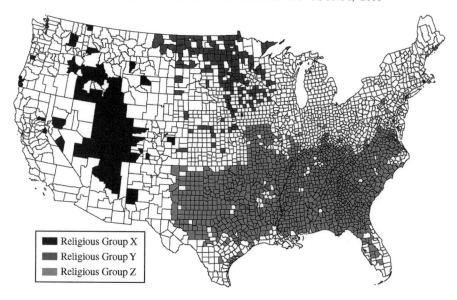

Religious Group X
Religious Group Y
Religious Group Z

Use the map above to answer questions #56 to #58.

56. Religious group X are:
A. Southern Baptist
B. Catholic
C. Church of Jesus Christ of Latter-Day Saints
D. Amish
E. Episcopalian

57. Religious group Y are the:
A. Lutheran
B. Catholic
C. Church of Jesus Christ of Latter-Day Saints
D. Amish
E. Episcopalian

58. Religious group Z are the:
A. Southern Baptist
B. Catholic
C. Methodist
D. Amish
E. Episcopalian

59. What accounts for the large distribution of Episcopalian/Anglican adherents in the upper New England region?
A. History of slavery united the people in a common area and faith.
B. Migration of the original population to areas outside of US government control so they could practice their faith.
C. Area of original settlement of English colonists who brought the faith with them.
D. Isolation and discrimination forced their concentration into the region.
E. Early laws in the Thirteen Colonies forced these observers into the region.

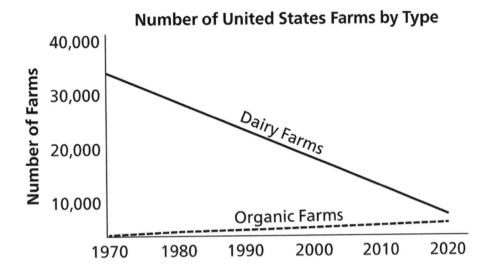

Number of United States Farms by Type

60. What has contributed to the decline of dairy farms since 1970?
A. Extensive & consolidation into large scale dairy farming in order to produce a higher yield and increase revenue
B. Growing number of lactose intolerant immigrants
C. The USDA, FDA, and public peoples have revealed that dairy products are the #1 cause of life-threatening diseases
D. cows are performing better with increased production on organic farms
E. public awareness of the impact on greenhouse gases from the amount of food and water used in raising the cows.

End of the multiple-choice portion of the practice test.

Free-Response Questions

Directions: *Answer each of the three free-response questions in 75 minutes or less.*

1. Use the following table to respond to the following free-response question.

Stage	Demographic Transition	Migration Transition
1	Low NIR, high CBR, high CDR	High daily or seasonal mobility in search of food
2	High NIR, high CBR, rapidly declining CDR	High international emigration and interregional migration from rural to urban areas
3	Declining NIR, rapidly declining CBR, declining CDR	High international immigration and intraregional migration from cities to suburbs
4	Low NIR, low CBR, low CDR	Same as stage 3

A. Describe the economic sectors of development in countries at stage 2 of the Demographic Transition
B. Describe the economic sectors of development in countries at stage 4 of the Demographic Transition
C. Identify a country that meets the criteria for stage 2,3 and 4;
D. Using one of the countries selected, explain the social political and economic conditions that place the country in the stage identified.
E. Compare stage 3 of the Demographic Transition model with Rostow's stages of development and Ravenstein's theories on migration.

2. According to the UN Sustainable Development Goals, one in five people lack access to electricity however, fossil fuels used to generate electricity are the principal contributor to climate change.
A. Describe how production and accumulation of greenhouse gases has led to climate change
B. Explain how climate change impacts agricultural crop production.
C. Explain how development leads to production of greenhouse gases.
D. Identify 2 alternative energy sources that do not require fossil fuels to produce electricity.
E. Explain how the access to electricity can lead to an improvement in social development.
F. Explain how the access to electricity can lead to an improvement in economic development.
G. Describe how climate change can cause forced migration of a population.

3. Ecotourism is tourism based in natural environments that frequently helps to protect the environment in question while also working with the local population
A. Define ecotourism
B. Explain the difference between ecotourism and tourism.
C. Describe a strategy for development based on ecotourism
D. Explain a strategy for environmental preservation through ecotourism.
E. Describe two ways ecotourism places stress on the environment.
F. Explain how ecotourism can support the UN Sustainable Development Goals

END OF PRACTICE EXAM

Answer Key to AP Human Geography Practice Test 1

Multiple Choice Answers Explained

1. **C.** The other choices deal with absolute location and site.

2. **C.** Spatial association identifies cultural, economic, and environmental factors that display similar distributions.

3. **E.** More than 95 percent of the natural increase is clustered in developing countries. This has significant future implications.

4. **D.** Physiological density is the number of people per area suitable for agriculture.

5. **D.** Arithmetic density is total number of objects in an area, so it tells us nothing more than the number of people per area of land.

6. **E.** All of these statements are true.

7. **D.** By the time countries reach stage 4 they have very low rates of natural increase. For example, this is true of western European countries today.

8. **A.** See Figure 2-5 on page 51. This is a population cartogram, which displays countries by size of population rather than land area.

9. **A.** The statement in A is premises of Malthus's prediction regarding future world population.

10. **A.** Economic opportunities and the ability to provide for one's family is the primary motivation for migration.

11. **C.** See Figure 3-18 on page 90. This map shows migration from one region to another in Brazil. This is interregional migration.

12. **E.** An increasing trend with migration from Asia to the United States is brain drain followed by chain migration. This allows well-educated Asians to take advantage of the priorities set by the U.S. quota laws.

13. **C.** Counterurbanization, which is becoming more common in the United States, is the migration from urban areas to rural areas and small towns. It results in part from very rapid expansion of suburbs.

14. **C.** Unlike popular culture, folk culture is transmitted from one location to another more slowly and on a smaller scale, primarily through relocation diffusion.

15. **A.** Soccer originated as a folk culture in England, and has since been transformed into a part of global popular culture.

16. **D.** Popular culture tends to create a more uniform environment and provides access to electronic media. It wouldn't necessarily prevent the diffusion of folk culture, and it certainly modifies the physical environment.

17. **E.** See Figure 10-28 on page 366. The Gender Inequality Index map shows the least inequality in Europe and the most inequality in sub-Saharan Africa.

18. **D.** Sustainable development is development that meets the needs of people in the present, without compromising the ability of future generations to meet their needs. It can only be effectively achieved through international cooperation.

19. **E.** A language family is a collection of languages related through a common ancestral language that existed long before recorded history.

20. **E.** A creole language is one that results from the mixing of a colonizer's language with the indigenous language of the people being dominated.

21. **E.** All of these statements about the relationship between culture, religion, and the physical environment are true.

22. **B.** This is the only true statement that can be made from the population pyramids shown.

23. **B.** A universalizing religion is global and seeks to appeal to all people regardless of culture or location. Christianity has more than 2 million adherents, more than any other universalizing religion.

24. **C.** An ethnic religion is one that is relatively geographically concentrated, and likely to be based on the physical characteristics of a particular location. Hinduism is by far and away the world's largest ethnic religion, with more than 900 million adherents.

25. **B.** See Figure 12-42 on page 456. Most of the world's largest urban settlements are in developing counties.

26. **A.** A nation-state is a state whose territory corresponds to that occupied by a particular ethnicity.

27. **D.** The word comes from the Balkans region of South Eastern Europe where there has been so much national and ethnic conflict. It is the process by which a state breaks down through conflicts among its ethnicities.

28. **C.** Reduce, reuse, recycle is the best strategy to reduce solid waste.

29. **A.** See Figure 7-43 on page 252. This is the only statement that can be supported from that map. Armenia is a homogeneous state.

30. **D.** Ethnic cleansing is the forcible removable of one group by another ethnic group, and it may sometimes involve genocide.

31. **A.** The United Kingdom consists of England, Wales, Scotland, and Northern Ireland. The other countries listed are nation-states.

32. **C.** All of the other options involve some level of dependence.

33. **D.** The United Nations Law of the Seas was initially signed by 158 countries, and it standardized the limits for most countries at 12 nautical miles.

34. **E.** Gerrymandering was named for Elbridge Gerry, an early nineteenth-century American politician from Massachusetts. It is the redrawing of legislative boundaries to benefit the party in power. It is illegal today.

35. **D.** Fragmented state is separated into nonadjacent areas or a collection of islands.

36. **E.** All of these statements are true of the Human Development Index.

37. **C.** A primary sector activity is the part of the economy concerned with the direct extraction of materials from Earth's surface, and includes agriculture, mining, fishing, and forestry.

38. **B.** Less developed countries have higher infant mortalities because of lack of prenatal care, quality food and water, young age of the mother, or poor medical care.

39. **B.** According to Rostow's development model, the process of development begins in stage 2, which he called "Preconditions for Takeoff." At that time, an elite group will initiate innovative economic activities.

40. **E.** In the self-sufficiency model, countries encourage domestic production of goods and discourage opening themselves up to foreign investment and international markets.

41. **D.** Nuclear power is not renewable. All of the others mentioned are renewable.

42. **B.** Whether crops are grown or animals are raised has nothing to do with the distinction between commercial and subsistence agriculture. All of the other options are features that help to make that distinction.

43. **A.** Intensive subsistence agriculture tries to produce the maximum feasible yield from a parcel of land. It is the form of agriculture that feeds most people in the developing world.

44. **B.** Pastoral nomadism is a form of subsistence agriculture based on the herding of domesticated animals. It is adapted to dry climates, where planting crops is impossible.

45. **E.** According to this model, when choosing an enterprise, the farmer compares two costs: the cost of the land and the cost of transporting products to market.

46. **C.** Plantation agriculture is the most important form of commercial agriculture in the developing world.

47. **C.** Some European policies to help preserve the countryside from development and avoid the sprawl that characterizes American suburbs have resulted in the clustering of people with social and economic problems in high-density and remote suburbs.

48. **B.** A bulk-reducing industry in one in which the final product weighs less or comprises a lower volume than the inputs. Copper production is an especially good example of this.

49. **E.** All of these statements about maquiladora plants are true.

50. **A.** Break-of-bulk points are locations where transfer is possible from one mode of transportation to another.

51. **D.** The map shows that the largest toxic chemical release sites in the United States are in the west, and these are mostly mines.

52. **E.** Accessibility attracts services to the Central Business District. None of the other options do that.

53. **C.** Some European policies to help preserve the countryside from development and avoid the sprawl that characterizes American suburbs have resulted in the clustering of people with social and economic problems in high-density and remote suburbs.

54. **B.** Urban settlements are centers for consumer and business services, whereas rural settlements are centers for agriculture and provide a small number of services.

55. **D.** Linear rural settlements comprise buildings clustered along a road, river, or dike to facilitate communications.

56. **E.** The purpose of the enclosure movement was to promote agricultural efficiency, by consolidating small landholdings into a smaller number of large farms in England during the eighteenth century.

57. **D.** A metropolitan statistical area in the United States is an urbanized area of at least 50,000 people, the county within which the city is located, together with adjacent counties that have a functional connection to the central city.

58. **B.** The range is the maximum distance people are willing to travel to use a service. The range is the radius of the circle (or hexagon) drawn to delineate a service's market area.

59. **A.** The gravity model holds that the potential use of a service at a particular location is directly related to the number of people in a location and inversely related to the distance people must travel to reach the service.

60. **C.** The primate city rule is when the largest settlement in a country has more than twice as many people as the second-ranking settlement. Argentina and the Republic of Korea are examples of countries that follow this rule.

Free Response Questions Explained

7 points total

1. Topic: Unit 2, Population and Unit 12 Development
The three types of density used in population geography are arithmetic, physiological, and agricultural.
A. 1 point Arithmetic density is simply the total number of people per square kilometer (or unit of land).
B. 1 point Agricultural density is the number of farmers per unit of arable land.
C. 1 point Physiological density is the number of people who are supported by a unit of arable land.
D. 1 point The lower the agricultural density means that there are fewer farmers farming the land. If they are able to supply the food needs of the population with very few farmers they are using heavy machinery to assist in the planting, maintenance and harvesting of the crops.
E. 1 point The land has to be able to provide food and shelter for the population. As the population becomes larger and denser the carrying capacity of the land has to increase to support this population.
F. 2 points The population in more developed countries are concentrated in urban areas compared to less developed countries where significant portions of the population live in rural areas and cities are ringed with squatter settlements from rural to urban migrations.

7 points total

2. Topic: Unit 8 Political Geography
A. 1 point An autocratic government is a country run by ruler who makes decisions based on his/her self-interests.
B. 1 point An anocracy, which is not autocratic, nor is it a democracy, but rather a mix of both an autocracy and a democracy.
C. 1 point A democracy allows citizens to vote to elect leaders and can participate in elections.
D. 1 point Based on the map, there is a high concentration of autocratic regimes in the area of North Africa and the Middle East.
E. 1 point North Africa and the Middle East has a history of conquest, colonialism, and imperialism. When set on a path of independency, many fell to autocratic rulers because they had a history of loyalty to the royal families regardless of their autocratic rule. In other cases, the elected leaders took control of the government and the military and seized control of the state.
F. 2 points Devolution of a state begins with civil unrest from nationalist, cultural, economic or political disagreement with the current governmental system. When powers typically held by the central government are distributed to regions of the country to satisfy the demands of that population the control of the government begins to diminish. If more groups are granted the ability to control their areas outside of the central government eventually the central government has no power or support and the government fails to have any control over the state.

7 points total

3. Topic: Unit 13 Urban Geography

See Figures 13-9, 13-11, and 13-14 for diagrams of the models.

A. 1 point Burgess, Concentric Zone Model

B. 1 point Hoyt, Sector Model

C. 1 point Harris-Ulman Multiple Nuclei Model

D. 2 points The Hoyt sector model has only five sectors for a city, where as the Multiple Nuclei has nine. Each shows the CBC near a central point and both has middle-class residential next to the CBD. Low-class residential is also next to the CBD in both models. The areas of the concentric zones gave way to sectors of manufacturing, transportation arteries, and high-density housing.

E. 2 points All Spanish cities in Latin America were built according to the Laws of the Indies, drafted in 1573. The laws explicitly outlined how colonial cities were to be constructed—a gridiron street plan centered on a church and central plaza, walls around individual houses, and neighborhoods built around central, smaller plazas with parish churches or monasteries. The Burgess model is a series of rings circling the central business district. The outer ring is the area of wealthier and lower density. The Latin American model is rings that intersect to a spine or boulevard that leads to the central plaze and out to the edges of the settlement.

Answer Key to AP Human Geography Practice Test 2

Multiple Choice Answers Explained

1. **A.** A map is a two-dimensional or flat-scale model of Earth's surface, or a portion of it.

2. **A.** The biggest disadvantage of a Mercator projection is that the higher latitudes appear much larger than they actually are.

3. **E.** See Figure 2-30 on page 64.

4. **C.** The difference between the crude birth rate and the crude death rate is the rate of natural increase (or decrease). This does not take into account immigration or emigration.

5. **B.** This compares the number of people too young or too old to work with those in their productive years.

6. **B.** Internal migration is more important in countries at Stage 3 and 4.

7. **A.** An environmental or political feature that hinders migration is an intervening obstacle. U.S. quota laws are an example of a selective immigration policy that admits some types of immigrants but not others.

8. **A.** A dialect is a regional variation of a language distinguished by distinctive vocabulary, spelling, and pronunciation.

9. **A.** Asian Americans make up 40% of the population of Hawaii.

10. **C.** There are large numbers of Kurds in Turkey, Iraq, and Iran. There are not large numbers of the other ethnic groups in more than one country.

11. **E.** This was especially true of Mesopotamia and Greece.

12. **A.** All of the other choices are federal states.

13. **C.** Emigration and fertility rate are not part of the HDI. This index is used by the United Nations.

14. **B.** The literacy rate among females is the main reason the United Nation's HDI index is low in this petroleum rich region.

15. **A.** It is practiced by roughly 250 million people, predominantly in tropical regions.

16. **A.** See Figure 7-40 on page 252.

17. **D.** This is an important type of farming in the developed world. It is the most common form of commercial agriculture in much of the United States and Europe.

18. **E.** This agricultural practice preserves and enhances environmental quality.

19. **B.** Most smart growth is due to legislation and regulation.

20. **E.** These four types of distortion can result, and are especially severe for maps depicting the entire world.

21. **C.** Situation is often referred to as relative location, and grid coordinates is the same as absolute location.

22. **A.** GNP and literacy rate are more associated with levels of development.

23. **A.** Natural increase is the difference between the crude birth rate and the crude death rate.

24. **B.** Ethnicity is identity with a group of people that share distinct physical and mental traits as a product of common heredity and cultural traditions.

25. **D.** A country like Chile or Italy has many areas isolated from the capital because they are elongated states.

26. **D.** See Figure 8-30 on page 282. Geometric boundaries are simply straight lines drawn on a map. The boundary between Chad and Libya was drawn by European countries early in the twentieth century, when the area comprised a series of colonies. This boundary is now disputed.

27. **E.** The purpose is to benefit the political party in power, although gerrymandering is now illegal.

28. **B.** This index looks at GDP, life expectancy, literacy rate, and educational level to determine a country's level of development.

29. **C.** Truck comes from the middle English word meaning bartering or the exchange of commodities. Truck farmers may sell their crops at a farmer's market, from the back of their trucks, or may sell to a large corporation.

30. **E.** Scientists agree that agriculture originated in multiple hearths around the world.

31. **D.** There are currently 362 metropolitan statistical areas in the United States.

32. **A.** This is sometimes called a beltway.

33. **D.** Because of housing shortages, a large percentage of poor immigrants to urban areas in developing countries live in squatter settlements.

34. **D.** Research and development and information technology grow with postindustrial economies.

35. **A.** The data supports that the share of the GDP from agriculture was 1 percent, and the service sector had 82 percent in 2016.

36. **E.** all are correct statements

37. **C.** Transnational companies outsource labor costs to countries with lower wage pricing

38. **C.** According to the map industrial production has shifted from the Northeast to the South and West.

39. **B.** According to the map on pg. 369 more then 50% of women work outside of the home.

40. **B.** The origin of point source pollution can be clearly identified.

41. **D.** Brownfields are abandoned or neglected former industrial sites in urban areas.

42. **D.** The largest number of international migrants (49.8 million, or 19% of the global total) reside in the United States. Saudi Arabia, Germany and the Russian Federation host the second, third and fourth largest numbers of migrants worldwide (around 12 million each), followed by the United Kingdom (nearly 9 million). https://www.un.org/development/desa/publications/international-migration-report-2017.html

43. **E.** Harris considered the peripheral model to be a modification of the multiple nuclei model (which he co-authored), reflecting the growth of suburbs. The nodes of consumer and business services around the beltway are called edge cities.

44. **A.** a food desert contains primarily low income residences the distance from the center of the square to the nearest grocery store was greater than 1 mile in an urban area and greater than 10 miles in a rural area.

45. **A.** a low-income resident in an urban area may not own a car and may not live near a bus or subway.

46. **D.** Only 3 of the 11 metacities are in developed countries—Tokyo, Seoul, and New York.

47. **B.** 4 in developed countries included 3 in the United States (Las Vegas, Austin, and Atlanta) plus Suwon, South Korea.

48. **B.** a metropolitan statistical area

49. **A.** Iceland has the lowest GII of the countries listed.

50. **B.** Western Sahara discussed is by far the most extensive (266,000 square kilometers [103,000 square miles]) and most populous (around 540,000). "non–self-governing territory"

51. **A.** a three dimensional feature loses accuracy when transferred to a two-dimensional perspective.

52. **C.** High infant mortality rates indicate lack of maternal prenatal health care, adequate nutrition, and lack of medical care at birth and infancy.

53. **C.** Improved access to medical care and medicines and sanitary conditions reduces the spread of life-threatening disease increasing life expectancy.

54. **C.** Buddhism is located in very large numbers southeast Asia, Tibet, China, Mongolia and Japan

55. **D.** Resourcs are extracted where they exist, shipped to lower labor cost manufacturers and sent to large markets in developed countries

56. **C.** the Church of Jesus Christ of Latter Day Saints, settled in the Salt Lake Valley of Utah and have spread around the region.

57. **A.** The upper Midwest is predominately Lutheran in the area indicated as a result of the Scandinavian and German populations that settled the area in the late 1800's-early 1900's.

58. **A.** Southern Baptist are concentrated in the Southern United States as a result of their original pro-slavery position during the Civil War period.

59. **C.** The Anglican church was brought to the area of New England by original English settlers.

60. **A.** The number of dairy farms have decreased as the size of the commercial dairy farm has grown over the last 50 years as mechanization has streamlined the process of raising dairy cows.

Free Response Questions Explained

7 points total

1. **Topic: Development, Migration, Demographic Transition Units: Population Geography, Migration, Development**

    A. 1 point   Stage 2 are less developed countries that are starting to urbanize. Development would come from outside sources and be a source of jobs for citizens there. These countries are predominately in the primary sector of subsistence agricultural and mineral extraction to the secondary sector of limited manufacturing.

    B. 1 point   Stage 4 countries are advanced MDCs whose patterns of urbanization continue to be urban to suburban and who provided tertiary services the most while supporting quartinary and quinary sectors as needed.

    C. 1 point   Must have both answers correct for 1 point. Stage 2 any lower developing country, Stage 4 United States, any western and northern European country, Japan, South Korea, Singapore, Australia, New Zealand, Uruguay, others acceptable if they fit the criteria

    D. 2 points   Depending on country, answer must address a social, a political, and an economic characteristic that places the country in the DTM stage. For example: Japan,
    Social: Japan has a negative population pyramid with a very low natural increase rate due to a low crude birth rate and a very large aging population.
    Political: The government supports education which leads to better family planning and encourages women to complete college level education and go into the work force, further influencing the declining birth rate.
    Economic: The government supports the funding of the infrastructure to provide for safe water, access to quality foods, mobility networks and economic stability for industry to operate.

    E. 2 points   A country in stage 3 is experiencing (Ravenstein) a high degree of international migration, and intraregional migration from rural to urban and urban to suburban as economic wealth increases. Economic development falls into the "take-off" toward the "drive to maturity" stage of Rostow's model. Increased manufacturing in the secondary sector, predominately textiles and apparel is leading to global exports. Mechanization and technology is improving the manufacturing and production.

7 points total

2. **Topic: Development, Sustainable Development Goals, Climate Change**

    A. 1 Point   Greenhouse gases, predominately carbon dioxide, methane, nitrous oxide and water vapor, traps reflected UV light and energy from dissipating into the atmosphere increasing the warming of the earth's surface. The increased heat energy has increased the intensity of storms, caused glacial and snow melt and increased the heating temperature.

    B. 1 point   Climate change causes a shift in the areas that plants can grow in. Some areas have become too warm and more northerly areas have warmed up enough that plants can be raised there.

C. 1 point   Development brings a shift from primary sector activities to secondary sector of manufacturing. Manufacturing and processing industries require electricity frequently generated from oil, gas or coal which produces greenhouse gases in the process. Development standards of the population are dependent on improved living conditions, mobility and education. Each of these areas increase development with the access to electricity and manufactured products.

D. 1 point   Alternative sources can include: solar power, hydroelectric power, tidal power, wind power, nuclear power, and geothermal. Pick 2

E. 1 point   Access to electricity allows for indoor light at night for school work or chores. Electricity allows for the use of machinery for production of domestic goods, medical facilities, foods and necessary items. Any of these areas contributes to the improvement of the individual and the family.

F. 1 point   Access to electricity allows for the manufacturing of products that can be sold leading to an increase in income and further development.

G. 1 point   Climate change causing sea level rise has caused populations on very low lying areas to move inland or to other coastal areas. Areas of increased desertification in sub-Saharan Africa has caused migration of populations further south. Other migrations have been caused by the destruction of areas from intense storms that have destroyed homes and livelihoods.

7 points total

3. Topic: Ecotourism, development

A. 1 point   Ecotourism is a form of tourism into pristine, fragile, natural areas. The cost of the experience is used in the maintenance, protection of the area and local community. The cost is designed to help preserve and protect the area from commercial development.

B. 1 point   In general tourism is the experience of temporary immersion in another culture, recreational activities away from home, or the exploration of areas under controlled access. Ecotourism seeks to provide the tourist with an experience in a small scale remote and natural location.

C. 1 point   Ecotourism can contribute income into local economy by providing jobs to support the ecotourists.

D. 1 point   Restrictions on development of commercial operations can be restricted by governments allowing only ecotourist operators. Funds from operating the ecotours can be dedicated to preservation programs and access restrictions to further protect the environment. Limitations on the number of visitors can also be regulated through the ecotour operators.

E. 1 point Two stresses are required for the answer. Possible answers can include: pollution, increased waste and sewage waste, noise, traffic, construction of roads and buildings, poaching, migration of local workers into the area, and other reasonable answers.

F. 2 points UNSDG # 10, #14, and #15 address aspects that are related to local development and attention to the preservation of the natural environment. Development of ecotourism in areas that would be suitable for this type of controlled tourist experience can provide monies to local villages through working with the ecotourism companies. Additionally, protection of ocean areas and fragile forests, deserts, and wilderness areas can be managed through controlled access under ecotourism operations operating under the laws of those countries, thus supporting the goals of sustainable development.

Chapter Quick Quiz and Free Response Answers

Chapter 1:

1.1.1. B	1.2.3. D	1.3.7. D
1.1.2. D	1.3.1. C	1.4.1. D
1.1.3. B	1.3.2. B	1.4.2. E
1.1.4. D	1.3.3. C	1.4.3. C
1.1.5. A	1.3.4. C	1.4.4. C
1.2.1. C	1.3.5. E	
1.2.2. C	1.3.6. D	

Quick Quiz Answers:

1.1. E	1.5. D	1.9. E
1.2. C	1.6. C	1.10. B
1.3. C	1.7. B	
1.4. A	1.8. D	

Free Response Chapter 1

Question 1.

1. The four types of distortion that can occur when you are creating a map deal with shape, distance, relative size, and direction.

Geographers recognize that distortion will occur, and have created maps that adjust for each:

1. Shape—the best map projection to deal with exaggerated shapes of countries would be a Mercator projection.
2. Distance is also best on a Mercator projection, especially near the equator.
3. Relative size is best projected on equal-area projections.
4. Direction is consistent on Mercator projections.

2. The **Mercator projection** is best for use as a maritime map of the mid-latitudes.

The **Goode's Homolosine** map is an equal-area projection used to present accurate spatial distribution of land or oceans in each section. The **Robinson projection** is a compromise projection showing the entire world with low distortion within 45 degrees of the equator.

Question 2.

1. Possible answers for Africa: Angola, Egypt, Chad, Nigeria, Ghana, Mali, Burkina Faso, Mauritania, Morocco, Algeria

   Possible answers for Asia: Pakistan
2. Social Reason: cultural traditions, patriarchal societies, religious practices
3. Economic reason for high gender equality: Women can increase the family income and bring up the level of development; men are involved in pastoral nomadism; men are working away; laws require women to be paid the same as men.
4. Political reason for high gender equality: value placed on representation of women, women are able to vote, and women can be elected to office.

Note: Answers to #2, 3, 4 should be generalized at this time. The student is beginning this course of study and detailed examples in these areas have not been addressed. Other reasonable responses are acceptable.

Chapter 2:

2.1.1. C	2.2.3. D	2.4.1. C
2.1.2. E	2.3.1. B	2.4.2. A
2.1.3. A	2.3.2. C	2.4.3. B
2.2.1. C	2.3.3. C	2.4.4. C
2.2.2. C	2.3.4. A	

Quick Quiz Answers:

2.1. B	2.5. A	2.9. B
2.2. C	2.6. D	2.10. A
2.3. D	2.7. A	2.11. E
2.4. E	2.8. D	

Free Response Chapter 2:

1. **A.** The economic sectors at this time could be facing a potential job shortage unless the demand for workers increases possibly in an expanding manufacturing complex, which would provide a large number of jobs. A shift in the demand for workers will employ the increased labor force as it comes of employment age.

B. Social support would require more facilities for young children, including daycare and preschool programs. Planning to extend social support for a large number of young adults is essential to meet the increasing demands of a large population in their twenties.

C. Education facilities for increasing elementary age and expanding high school facilities need to be planned. Health concerns focus on the needs of a youthful population, including childhood diseases. A large emerging young adult population may necessitate increased family planning programs and increased maternal facilities.

2. Potential economic challenges are the result of a decreasing young population. With this kind of decline, it is presumed that there are not enough potential workers to replace the current working population. As a result, the economy will need to shift to businesses that use more automated labor, outsourcing in some industries, or shift to increased imports to make up for lack of goods due to a decline in workers. The economy will also experience an increased number of people remaining in the workforce beyond a normal retirement age, since replacement workers are not readily available. More goods and services will be provided that address the needs and wants of an aging population.

3. **A.** The economic sectors will have to be less dependent on an abundance of low-skilled workers. Typically, this economy will predominately be tertiary and quaternary sector jobs. The workforce will contain a significant number of older people still working past the retirement age.

B. The government infrastructure will focus on social spaces designed for an older and aging population. This would include handicap access and assistance. Other facilities would include retirement living facilities, medical services for aging populations, and day facilities for those who do not have family during the day and can no longer stay by themselves.

C. Education facilities will need to consolidate and close due to a declining youth population. Health services will need to shift to care for the problems more commonly associated with an aging population. In particular, a population with more than a million people over 100 years of age will be in need of medical treatments and care specifically designed for their specific needs.

Chapter 3:

3.1.1. C	3.2.2. C	3.3.4. E
3.1.2. E	3.2.3. B	3.4.1. D
3.1.3. A	3.3.1. D	3.4.2. C
3.1.4. B	3.3.2. C	3.4.3. A
3.2.1. D	3.3.3. C	3.4.4. B

Quick Quiz Answers:

3.1 E	3.4 C	3.7 D
3.2 F	3.5 G	3.8 A
3.3 B	3.6 H	

Free Response Chapter 3:

A. Two countries that experience interregional migration: Brazil, Mexico, Canada, Russia, China, and the United States.

B. Discuss two push and two pull factors for interregional migration in an identified region of a country.
   Pull: Russia, to the west for job opportunities
   Pull: Brazil, interior development
   Pull: China, to the coastal cities for jobs
   Pull: Canada, westward to new regions of development
   Pull: United States, westward for land and southward for industrial jobs
   Push: Russia, decline in factory and mining jobs
   Push: Brazil, overpopulation in the coastal cities
   Push: China, lack of jobs in rural areas
   Push: Canada, lack of jobs in Ontario and Quebec
   Push: United States, available land for farming and jobs in the newer cities

C. One result of interregional migration occurring in both countries can include:
   o growth of new cities
   o relocation of industries to growth areas
   o shift in population as people leave cities in one region and move to jobs in another
   o rapid urbanization in China
   o changing traditional migration patterns
   o clustering of population into new regional areas

Chapter 4:

4.1.1. E	4.2.3. B	4.3.3. E
4.1.2. E	4.2.4. D	4.3.4. B
4.1.3. B	4.2.5. C	4.4.1. C
4.2.1. D	4.3.1. A	4.4.2. B
4.2.2. B	4.3.2. C	4.4.3. A

Quick Quiz Answers:

4.1. A

4.2. D

4.3. D

4.4. D

4.5. Social media has more of an impact on both folk and popular culture today because of the easy access to it. During the Arab Spring in North Africa and West Asia, even Bedouins had smartphones and access to the situations/uprising during the government overthrows. In Amish communities in the United States, it is not unusual to see teenagers and young adults with cell phones connecting them to the events outside of their community in addition to others within. These folk cultures are no longer kept in the dark about things that are going on in their country; they can actually watch them unfold in "real time."

Free Response Chapter 4:

A. By looking at the map, it is clear that soccer is truly taking off. What once was a sport mainly found in England, as a folk culture in small villages, is now turning into a global phenomenon. The map illustrates how many years a country has qualified for the world cup.

B. While Europe and South America clearly have qualified for the World Cup for the most years, countries such as the United States, Australia, China, and Russia are gaining ground. Even countries in Africa are catching up. What becomes clearer when looking at the map are the host countries; this is when we see the "snowballing" effect, where host nations are located all over the globe.

Chapter 5:

5.1.1. B	5.2.2. E	5.3.5. B
5.1.2. B	5.2.3. E	5.4.1. E
5.1.3. D	5.3.1. C	5.4.2. D
5.1.4. C	5.3.2. D	5.4.3. B
5.1.5. C	5.3.3. E	5.4.4. B
5.2.1. B	5.3.4. A	

Quick Quiz Answers:

5.1. C

5.2. D

5.3. A

5.4. A

Free Response Chapter 5:

1. Languages in Switzerland are divided by the cantons, which are culturally divided in four distinct regions of the country. Two languages divide Belgium along cultural identification but contribute to economic and political tensions.
2. The four official languages are associated with their regional areas. Students are required to learn two of the four languages in school. A long tradition of a decentralized government allowing locally made decisions reduces socio-cultural tensions.
3. A dual-language country can appeal to foreign visitors and companies, encouraging trade relations and foreign investment. Tourism is always enhanced when there is something unique about a country, making it a place people want to come and visit.
4. Language is a centrifugal factor when it causes ethnic separation or economic isolation when a country's population is unable to effectively communicate.

Chapter 6:

6.1.1. A	6.2.2. B	6.3.4. C
6.1.2. D	6.2.3. A	6.3.5. C
6.1.3. A	6.2.4. C	6.4.1. D
6.1.4. A	6.2.5. B	6.4.2. D
6.1.5. D	6.3.1. D	6.4.3. B
6.1.6. C	6.3.2. A	6.4.4. D
6.2.1. D	6.3.3. A	

Chapter Quiz:

6.1 B	6.3 E	6.5 A
6.2 D	6.4 C	

Free Response Question Chapter 6:

A. The Dome of the Rock, sacred to Islam, is situated just above the Western Wall, which is the remains of the original Jewish temple.

B. Any of the religious places identified are sufficient. They are sacred if they are declared as such by the adherents.

C. Religious places encourage pilgrims to visit. The flow of pilgrims have to be managed and the surrounding area has to be able to accommodate the itinerate visitor with shelter and food. Markets for the sale of religious souvenirs expand the economic landscape of the area supporting the religious site. The flow of pilgrims creates a cultural diversity in the area, exposing visitors to different cultures of fellow adherents.

Chapter 7:

7.1.1. B	7.2.2. B	7.4.1. C
7.1.2. A	7.2.3. B	7.4.2. A
7.1.3. B	7.2.4. D	7.4.3. E
7.1.4. C	7.3.1. B	7.4.4. D
7.1.5. B	7.3.2. C	7.4.5. C
7.2.1. D	7.3.3. B	

Quick Quiz Answers:

7.1. E	7.3. A
7.2. B	7.4. A

Free Response Chapter 7:

1. Socioeconomic impact could include: Emigrants leaving their home country causes a loss of labor force, loss of culture, change in age structure with a larger number of older population left behind, and decline in taxable residents. Immigrants entering a new country can cause a demand for jobs, increased unemployment, cultural discrimination, development of cultural enclaves, increase in population, shift in dependency ratio, and increased demand on social services and living accommodations.

2. Political impact: Migrants leaving and entering can be significant enough in numbers to shift political elections at local levels and in national governments. Election of migrants and descendants can lead to nationalist and opposition movements. When many ethnicities are made to live within one area, ethnic conflicts can occur leading to ethnic cleansing and civil wars. Other plausible answers are acceptable.

3. Centripetal factors affecting sociopolitical development of a multiethnic society: democratic government, voting rights, equal rights to minority populations, process for citizenship, equal protection under the law, nationalism for the goals of the State, opportunities to serve in elected offices. Centrifugal factors affecting the sociopolitical development of a multiethnic society: inability to achieve citizenship, segregated settlements, discriminatory laws, no government representation by elected officials.

Chapter 8:

8.1.1. D	8.2.5. E	8.3.6. B
8.1.2. D	8.3.1. C	8.4.1. B
8.2.1. C	8.3.2. A	8.4.2. B
8.2.2. A	8.3.3. E	8.4.3. E
8.2.3. D	8.3.4. E	8.4.4. D
8.2.4. D	8.3.5. A	8.4.5. B

Quick Quiz Answers:

8.1. D	8.3. A
8.2. B	8.4. B

Free Response Chapter 8:

1. Four of the following countries have claims to the Arctic: Denmark, Finland, Norway, Russia, Canada, the United States, Iceland

2. Countries have exclusive economic rights within the 200 nautical mile zone of their territorial areas. This means that all mineral extraction, fishing, and shipping access is under the control of the country who claims that territorial area.

3. The economic impact of melting Arctic ice includes better access to mineral deposits, including potential oil reserves. It also allows for shorter shipping routes from northern ports to other ports. Political impacts of melting Arctic ice creates more direct conflict with competing countries for claiming land areas previously inaccessible or covered in sea ice. The potential economic gains will drive the political conflict.

Chapter 9:

9.1.1. D	9.3.3. A	9.4.2. B
9.1.2. A	9.3.4. D	9.4.3. B
9.1.3. E	9.3.5. B	9.4.4. A
9.2.1. B	9.3.6. C	9.4.5. B
9.2.2. C	9.3.7. A	9.4.6. C
9.3.1. B	9.3.8. E	
9.3.2. E	9.4.1. E	

Quick Quiz Answers:

9.1. B	9.5. E	9.9. E
9.2. A	9.6. C	9.10. A
9.3. C	9.7. D	
9.4. A	9.8. D	

Free Response Chapter 9:

1. Answer requires the student to evaluate both the advantages and disadvantages of GMO crops. The command term *evaluate* requires discussion of both sides of the issue.

Advantages of genetically modified crops in a developed country include, but are not limited to the following:
- create a resistance to certain pests, diseases, or environmental conditions
- Achieve a reduction of spoilage in the field and after harvesting,
- Provide a resistance to chemical treatments (e.g., resistance to a herbicide)
- Improve the nutrient makeup of a crop
- Improve the yield, through the introduction of resistance to plant diseases increasing profit
- Increase tolerance of herbicides
- Reduce crop damage from adverse weather conditions
- Reduce fossil fuel use.
- In the future, genetic modification could be aimed at altering the nutrient content of food, reducing its allergenic potential or improving the efficiency of food production systems.

Disadvantages of genetically modified crops in a developed country include, but are not limited to:
Environmental disadvantages:
- causing a lower level of biodiversity with fewer strains of seeds.
- potential danger to other insects that are important to the ecosystems.
- creating herbicide resistant weeds.
- cross pollination between GMO and non-GMOs.
- increased funding for more research.
- concerns on changing the field of agriculture.
- trade concerns with countries that will not allow GMO products.
- allergic reactions to new proteins and unknown genetic material.
- potential decreased antibiotic efficacy

2. The impact of the Green Revolution is of interest to geographers because of the role agricultural productivity has in economic development, global trade, and health of the population. Answers can include Philippines, Mexico, or India as examples.
- The Green Revolution initially prevented potential famines in countries that were experiencing high total fertility rates and expanding life expectancies, which led to rapid population growth.
- Commercial productivity has increased yields on decreasing amounts of land as a result of the Green Revolution and the changes in agricultural production.
- The Philippines became a supplier of rice in the global market within 20 years by doubling its rice production.
- India experienced a surplus of several million tons in its wheat production and by 2006 was a major exporter of rice in the global market.

3. Truck farming is located within driving distance of the major market. Extensive grain farming is located far away from the manufacturing center and the market. Extensive grain farming involves mechanical cultivation of thousands of acres, while truck farming involves smaller amounts of land with limited mechanical use due to the fragility of the crops.

4. Plantation farms are located away from the market and require the deliberate cultivation of plants that are not tilled or cut down every season. Organic farming tends to be closer to the market, use smaller acreage, and require less inputs due to maintaining an organic status.

5. Community gardens provide a place to raise smaller quantities of preferred plants. The gardens are aesthetically pleasing, function as a social place, provide the possibility of additional income, provide locally grown fresh vegetables that might not otherwise be available, and offer the opportunity to do physical work for a rewarding benefit.

Chapter 10:

10.1.1. D	10.2.2. A	10.3.2. A
10.1.2. D	10.2.3. C	10.3.3. C
10.1.3. C	10.2.4. C	10.3.4. B
10.1.4. A	10.2.5. B	10.4.1. B
10.2.1. C	10.3.1. D	10.4.2. B

Quick Quiz Answers:

10.1. C	10.3. C
10.2. B	10.4. A
10.5. A	
10.6. D	
10.7. D	
10.8. C	
10.9. A	
10.10. D	

Free Response Chapter 10:

1. Countries with the highest income include The United States, Canada, Saudi Arabia, Australia, the Scandinavian countries, and countries in Western Europe. Countries with a low Gender Inequality Index would also include the United States, Canada, Western Europe, Australia, the Scandinavian countries, but also China, and Tunisia.

2. In comparing the data, countries with high income also appear to have lower gender inequality.

3. A major exception to this rule would be found in China.

Chapter 11:

11.1.1. B	11.2.3. B	11.3.4. B
11.1.2. A	11.2.4. A	11.4.1. A
11.1.3. B	11.2.5. C	11.4.2. B
11.1.4. A	11.2.6. A	11.4.3. A
11.1.5. B	11.2.7. D	11.4.4. C
11.1.6. B	11.3.1. E	
11.2.1. E	11.3.2. D	
11.2.2. A	11.3.3. D	

Quick Quiz Answers:

11.1. B	11.5. E	11.9. A
11.2. B	11.6. A	11.10. B
11.3. A	11.7. C	11.11. D
11.4. E	11.8. C	

Free Response Chapter 11:

Sustainable development integrates economic development with environmental sustainability.

1. Define: Sustainable development seeks to improve development levels of populations while managing demands on resource and environmental resources today in order to have sufficient resources for future generations. Sustainable development addresses issues of natural resource depletion, mass consumption, the costs and effects of pollution, and the impact of climate change, as well as issues of human health, well-being, and social and economic equity.

2. The purpose of focusing on sustainable development in industry is to reduce waste, reduce the use of nonrenewable resources, and develop better products that allow resources to be available for future generations. Examples (other plausible answers are acceptable) of sustainable development in:

a. Agriculture: No-till agriculture; genetic modification to use less water, produce higher yield with less fertilizers; and shift in production areas

b. Energy: Use of renewable resources (sun, wind, hydroelectric) for energy production; more efficient use of energy-consuming appliances and lightbulbs; use of rechargeable energy sources; energy-efficient building practices (LEED)

c. Textile manufacturing: Alternative energy sources; use of recycled materials; reduce consumption

3. These are the components of the "Reduce, Reuse and Recycle" waste hierarchy and part of the goals for sustainable development.

a. Recycling: The process of converting waste materials into reusable objects to prevent waste of potentially useful materials. Recycling reduces the consumption of new raw materials, energy usage, air pollution, and water pollution by decreasing the need for "conventional" waste disposal and lowering greenhouse gas emissions compared to plastic production.

b. Reducing: The process of using fewer natural resources, creating less waste and less pollution; consumption patterns demand fewer products; changing manufacturing process; using less packaging

c. Reuse/remanufacturing: New products require a lot of materials and energy. Buying used and repurposed items such as clothing, energy efficient appliances; plastics reused in manufacturing walkways and furniture; textiles remanufactured into new carpets and furniture materials

Chapter 12:

12.1.1. B	12.2.4. B	12.4.2. B
12.1.2. C	12.3.1. E	12.4.3. E
12.2.1. E	12.3.2. C	12.4.4. C
12.2.2. A	12.3.3. A	
12.2.3. C	12.4.1. B	

Quick Quiz Answers:

12.1. D	12.5. E	12.9. D
12.2. A	12.6. A	12.10. A
12.3. C	12.7. C	
12.4. A	12.8. B	

Free Response Chapter 12:

The situational factors of dispersed rural settlement, clustered linear rural settlement, and the circular clustered rural settlement.

The expected answer needs to analyze the strengths and weaknesses of each settlement pattern, not just provide a description of the settlement. Answer may include the following:

- In dispersed rural settlements, farmers live on individual farms and are more isolated from their neighbors. Dispersed rural settlements are associated with more recent agricultural settlements in the developed world such as the United States.
- Linear rural settlements are clustered along transportation like roads or rivers. These are commonly found in areas settled by the French in North America. This allows access to transportation for distribution and access of goods.
- Circular rural settlements consist of a central open space surrounded by buildings. This type of settlement allows for a small communal setting for protection and personal relationships.

Chapter 13:

13.1.1. C	13.2.5. C	13.4.1. B
13.1.2. E	13.2.6. C	13.4.2. B
13.1.3. C	13.3.1. E	13.4.3. A
13.2.1. B	13.3.2. E	13.4.4. E
13.2.2. C	13.3.3. A	
13.2.3. A	13.3.4. E	
13.2.4. B	13.3.5. D	

Quick Quiz Answers:

13.1. A
13.2. B
13.3. E
13.4. C
13.5. E

Free Response Chapter 13:

A. Gentrification is the process of converting low-income rental properties near the CBD to middle-class owner-occupied homes and involves repurposing older buildings, particularly with historic architecture. These buildings are usually refurbished and repaired, and the space is reapportioned into offices, modern apartment-style housing, or eclectic markets for urban consumers.

Urban renewal is the process of gentrifying older buildings and building new structures. It is an ongoing process in urban areas. Areas of urban renewal are typically designed to maintain the traditional architectural style of the area while making the buildings usable in a modern society.

B. Gentrification is an alternative to suburban sprawl. The purpose of urban renewal is to bring residents with money back into a central city and create unique shopping and housing areas. Bringing residents back into the urban center also helps with the ongoing environmental challenges of air quality and mobility and provides an alternative to suburban sprawl. Revitalized areas in the central city provide the same conveniences and services found in suburban areas without the commuting and vehicle pollution.